HERO FOUND

"[Dieter] Dengler's actual POW experiences are the centerpiece of the book, and, thanks to Henderson's storytelling skill, these scenes often read like a first-rate suspense novel . . . poignant in its details. An engaging tale of a harrowing POW experience." —*Kirkus Reviews*

"Any American who has ever gone to war, or has known people who have, will be deeply moved by this unforgettable story of escape and survival against all odds."
—John Warner, former U.S. senator and Secretary of the Navy

"In *Hero Found*, Bruce Henderson's writing is meticulous and compassionate, the kind of writing that comes from observing a moment in history up close, wondering about it for decades, and then returning to the scene to understand it once and for all."
—Amanda Ripley, contributing writer at *Time* and author of *The Unthinkable*

"The subtitle gives it away, but the story . . . will still keep you up at night." —Sam Whiting, *San Francisco Chronicle*

"This account of one of the most remarkable and thrilling episodes of the Vietnam War has been written with the understanding and feel of a shipmate of Dengler's aboard the carrier *Ranger*. But there is no gold plating or false heroics. In his tough and gritty narrative, Henderson has deftly captured the pungent environment of the navy's carrier pilots at war. Among the very best of its genre."
— Admiral J. L. Holloway, U.S. Navy (Ret.), Chief of Naval Operations, 1974–1978

ABOUT THE AUTHOR

Roger Tully

BRUCE HENDERSON is the author or coauthor of more than twenty nonfiction books, including the #1 *New York Times* bestseller *And the Sea Will Tell* (with Vincent Bugliosi) and *Down to the Sea: An Epic Story of Naval Disaster and Heroism in World War II*. Henderson served as a U.S. Navy Seventh Fleet weatherman from 1965 to 1967. He lives in Menlo Park, California.

HERO FOUND

HARPER

NEW YORK • LONDON • TORONTO • SYDNEY

HERO FOUND

The Greatest POW Escape of the Vietnam War

BRUCE HENDERSON

HARPER

A hardcover edition of this book was published in 2010 by Harper, an imprint of
HarperCollins Publishers.

HarperCollins books may be purchased for educational, business, or sales promotional
use. For information, please e-mail the Special Markets Department at
SPsales@harpercollins.com.

FIRST HARPER PAPERBACK PUBLISHED 2011.

Map illustration on pages 202–203 by Susan Sugar
Designed by Janet M. Evans

Library of Congress Cataloging-in-Publication Data is available upon request.

ISBN 978-0-06-157137-4 (pbk.)

16 17 18   OV/RRD   10 9 8 7 6 5 4

For Conrad "Connie" Liberty,
Ranger shipmate and friend for life

Contents

Author's Note

I grew up believing in heroes. For me, they were always pilots.

It began with U.S. Army Air Corps pilot, 2nd Lt. Robert G. Silva, my maternal grandmother's youngest offspring. Bob went missing on March 4, 1944, when his P-51-B Mustang—named *Hi-Yo Silva*, mimicking the Lone Ranger's command to his steed Silver on the popular radio show—dropped out of formation at 22,000 feet in a heavy overcast above the North Sea. His squadron—the 353rd Fighter Squadron of the 354th Fighter Group, which finished the war as the highest-scoring fighter squadron in the European theater, with 295 air victories—was returning to Boxted airfield in eastern England after escorting B-17 Flying Fortresses on the first daylight bombing raid over Berlin. The daring mission, involving hundreds of Allied bombers and fighters, marked a "turning point of the war," according to the mission's bomber wing commander, Col. H. Griffin Mumford. Thereafter, bombing runs flew day and night over the heartland of Germany until that country's unconditional surrender seventeen months later. The March 4 mission, the subject of a six-column front-page headline in the *New York Times* ("800 U.S. Bombers Smash at Berlin by Day"), proved historic for another reason: with the loss of twenty-three fighters, "most due to the [bad] weather rather than the enemy," it was to be the costliest day of the war for U.S. fighter squadrons in the skies over Europe.

Born the year after the war ended, I spent the fondest days of my youth at my grandmother Daisy's rambling and always welcoming Victorian home at 1522 Lincoln Avenue in tree-lined Alameda, California, a small island community in the San Francisco Bay next to Oakland. I was no more than eight or nine years old when I first opened a brown-striped suitcase kept in a closet in the middle bedroom, formerly my grandfather's room but after his death a place to keep trunks, boxes, and a treadle sewing machine at which my grandmother mended, shortened, and cuffed. The suitcase had been Bob's—used in his travels from home while he attended the College of the Pacific in Stockton, California, where he finished a civilian pilot training course before joining the Army Air Corps as an aviation cadet in the summer of 1942 at age twenty-two.

The old suitcase was a boy's treasure trove. Initially, what interested me the most was the pilot paraphernalia: leather-rimmed goggles, a helmet of soft leather with padded chamois lining, leather gloves, a silk scarf, silver aviator wings, and two padded boxes each containing a tiny, folded U.S. flag atop a shiny military decoration. One was the Purple Heart, given to any member of the military wounded or killed in action. The other was an Air Medal, awarded "for heroic or meritorious achievement while participating in aerial flight." I was particularly taken with the design of the latter: the bronze medallion had a swooping eagle clutching a lightning bolt in each talon. Also in the suitcase was my uncle's pocket-size address book. Tucked inside the back flap was a stick of Dentyne gum, hard and no doubt unchewable. My grandmother always had a new pack of gum waiting for me whenever I arrived, and despite the many brands of gum in the world it was always Dentyne. I never knew why until that moment.

Throughout the years I would regularly slip into the middle bedroom and open the suitcase. In time, I read all the letters my grandmother kept inside—more than 100 of Bob's letters home from his earliest days in army flight training until his last letter written three days before his final mission. On the front of that envelope my grandmother wrote that she had received it on March 13, 1944, and added, "My last letter from my darling."

March 1, 1944

Dear Mom—

Received two letters from you today—I'm happy again! I'm glad you're all so proud—but like I told you once before Mom—everything I am, or hope to be, I owe to you and Pop. Think Abe Lincoln said that once, regardless—I mean it too!

Another medal today to my credit—I now can wear the "Oak Leaf Cluster." It's a little bronzed leaf you wear on your Air Medal, signifying you've earned the Air Medal a second time. Two more Oak Leaf Clusters to go, and then the D.F.C. (Distinguished Flying Cross), the highest aviation award there is. But that's wishful thinking—better not cross my bridges 'till I get to them.

Well, angel—late again—and expect another date in the clouds with Jerry tomorrow—so I'd better get some sleep.

All my love,
Bob

Three days after opening Bob's last letter my grandmother received the dreaded Western Union wire from Washington, D.C., expressing the secretary of war's "deep regret that your son has been reported missing in action." That telegram, yellowed and wrinkled, was also in the suitcase. So was a typed letter from Bob's commanding officer, Col. Jack T. Bradley, dated April 12, 1944, in answer to a letter my grandmother wrote seeking further information about her missing son. "Bob was missing after a Berlin raid and was last seen as the squadron was climbing through the clouds near the French coast," wrote Bradley, who would finish the war as one of the top P-51 aces, with fifteen confirmed aerial kills. "We ran into some terrible weather that day and feel sure that Bob lost control of his ship in the clouds, as did several others. We broke into the clear to find that he was no longer with us. We were at a very high altitude and Bob had a good chance of getting out safely, even under the worst circumstances. Therefore we are all hoping to hear that he is a prisoner of war. Several men who did not seem to have as good a chance of surviving as Bob did have been reported captured by the enemy. Bob's loss is greatly felt by the squadron. He has completed many successful missions against the enemy and has been awarded the Air Medal and Oak Leaf Cluster. His promotion to First Lieutenant came through only a few days after his last flight. The loss of a pilot with Bob's experience and ability is in itself telling, but more than that we miss Bob himself, as he was everyone's friend and never seemed to lose his cheerfulness. If we receive any information at all about Bob, we will forward it to you without delay."

The hope given to the family by the commanding officer's letter dissipated when Bob was declared killed in action, although neither his body nor the wreckage of his aircraft was ever found. When the war ended, Bob's wingman, David B. O'Hara, visited my grandparents in Alameda and filled in some details about Bob's last flight. Bob had problems with his plane's oxygen system, which had sent him back to the airfield shortly after takeoff for a quick repair. Taking off a second time, he rejoined the aerial armada bound for Berlin. O'Hara thought Bob's oxygen problem might have recurred on the flight back to England as they crossed the North Sea at high altitude, causing him to lose consciousness. O'Hara saw Bob's plane "oscillating more-or-less in a pendulum motion from one side of the formation to the other," then shoot upward "at least 100 feet and stall out." Trying to stay with his wingman, O'Hara hit full throttle and yanked on the stick, resulting in a snap roll and spin. When O'Hara regained control of his plane, Bob was gone.

My spirited and indomitable grandmother, who chased fire engines in her bright red 1952 Chevy coupe and at Christmas gave the best gifts under the tree, lived another forty years, to the venerable age of 101, but not once did I see her speak about her lost son without her eyes brimming with tears. In truth, it was not something I fully comprehended until I had my own children. Although my grandmother had three other children, including my mother, it was no secret that her youngest, Bob, to whom she gave birth in the front bedroom twenty-four years before his death, was special. Relatives and family friends shared similar feelings about Bob, who in a short span went from winning swimming and boxing medals in high school to flying combat missions over Europe. His was, of course, a generation of young men who died before their time in faraway places. My grandmother belonged to the Gold Star Mothers Club, a support group begun in the waning days of World War I by the mother of an airman killed in France. She hung in the front window a rectangular banner with a single gold star signifying her loss. I remember us visiting the nearby home of her friend

Violet Newhouse, who in her window had a banner with three gold stars. For my family, whose other menfolk returned from war unscathed, it began and ended with Bob. By all accounts he was our best, most likable, and most promising. Everyone could only speculate: what *would* Bob have done with his life? He was irreplaceable, and his loss unfathomable.

One day when I was in the fifth grade I created a fantasy about the uncle I never knew. It was one that I would secretly hold for years, and only reluctantly outgrow. The teacher, introducing the topic of world geography, passed out several books containing colorful maps. When one reached me, I found the page that showed the North Sea. With my fingertip I traced a line from Germany to England, and saw where the North Sea narrowed between landmasses. On the map, it looked as if Bob could not have gone down very far from a coastline. If he had parachuted from his plane, could he have made it ashore? Had he managed to float or swim to England he would probably have been identified, but what if he had washed up on the coast of occupied Europe? I looked out the bank of windows lining one side of the classroom. Gazing at the sky dotted with white cotton-candy clouds, I daydreamed. What if Uncle Bob had parachuted safely and made it ashore? Suppose he was injured and unable to talk? What if he had amnesia and didn't remember his name? Suppose he had been picked up by friendly locals? Had he, without any memory of his past, settled in a small village after the war? I looked again at the map, studying the possibilities. It soon became clear what I must do. When I grew up, I would search for my lost uncle in France and elsewhere, showing people his picture. Somewhere, somehow, I would find him, and bring him home to my grandmother. Of course, I also very much wanted to find him for myself, so I could have the uncle I had never known.

One day not long afterward, I was on the playground of Dayton Elementary School during recess when a roar in the sky caused everyone to look up. A huge plane appeared overhead, lower than I had ever seen one fly. The pilot was visible in the cockpit. It seemed as if the plane would plunge into our schoolyard. As the deafening noise intensified, the nose suddenly came up and the aircraft passed above our heads. In no time there was a tremendous explosion, and a fireball rose from a nearby empty marsh.

The crash site was cordoned off by the police and then by the military for two days, as investigators and cleanup crews did their work. The local newspaper carried details of the incident. The plane was a two-engine air force C-119 Flying Boxcar with a pilot, a copilot, and three crewmen. The pilot was credited with guiding the cargo plane, which had lost an engine and was on fire, away from the school before crashing into a wide field near the eastern edge of San Francisco Bay. The heroic pilot and his crew died instantly.

At the first opportunity, I wandered through the field where the plane had crashed. Although no large pieces of wreckage remained, I was amazed at how many small metal, rubber, and nylon fragments were strewn on the ground. I picked up several, finding some scorched and bent but others as smooth and perfect as the day they were made. A fear gnawed at me: what if I found part of a human body? I decided they must have taken all that away. I came back to the field many times after that, always taking a small piece of the crash home with me. Airmen had died, suddenly and violently, here in a field where my friends and I played army with gas masks, helmets, and backpacks from a war surplus store. I thought about the pilot who had saved lives—my own included. Did his family miss him as much as mine missed Bob? Had he survived the war only to die in a field next to a school in peacetime? Still, I held on to my fervent hope that Bob had not come to a such a tragic end, but had somehow survived.

By the seventh grade, I had found my very own pilot living right next door. In the habitual absence of my father—a salesman who worked week-ends and spent most nights drinking at a neighborhood bar until past my bedtime—and any other adult male relatives in my sphere, I followed around like a lost puppy one Richard "Dick" Templeton, a husky former U.S. Navy fighter pilot. After serving in World War II, he had stayed in the reserves; he flew one weekend a month at Alameda Naval Air Station. Like many reserve pilots, Dick got his monthly flight time in a twin-engine Beechcraft utility plane. One Saturday morning as he was leaving in uni-form, Dick, a gregarious, full-of-the-devil type—one Halloween he came trick-or-treating to our door holding an empty martini glass—told me to be outside at high noon. Waiting expectantly, I heard the airplane before I saw it. Then, it buzzed over low, banking sharply. Round and round it circled overhead. Kids and adults alike on the block joined me in waving at the plane being flown by *my* pilot. I was overjoyed, and very proud. Dick had a great way of topping himself, and before long I was with him in that navy utility plane taking my first airplane ride, buzzing my house.

When I was thirteen Dick invited me to my first air show, to see a performance of the navy's Blue Angels. A few days before the event, I purchased a model kit of a Blue Angels' Grumman F-11 Tiger. After I had glued together all the pieces, it was time to affix the decals, which included "U.S. Navy" and white pinstripes. Because there were six Blue Angels, the kit contained decal numbers 1 through 6 to put on the tail. I chose 3.

When we arrived at the Oakland Airport on Doolittle Drive, named after another heroic pilot—General Jimmy Doolittle, born in Alameda, who won the Medal of Honor for leading the first U.S. bombing attack of Japan only four months after Pearl Harbor—Dick took me to the front of the crowd. We stopped at a rope that cordoned off an area for the parked aircraft. The six Blue Angels were lined up in a row, the sun glinting off their polished navy-blue fuselages. Behind the rope stood their pilots in matching blue flight suits.

"Hey, Herb!" Dick yelled.

One of the pilots turned, and said, "Dick! Come on over!"

Someone lifted the rope for us. The Blue Angels pilot named Herb, it turned out, was a navy buddy of Dick's. The two men shook hands, and Dick introduced me. I looked up, wondering how Herb could fit inside a cockpit. He looked eight feet tall. A lieutenant's gold double bars were pinned on a foldable khaki cap that sat smartly on his head, and he wore aviator dark glasses.

"You want to sit in the cockpit?" Herb asked me.

I answered quickly before he could change his mind, and he led us down the row of planes. We stopped at the one that had his name painted under the open canopy: "Herb Hunter LT. USN." On the tail was number 3.

A new pilot was now in my life, and I read stories, wherever I found them, about the Blue Angels, always looking for a picture of number 3—which of course became my lucky number—and any reference to Herb

Hunter, who flew with the navy's elite demonstration team for three seasons (1957–1959).*

I joined the navy reserve while still in high school so I could go out to Alameda Naval Air Station for monthly drills and be around airplanes. After a restless year in college, I volunteered for two years of active duty. That is what brought me in June 1965 to the aircraft carrier *Ranger* (CVA-61). And while I was serving aboard ship as a weatherman (aerographer's mate)—taking observations, plotting maps, and launching weather balloons—another pilot came into my life.

Things started off badly for *Ranger* pilot Lieutenant (j.g.) Dieter Dengler, however. He was shot down over Laos; there was a violent crash in the jungle; the wreckage of his plane was found deep in enemy territory but there was no sign of his whereabouts. For long months we heard nothing of him. I well knew that aviators could be lost just that way: falling to the ground or sea, never to be seen or found; no corpse; gone forever; only distant memories for those who knew them. Emotionally, those unfulfilled hopes of finding my lost uncle had followed me to the fleet. And in 1966 off the steamy coast of North Vietnam, there were many pilots who went missing. Most, like Uncle Bob, did not return.

The fate of Dieter Dengler, however, was to be different. Already a legend in the navy for his escape and evasion skills—amply demonstrated during training in the California desert—he would initiate, plan, and lead an organized escape from a POW camp, becoming the longest-held U.S. pilot to escape captivity during the Vietnam War. Caught in a desperate situation, imprisoned not only by the enemy but by the jungle itself, Dengler was impelled not only to get himself out but to help free the other POWs—American, Thai, and Chinese—some of whom had been held for years.

In a surreal scene of brotherhood and celebration, Dengler returned to

---

* On July 19, 1967, I lost my Blue Angels pilot. Commander Herbert P. Hunter, second in command of fighter squadron FV-162 deployed aboard the aircraft carrier *Oriskany* (CVA-34) in the Gulf of Tonkin off North Vietnam—a man who "made piloting a jet plane look effortless"—crash-landed his battle-damaged F-8 Crusader, which plunged off the flight deck into the water. Hunter's lifeless body, attached to his partially deployed parachute, was recovered by a rescue helicopter.

The author aboard *Ranger* off the coast of North
Vietnam in the Gulf of Tonkin, 1966. *Family photograph.*

Ranger six months after being shot down—emaciated, ravaged with several
tropical illnesses but very much alive and joyous to be so—only two weeks
before we were due to leave the Gulf of Tonkin and return home.

True, Dieter Dengler was but one lost pilot and hero found. Yet for his
fellow fliers and shipmates, and for me personally, his story of unending
optimism, innate courage, loyalty, and survival against overwhelming odds
remains our best and brightest memory of our generation's war.

HERO FOUND

1

"BORN A GYPSY"

WARTIME GERMANY

On February 22, 1944, in the Black Forest village of Wildberg, a small peaceful town nestled between rolling green farmlands and wooded mountains, an SS officer in a dove-gray uniform arrived at the home of the widow Maria Dengler and her three young sons. When she came to the door, the officer told her that the fatherland was confiscating her late husband's bookbinding machinery. Metal was so scarce in Germany that residents had been ordered, "under penalty of death," to remove and turn in all brass door hinges, which were to be melted down into shell casings for ammunition.

"You must not take the machines," Maria protested. "One of the children might become a bookbinder."

"I have my orders. A truck will be here in the morning."

Maria said she would be speaking to Wildberg's mayor about the matter. A local *Bürgermeister*, or mayor, held such authority over his township and its residents that the SS officer seemed unsure what to do or say next.

At that moment, the town's air raid siren went off.

"We have to get out!" Maria yelled to her sons.

"Don't worry," said the SS man. "They don't bomb small villages."

Wildberg, Germany, in the 1930s. *Family photograph.*

"We're leaving," said Maria, gathering her boys to her side.

The oldest, Klaus, eight, serious-minded and a loner, showed a bent for academics and music. Dieter, six, a tousled-haired rebel, was always into so much mischief that Maria worried her middle son was "born a Gypsy." The youngest, Martin, four, was a good-natured boy who idolized Dieter and tagged after him.

Maria and her sons ran from the house. She prayed she was doing the right thing to keep them safe, as she had promised Reinhold on his last leave home before he returned to the Russian front. As the drone overhead grew deafening, they ran past the butcher shop and across a narrow bridge, then disappeared into the long shadows of pines and firs. For some time now she had been taking the boys into the dark forest to show them how to survive in case they were ever homeless and on their own. She taught them which wild berries to pick and which mushrooms were safe to eat, how to pick stinging nettles that could be boiled, and how to burrow into the ground at night and cover themselves with branches and leaves for protection from the elements.

The formation of planes appeared as countless black dots stretching from one horizon to the other. Such massive overflights were on the increase as Allied air power hammered Stuttgart, an important German industrial center thirty miles away. Although up to now Wildberg had been spared, sometimes at night distant fires burned so intensely that it was bright enough on the village's unlighted streets to read a newspaper. Today, for the first time, a flight of heavy bombers dropped out of formation and circled overhead.

As the siren wailed, bombs began dropping on the small village which had on its outskirts a glider school where new Luftwaffe pilots were trained.

✪ ✪ ✪

Maria Schnuerle and Reinhold Dengler, ages twenty-eight and thirty-one respectively, were married in 1936. Shy and religious, Maria, the daughter of a baker in Calw—ten miles north of Wildberg—had never been courted. Reinhold, however, had "an eye on her for a long time," as Maria was a member of her church choir, which occasionally visited Wildberg, where he sang in the local choir.

For years, Reinhold had been unable to look for a wife. His father had died when Reinhold, the oldest of four children, was sixteen. On his deathbed, the father asked Reinhold to support his two sisters and brother until they were on their own. That time had arrived—with one sister married, another a schoolteacher, and his brother having completed training as a notary.

One spring day after the church choir from Calw sang in Wildberg, local families were asked to take a visiting choir member home for lunch. To Reinhold's delight, the Denglers hosted the rosy-cheeked blonde he had eyed: Maria, the baker's daughter. After lunch, Reinhold and Maria went for a walk. Along a meandering trail through woods carpeted with wildflowers, he showed off his impressive skills as a gymnast with handstands and backflips.

"Maria Schnuerle, I have something for you," he announced. "This is the first present I can give you."

He pressed into her hand several bright blue forget-me-nots.

An embarrassed Maria smiled, although she wondered if the dashing Reinhold Dengler "talked to all the girls" in such a pleasing manner.

Reinhold was a man of many talents. He had taught himself the book-binding business and photography, and he was also a skilled artist who created detailed landscapes in pencil and water colors. He was admired by those who knew him for his kindness, creativity, and devotion to family.

The couple made a plan to meet midway between Calw and Wildberg the following Sunday. They both bicycled to the rendezvous, and after pedaling for a couple of miles they left their bikes inside a small factory and walked along a well-worn path. That afternoon they encountered numerous passersby, most of whom greeted Reinhold warmly. Maria was struck by how many people knew her suitor and how well liked he seemed to be.

After a while, Reinhold said, "Maria, I have to say something to you."

"What is it, Reinhold?"

"I want you to be my wife."

Surprised and overwhelmed, Maria did not immediately respond.

Reinhold was undeterred. "When you get home, I want you to tell your mother and father about our walk today. Tell them that I would like to meet them next Friday. I will come to your house."

When Maria delivered the message, her father was outraged. "Who the hell does he think he is, coming into the family like that?" He sat down and wrote a stern letter to Reinhold, rejecting the idea of a family visit.

Hermann Schnuerle the baker was a famously stubborn and principled man. Although he was a member of Calw's town council, he had refused to vote in the 1934 plebiscite that served as a referendum for Adolf Hitler. Nationwide, 95 percent of all registered voters had gone to the polls, and 90 percent of them had approved of Hitler becoming the *Führer*. The baker's wife and others beseeched Hermann to go to the town hall and at least give the appearance of voting. He refused, explaining that he believed Germany was headed in the wrong direction and that Hitler was not the man to lead it. Later that day a group of men came for Hermann, telling him to accompany them to the town hall. After they rounded the first corner they tied his hands and hung around his neck a placard declaring him to be a traitor. Marched through town in a solemn parade, Hermann was cursed and spat upon by some of the same people who came to his shop every morning for his fresh bread. Many thought the baker would simply disappear. Instead, he was sent for more than a year to a "rock refinery where they cut rocks." When he returned home to his family and baking business, he was steeled rather than broken by the ordeal.

When Hermann read his letter to Maria and her mother, Maria said, "Now I have something to tell you. Reinhold was sixteen when his father died and he had to support his family. He is thirty-one now. Many people know him. He is liked and admired. He is a good man and a hard worker. He is a bookbinder and photographer, and people from as far away as Hamburg hire him."

Her father tore up the letter and wrote a new one, telling Reinhold Dengler, "Since I only hear wonderful things about you we are looking forward to meeting you next Friday." Reinhold made his visit, and won over Maria's family: not only her father, but also her mother and siblings, including her brothers, Harold and Theo. Maria and Reinhold's wedding soon followed.

Three years later, in 1939, Reinhold was drafted into the German army and went away for a year. When he came home on leave, he told Maria he was in charge of a library in Poland, and for her not to worry, as he was out of danger. "I'm not fighting," he explained, "and nobody bothers me." But as the war continued and the situation grew more desperate, Reinhold did become involved in the fighting. When he returned home in the summer of 1943 on his last leave, Reinhold told Maria that Germany was losing the war. She was shocked, since the only news the civilian population received told of great victories for Germany and crushing defeats for the Allies. "I may not be back," he said frankly. Reinhold made out his will. Expecting difficult times ahead—including food shortages—he implored Maria not to "tie the boys to her apron" but rather to teach them self-sufficiency. Near the end of his leave, he told Maria, "Let's take a picture. It will probably be the last one we have of us." That winter, Reinhold's prophecy came true when the Soviet Union recaptured Kiev in the Ukraine and pushed the Germans into retreat. Reinhold was killed when his bunker was hit by an exploding grenade. He was thirty-eight years old.

Reinhold Dengler. *Family photograph*

After receiving notification of Reinhold's death, Maria proclaimed her life "now in God's hands." She kept her pledge to Reinhold to show their sons how to survive on their own, but she believed that whatever happened to her and the boys was preordained by God. In an opposite reaction, Maria's brother Theo, who had come to love Reinhold like his own brother, threw away his Bible because "there cannot be a God if a man like Reinhold is killed."

The war came to Wildberg not long afterward. At the precise moment it arrived, Dieter and Martin were at home, peering out a third-story window. A single-engine fighter with a big white star on its fuselage swept so low and so close to the house that the boys could see the pilot in the cockpit. The canopy was open, and they clearly saw the pilot's goggles atop his head and the white scarf around his neck. The plane roared past, aiming for the train station down the hill, its loud guns spitting out yellow flashes. The aircraft then pulled up abruptly in a steep climbing turn, and was gone as quickly as it had appeared.

For Dieter, the close encounter would be unforgettable and life altering. He had never seen anything so exciting. Not at all fearful, he had been mesmerized by the flying machine that soared above the earth with the freedom of a bird. Years later he would describe it as "like an Almighty Being that came out of the sky." He decided then and there that he would grow up to fly a plane just like that one. From then on, he later explained, "little Dieter needed to fly."

Attacking Allied planes would return on other days, making quick low passes over the town's train station. Railroad workers learned to keep only the older locomotives on the tracks, while parking the newer rolling stock inside a nearby tunnel. The children came to regard the flyovers more as amusement than as danger, for they lasted such a short time and inflicted no casualties or damage on homes and shops. Before the smoke and dust cleared, older boys would be eagerly running along the railroad tracks picking up spent bullets, and, if they were really lucky, "an entire cartridge belt to wear proudly."

For the youth of Wildberg, their enjoyment would be short-lived.

Maria and her sons neared the top of a steep hill when the "ground erupted." Never before had they heard the high-pitched whistling sound of bombs dropping or the "deafening booms from their explosions." They scrambled under the cover of old, fallen timber, and hugged the ground. Covering their ears, they prayed as the earth shook beneath them.

They did not emerge until after the bombers were gone. When they did they looked anxiously in the direction of Wildberg but could not make out anything through the dense foliage. All around them was silence, not even the chirping of a sparrow. On their way back they met a group of armed men with leashed German shepherds. They said they were looking for an enemy pilot who had landed nearby in a parachute, and asked Maria if she had seen anyone. Maria said no, and hurried on with her boys.

As Maria and her sons left the woods, they entered a sunlit meadow where they came upon a stunned villager standing with two tethered cows. "Everything is gone," said the woman. "Everything."

At the outskirts of Wildberg, the first dead bodies they saw were those of horses and cows lying stiffly on their sides or backs. The heat and smoke grew intense as they entered town. Many structures were flattened and in cinders; others were ablaze, including the shoe repair shop, which filled the air with the pungent smell of burning leather. Wildberg's seventeenth-century castle had burned to the ground, and the village church and school were also destroyed, as were rows of houses and shops.

Maria and her sons realized with horror that the debris on the ground included arms, legs, heads, and other human body parts. They dared not look closely for fear of recognizing the remains of friends and neighbors.

Turning a corner, they were surprised to see in the distance that their home was still standing, although the houses on either side were gone.

Their next-door neighbor Mrs. Bohler had been visiting a friend in the hospital when the bombs fell. She had hurried home to find her husband and nine children dead. Her husband—still with binoculars around his neck—and the children had been outside watching the planes fly over.

As they came closer, Maria saw that the wooden frame of their house was intact but most of the plaster walls were gone. Pieces of their tile roof lay across the street. Although the house was uninhabitable, Maria declared it "God's gift" that there was no fire. Unlike many residents, who had lost their worldly goods, the Denglers were able to recover most of their belongings, although everything had "a million pieces of glass in it." White-hot shrapnel had ripped through the house, singeing fist-size holes in furnishings and clothing. Digging through the rubble, the three boys dropped down into the pitch-black cellar and retrieved most of the remaining canned goods their mother had put up.

Looting had begun, with townsfolk who had lost their homes and belongings scavenging through wrecked and deserted structures whose owners were gone, taking food, clothing, blankets, tools, and utensils.

Finding a working phone, Maria called her parents. Upon hearing that their home and most of Wildberg had been destroyed, her mother said, "You and the boys are welcome here." A plan was made for Maria's brother Theo, who was home from the army on medical leave, to come to Wildberg to help with the move to Calw. The next day, Theo showed up in a horse-drawn wagon.

The Schnuerles were already feeding and housing more than a dozen relatives and friends, including several Jews, such as Mrs. Hess, who was fearful of being "resettled" after her Swiss husband was drafted into the army. Although Hermann and his family did not suspect the ghastliness of Hitler's Jewish plan, they knew that Jews in Calw—such as the butcher, who had owned his own shop that was now boarded up—had disappeared. Having once been forcibly taken from his own home, Hermann did not hesitate to help others.

Maria Dengler with her three sons, 1942. Right to left: Dieter, Martin, and Klaus. *Family photograph.*

A year passed, and before all the wildflowers of the Black Forest bloomed that final spring of the Third Reich, the war in Europe was over. The German economy went into free fall. With store shelves empty, hungry people canvassed the countryside, going from farm to farm trading their silver, Persian carpets, and other heirlooms for eggs, milk, and potatoes.

For many German civilians—mostly women, children, and the elderly, as men between eighteen and fifty years old were scarce—the Allies' occupation of their homeland meant a fight for survival far worse than any they had endured during the war years. The next two winters were bitterly cold. With so many houses damaged or destroyed, there was inadequate shelter, and there were shortages of coal and food. Many people starved or froze to death.

Under the Allies' division of occupied Germany, the southwest corner of the defeated country—where Calw was located—was in the French zone. It was not long before the residents of Calw met their occupiers: the rugged Moroccan Goumiers, who carried long daggers in their belts and were frightening in appearance and by reputation. In the final weeks of the war, the Moroccans had breached the fortified Siegfried Line and fought their way through the Black Forest all the way to the Austrian border. They specialized in night raids and were also used to man the front lines in mountainous and other rough terrain. With the spoils of war in mind, these wild and fearless combat veterans arrived in Calw "like a conquering army."

Young Dieter would never forget the first time he saw the Moroccans. He was standing at his mother's side in his grandfather's bakery, "wide-eyed and scared," when three of the hardened fighters, wearing turbans and striped cloaks, entered with axes and commenced to smash open storage bins, cabinets, and closets, taking anything they fancied. When they left, his grandfather hurried everyone into the cellar where he stored potatoes and made cider. They sat silently on crates and barrels stacked against earthen walls, the only light coming from a single candle. Suddenly, the door flew open and several Moroccans rushed inside. Looking over the huddled group, they chose Maria's younger sister and another woman hiding with the family, and hauled them away, leaving Maria with her three boys clinging to her. In a while the two women returned to the cellar, weeping but saying nothing about their ordeal.

A postwar routine soon descended over Calw and its 20,000 residents. A contingent of Moroccans moved into an empty schoolhouse next to Hermann's bakery. The soldiers required the local women to do their laundry, and Hermann was forced to bake for the occupiers, who supplied him with the necessary ingredients that for a time were difficult to obtain. Hermann, whose ancestors had been bakers since 1620, managed to skim some yeast, flour, and butter for his own baking.

Once a week, Maria bicycled into the countryside to trade small packets of yeast to farmers for food and produce. This type of private bartering with farmers was forbidden by new statutes put in place by the occupational forces. Maria, however, felt she had no choice; the family had to eat. Occasionally, she returned with an old, bony hen killed because it had stopped laying eggs. From the scrawny carcass she made a thin gruel that lasted for days.

Maria's two younger sons joined in the hunt for food, while the oldest, studious Klaus, was content to stay home with his books or practice the violin, which he would play for so many hours that his chafed neck would bleed. When it was apple season, Dieter and Martin rose before dawn. Although the new laws made it a serious offense to pick fruit from someone else's trees, it was permissible to take anything on the ground that rolled onto public property. By sleight of hand, the boys made sure some fruit went "rolling down the street." They also went into the woods to pick wild berries and mushrooms. Whenever they returned with food, they would be followed next time by "a herd of people" they would try to lose in the forest. "Martin, you go left and I'll go right," Dieter would order. "We'll meet where we found the berries."

Dieter curried favor with the Moroccans by delivering their laundry and running other errands. When the soldiers lined up for noontime chow, Dieter would squeeze through the smelly, jabbering foreigners and hold out an empty container toward the man with the ladle, who filled whatever was placed in front of him. Dieter took the soup home; his mother thinned it in order to feed more people. Once in a while she had a fresh egg to add—one egg stirred in the pot for a dozen people, and a treat for all.

Dieter watched whenever the Moroccans brought in sheep from the fields for slaughter. They first struck a bayonet in the sheep's throat, and after it slowly bled to death they beat the carcass with sticks prior to skinning it. They then cut up the carcass, throwing the heart, liver, and entrails into the bushes. Instantly, there would be kids coming out from all directions scrambling for the scraps. Whether the prizes were won by speed or fisticuffs, Dieter usually ended up with something, which he took home to his mother to cook. She also cooked wallpaper Dieter tore from bombed buildings, for the "nutrients in the glue."

As Dieter became an inventive scrounger, he found himself in trouble much of the time—for stealing, trespassing, truancy, fighting, and missing curfew. Growing into the Gypsy that his mother had feared, Dieter was "the most difficult" of her three boys. To punish him, she struck his backside with a rubber hose. Dieter took the blows stoically from the mother he loved, but he could not always find it in him to behave.

Gradually, conditions improved as the Marshall Plan went into effect. Each morning the children were lined up and given a cup of watery hot chocolate and a slice of bread, and once a week they were given a Hershey bar. The first time links of sausage reappeared in a butcher shop display window, Dieter stopped and stared. So did other passersby, although few could afford to buy any. For two years, until surplus clothing was distributed, Dieter wore the same pair of shorts his mother made from an old flag, and—when not barefoot—shoes with holes in the sole. "Cold and hungry" is how he would recall those years, his "first lesson in survival."

If those years in postwar Germany were about surviving, Dieter also flourished. He was the first boy in the neighborhood to have his own bicycle, which he built himself. He found the frame at the dump, bartered for one tire here and another there, and fashioned a seat out of a small pillow. During those years Dieter became a leader, too. It was a role that came naturally from his being capable and enterprising, as well as tough and never backing down. His brother Martin recognized that although Dieter was not always the most skilled fighter, he would "never give up or be defeated." By his early teens, Dieter was "always the leader," and had his own gang—one of two in Calw, each with more than 100 members. The gangs fought to defend their turf, divided by the Nagold River that ran through town. To his followers, including Martin, Dieter, fiercely loyal to friends, was "the hero of Calw" with "nothing getting past him." To Martin, Dieter "ran the town" and was "a hero to a lot of kids."

Martin wanted to grow up to "drive railroad trains," but he was selected at age five to become a baker and take over his grandfather's shop one day. As for Dieter, Maria signed him up at age fourteen, following four years of middle school and after he flunked the entrance test for high school, for an apprenticeship to a blacksmith and tool and die maker known as a stern taskmaster. She felt her middle son would benefit from a strong male figure in his life.

The blacksmith, Mr. Perrot, was not only strong but cruel as well. With "calloused hands that were accustomed to forging metal on an anvil" all day, he beat Dieter and the dozen other boys under his tutelage—sometimes bare-fisted, at other times with a metal rod across the back. Six days a week from morning till dark they labored, building gigantic clocks and faceplates for cathedrals across Germany. The boys did so mostly for the experience, as they received only the equivalent of $2 a month. Dieter worked some nights in a butcher shop, his only remuneration being the quantities of smoked bratwurst he could stuff down while working, and a bag of sausage ends to take home to his mother.

When Dieter was sixteen, an American bookmobile came to town. Browsing through a flying magazine, Dieter spotted an advertisement with a young man wearing wings on his chest standing next to a new airplane. Dieter's dream of flying had not diminished over the years, and the picture struck a chord. The ad read: "We Need Men to Fly These Planes." There was a coupon to tear out and send in, which Dieter did. It came back with information about how the U.S. military was training young men to fly. With both military and civilian aviation all but nonexistent in postwar Germany, Dieter decided the only way he could become a pilot was to go to America.

Not long afterward, when an in-law from New Jersey arrived for a visit, Dieter found a way to sit next to her at a banquet in her honor. In spite of being "interrupted a hundred times by everyone wanting to impress her or looking for a handout," he managed to tell her, in his fractured English (English was taught in German schools after the war), of his hope to come to America to fly planes. Taken with the charming youth with big ideas, Aunt Clara, a fortyish widow who had been married to the brother of Dieter's grandmother, volunteered to be his official sponsor. She suggested he work on improving his English. Also, he would have to pay for his steamship ticket. At the time, the lowest-class one-way fare to New York was $520—a fortune to Dieter.

It wasn't long before Dieter had a plan. Scrap metal was in short supply and brought a good price. He became a round-the-clock scavenger, collecting brass, lead, and other valuable metals wherever he found them. The blacksmith had a collection of old brass wheels in the attic of his shop and didn't seem to miss an occasional one. When Mr. Perrot wasn't looking, Dieter would toss a wheel into the river that ran next to the shop, then retrieve it late at night by wading in knee-deep water and feeling around for the treasure. He found the roofline of churches a good source of ornamental brass, which he snipped away under the cover of darkness. The phone company was laying lead-coated underground cable throughout the area; he'd sneak into a supply yard at night and unroll a portion that wouldn't be missed. Most of the pilfered materials he sold to an unscrupulous dealer in another village. For the first time in his life, Dieter made real money, and saved it for his steamship fare. Taking Aunt Clara's advice, he found an old soldier, a retired *Wehrmacht* general, willing to tutor him in English.

When he turned eighteen, Dieter received in the mail information about gaining entry to the United States, and was given a date to appear for an interview at the American consulate in Munich, 150 miles away. Wearing an old double-breasted suit of his grandfather's, Dieter set out hitchhiking for Munich the day before he was due at the consulate.

The immensity of Germany's third-largest city, which had 1 million residents, amazed Dieter. Heavily damaged by Allied bombing during the war, Munich had been completely rebuilt, preserving its prewar street grid. New low-slung modern buildings that looked out of place on grand royal avenues stood alongside magnificent nineteenth-century structures that had miraculously been spared.

Dieter arrived at the consulate several hours before dawn. It was winter, and the temperature had dropped overnight to below freezing. Sitting on the icy steps of the consulate waiting for it to open, he "nearly froze to death." Eventually, a group of employees arrived, among them a tall, bald man with the key to the front door. He looked down at the shivering Dieter with something akin to disapproval. Dieter followed behind them into a hall with a high ceiling, and went to the men's room to try to make himself look more presentable. Later, when Dieter's name was called, the tall man turned out to be the consular official who would interview him. After the man solemnly shook hands with him, Dieter eagerly began talking. When he said that he would soon finish an apprenticeship with a tool and die maker, the official became interested. "America needs craftsmen," he said. Smiling at last, he added that Dieter must be serious if he would sit outside the consulate "all night long" in the freezing cold waiting for his appointment. Dieter decided not to admit that he had no extra money to spend on a hotel, as he still had to pay off the balance of his steamship ticket after putting down a deposit. The rest of the day Dieter spent filling out numerous forms and taking a physical examination.

Back home, Dieter returned to Mr. Perrot's shop to finish his training before being permitted to take his final test. On the appointed day, he was grilled for nearly two hours by a panel of eight judges—headed by Mr.

Perrot—that included a master carpenter, a metalsmith, and other trades-men. He was asked about the qualities of zinc, copper, lead, steel, and other metals, as well as the use of various tools. Then, he was handed an intricate blueprint to follow at the lathe. When he finished, they examined his work. Asked not a single question about it, he was dismissed. Dieter left convinced he had flunked, an outcome that he had no doubt would have been the doing of his boss. Flunking the final test normally meant having to do another year as an apprentice—another year that Mr. Perrot would have him for "slave labor." Dieter, however, had other plans. Heading home, he bade his family farewell. Strapping on his backpack, which was already filled with everything he was taking, he grabbed his official documents and set out to hitchhike 400 miles to Bremerhaven, the North Sea port from which his ship would depart for America. He had already sold all his possessions, including his homemade skis, a newer bicycle he had built, and a kayak he had picked up in trade. In fact, Dieter sold the kayak "three times to three different people," all of whom showed up to retrieve it after he left.

Residents of Calw—the birthplace of the novelist and Nobel laureate Hermann Hesse, who had apprenticed years earlier in the same blacksmith shop for Mr. Perrot's brutally abusive father and used the experience as material for his book *Beneath the Wheel*—were in agreement that the cagey and charismatic Dieter Dengler would grow up to be either very successful and rich, or "the biggest gangster ever" and in prison.

2

AMERICA

For three weeks Dieter passed the time in Bremerhaven, lingering near the docks while he awaited the arrival of his ship. He slept in empty cargo crates and ate green bananas and other perishables that fell off the conveyor belts snaking from the holds of cargo ships. He also scavenged for edible leftovers in garbage cans behind waterfront restaurants. Having been assured by the shipping line that all the food he could eat was included in the price of his passage, he couldn't wait to get a decent meal aboard ship.

When the ocean liner SS *America* arrived, being pushed dockside by a cast of tugboats, its great size was beyond belief to the young man from the Black Forest. The 33,000-ton vessel was longer than a city block—more than 700 feet from bow to stern. Built in 1939 to carry 1,200 passengers in three distinct and separate classes (cabin, tourist, and third class), with a crew of 640, *America* had been converted to a troopship during World War II. Converted after the war to again carry civilian passengers, and painted in the iconic red, white, and blue of the prestigious United States Lines— even on the two finned smokestacks designed to minimize wind resistance in gales—*America* was the most graceful and well-appointed liner flying the U.S. flag.

Dieter watched in awe as the passengers filed down gangplanks, many of the men dressed in fine suits and the women in fancy dresses and feathery hats. Gleaming Cadillacs and Lincolns were hoisted from a forward cargo hold onto the pier, where well-heeled passengers waited to drive away.

When he finally boarded the ship for its return run from Bremerhaven to New York—with port calls at Le Havre, France, and Cobh, Ireland—Dieter was ecstatic about his future. As the mooring lines were released and the ship inched slowly away, a band on deck played *"Auf Wiedersehen."* Friends and relatives on the ship and pier waved tearful good-byes. The song beseeched travelers not to stay away too long, but Dieter "had news for them." He didn't want to come back. For him, an "era had come to an end," and he knew it. Nobody on the pier was waving good-bye to him, and he was ready for his adventure in America.

Compartments for third-class passengers were located in the bow section of the ship, where the motion at sea was most pronounced. Dieter was assigned to a room with three other men, and his first food aboard ship was a "strange American hot dog" on a bun with only ketchup. Not long afterward, when the ship hit the choppy waters of the North Sea, Dieter became seasick. He couldn't eat much after that—missing out on those all-you-can-eat meals he had so looked forward to. Miserable, he mostly stayed in the room "heaving for ten days." Occasionally, he dragged himself to the dining salon so he could bring back fruit and sandwiches. He marveled at the bowl of oranges kept filled on the table to which he was assigned. He had usually seen an orange only at Christmas in his stocking, along with cookies and a new pair of socks knitted by his mother. Although he was able to eat very little, he was unwilling to waste food, and hoarded what he could like a squirrel preparing for an early winter.

At four o'clock in the morning on May 12, 1957, passengers awoke as word spread that the Statue of Liberty would soon be in view. Although still weak, Dieter went topside on wobbly legs and joined a crowd at the railing. And then, "the most beautiful sight" he had ever seen appeared in the morning mist. Here, at the gateway to America, it did not escape Dieter that Lady Liberty's radiating torch was pointed in the direction he wished to go: skyward.

Back in his room, he put on a long shirt that had been his grandfather's. Keeping the tail out, he tied a length of string around his thighs, and filled the shirt with his collected foods. He slipped on a German army overcoat to conceal his stash. Grabbing his backpack, he went up on deck to stand in the long line for U.S. customs and immigration, which had set up processing stations on deck. When he finally made it to the front of the line, a customs official checked his documents. Looking hard at Dieter, the official yanked on his bulging shirt. All the fruit and sandwiches spilled out.

Everyone started laughing, and Dieter turned beet red.

He thought about the people back home who had laughed at his plan to go to America and become a pilot. Nobody lived such childish dreams in such difficult times. He had been selected and trained to be a tool and die maker, and that's what he was supposed to do. "You'll end up dead or in jail," one hometown skeptic had warned him.

Dieter was sure that a U.S. jail was exactly where he was now headed.

"No food allowed," said the official, waving Dieter on.

When he was finally off the ship, Dieter entered a "whole new world" filled with masses of people, porters, buses, trains, and taxis. He wandered until he found Aunt Clara—waiting with other sponsors in a large building—under the letter D. Off they went to New Jersey in her big car, which to Dieter's astonishment had windows that went up and down when a switch was pressed. Driving through a tunnel, Aunt Clara explained they were underwater, and that his ship had recently passed overhead. It was incomprehensible to Dieter.

One of the papers he had signed at the consulate in Munich directed him to report within ten days to a selective service office to register for the draft, required of foreign males between the ages of eighteen and twenty-six living in the United States. Dieter did so a week later in Elizabeth, New Jersey. He was processed as 1A—available for unrestricted military service. A short time later, in nearby Newark, he walked into a U.S. Air Force recruiting station with wall-to-wall posters of military aircraft in flight. Years later, Dieter well remembered the question he asked that day, and the answer he received.

"Will I be able to learn how to fly?"

"You will, son. You'll go to flight training in Texas."

That sounded fine to Dieter. He took the test, passed, and signed up as of June 7, 1957—twenty-six days after stepping off the ship from Germany.

No one told him that only officers became pilots in the air force, and to be an officer you had to go to college. Dieter entered the air force as the lowest-rank enlisted man—pay grade E1—on a four-year enlistment.

A few weeks later he took his first airplane ride: a charter flight with other recruits to Lackland Air Force Base in San Antonio, Texas. They arrived in July, in boiling heat, for basic training. That was as close to flying a plane as Dieter would get as an enlisted man in the U.S. Air Force.

By the time basic training ended, Dieter knew he had been "conned" and there would be no flight training for him; he also knew that there was "no way out." After a lengthy period in which he worked in the mess hall peeling potatoes, he was assigned to the motor pool at Turner Air Force Base in Albany, Georgia. He spent nearly two years washing cars and changing tires in the Peach State but "never saw a peach orchard." In Georgia, Dieter borrowed an officer's flight suit and posed in front of an air force jet for some "deceiving pictures," which he mailed to Germany. The skeptics there had been right: he was not flying planes in America. But he was not going to let them know that, because he had no intention of giving up his dream.

After two years Dieter was transferred back to Lackland, where he became a driver in the motor pool. After passing his high school equivalency test and receiving his GED, Dieter registered at a local community college, San Antonio College, and took several night classes, including introductory algebra. He was delighted to receive a B in algebra, since he had little math background. He next took college algebra, basic English, and history. He applied for citizenship and passed the test. He held up his right hand and was administered the Oath of Allegiance to the United States in a San Antonio courtroom packed with other new U.S. citizens from around the world.

At the behest of General Curtis E. LeMay, who believed that "every airman should be capable of defending himself and his country with small arms," the U.S. Air Force Marksmanship School was established at Lackland in 1958. LeMay, then the vice chief of staff of the air force, believed that its small-arms training was inadequate, and wanted a program to improve marksmanship. Initially, seven officers and twenty enlisted men were assigned to the school, among them the best competitive pistol and rifle shooters in the air force. A twelve-week course was developed to train new instructors who would return to their own bases and teach shooting to combat aircrews and security personnel.

In 1959, there was a search for airmen with shooting or gunsmithing experience to join the staff of the marksmanship school. Because of his training in tool and die making, Dieter was transferred to the school and assigned to the gunsmith shop for on-the-job training with firearms. He learned about the muzzle velocity of various types of rounds, their maximum range, and how to strip and reassemble firearms, and he was soon maintaining and repairing all types of standard and modified handguns and rifles. He found himself "surrounded by shooters in an organization dedicated to shooting," including one instructor (Frank Tossas) who became the first air force rifleman to fire a perfect score over the National Match Course, and another (Frank Green) who would go on to win a silver medal in shooting at the 1964 Olympics. All personnel assigned to the school were "allowed and encouraged to shoot," not only on the practice range but on teams that traveled to various matches. Dieter learned the techniques of great shooters, including controlled breathing, consistent aim, and trigger control—squeezing rather than pulling a trigger. By the time he was honorably discharged from the Air Force in 1961, Dieter was a skilled marksman.

Dieter headed for California in his 1938 Plymouth, which he painted fire-engine red with surplus paint given to him by the fire department. Unable to save anything on his pay of $72 a month, he camped along the way because he could not afford motels. He drove to San Francisco, where his younger brother, Martin, was living after coming to the United States a year after Dieter. Martin was a journeyman baker by then, and attending college.

To most people, Dieter and Martin sounded alike—their accented English was indistinguishable, seeming to come from the same source. Physically, however, the brothers were not alike. Dieter was lanky; five feet nine inches tall and weighing 150 pounds. Martin was two inches shorter and stockier. If they had played high school sports, Dieter would have been on the soccer team, and Martin on the football team. What one got with Dieter was lightness and quickness—sometimes in all directions at once—while Martin showed sturdiness and reliability. Both brothers had a fair complexion, light brown hair, and brown eyes; in Dieter, the eyes twinkled with mischief.

The brothers, who had grown up sharing a bedroom, were again roommates. For a time, Dieter sold advertising space for a magazine, then shoes; he took a string of other jobs to make ends meet. He enrolled at City College of San Francisco, where Martin was a student. When it was time to study, however, Dieter was "more interested in going to the beach with the California girls." In his first semester—spring 1961—he had a B-minus average for 12 units, but in the fall he flunked elementary French (even though he had taken French in middle school) and received a D in a business course and a C in intermediate algebra. It was no coincidence that he applied himself and received his highest grade in a course that would be helpful for piloting a plane: air navigation, an astronomy course, in which he received a B.

Dieter had a new plan for becoming a pilot. He had learned about the Naval Aviation Cadet (NAVCAD) program, which required an associate of arts degree. After that, upon completing more than a year of intense training—including learning to fly—he would be a commissioned officer and naval aviator. He now set his sights on graduating with a two-year degree.

Like most college students, Dieter also enjoyed himself, dating a bevy of girls and partying with Martin and lots of new buddies. There were surfing trips to nearby Santa Cruz and skiing trips to Lake Tahoe—a five-hour drive in an old VW van Dieter bought for $185 and kept running, thanks to his days in the motor pool. Everything was done on limited funds. Most of the time Dieter didn't have any money, and on those occasions when he did have cash he was too frugal to spend much. Before leaving home to go skiing, Dieter would wedge in, next to the engine, a couple of cans of Skippy dog food. When he arrived at the ski resort, he would park, raise the hood, and stand in the parking lot enjoying a hot meal before hitting the slopes. Dieter thought that with enough ketchup, Skippy tasted "like corned-beef hash." Among his friends, he soon earned a reputation as an "indiscriminate eater."

Rather than spend money on his clothing, Dieter collected unclaimed clothes left in classrooms, at the gym, on park benches, and at bus stops. Some days he returned home with a couple of shirts and a pair or two of pants or shorts. One Christmas, Martin wanted to buy Dieter new slacks and decided to confirm his size. In Dieter's closet were pants with waists ranging from twenty-eight to thirty-six inches.

When it came to car maintenance, Dieter could do it all, including rebuilding an engine or transmission. Certain items that had to be acquired from time to time, however, weren't always within Dieter's budget. He kept a can of spray paint that matched the blue-gray of his van. When he couldn't afford a new tire, he would take a cruise through neighborhoods at night looking for another VW. When he found one parked, he would jump out, remove a wheel from the other VW, and swap it for his own wheel with the worn tire. Then he would spray the new rim his color and drive away. It was the kind of scavenging he had often done in Germany. Dieter looked on it more as a form of barter than as thievery. After all, he gave up his own wheel and tire in trade.

Martin accompanied Dieter on many skiing, hunting, and fishing trips. At all three sports, Dieter excelled. Martin was especially impressed by Dieter's new proficiency with high-powered firearms—the only gun he had fired in Germany was an old BB gun—observing with his own eyes that his brother was a "fantastic shot." When they went to a rifle range in Pacifica, south of San Francisco, Dieter caused the gong to go off repeatedly by hitting the bull's-eye 300 yards away. Precision marksmanship combined with his outdoor experience made Dieter a great hunter. Too, when anyone downed game, he was ready with a sharpened hunting knife to do the cleaning, skinning, and butchering—skills he had learned working for the butcher in Calw. The brothers loved camping together. Harking back to their childhood days in the Black Forest, they often "played survival games." Dieter would set traps, using string, hooks, and bent branches to snare small game as their mother had taught them years earlier. They would soon be roasting rabbit or other wild game on a spit over a roaring fire. Then there were the wilderness scenarios on which Dieter would constantly challenge Martin. "Martin, what would you do if a bear came in from that direction?" Or: "People are chasing us, Martin. What do we do?" One time while skiing at Squaw Valley, Dieter dug himself into the snow and had Martin bury him up to his neck. It was an exercise to see how quickly he could get out of an avalanche, Dieter explained. Then he went to work extracting himself.

The brothers could disagree, and even fought, although when they were growing up it had always been Dieter who imposed his will on Martin. Their biggest fight as adults—a real donnybrook—was over a prized ski sweater from Switzerland that belonged to Martin. Seeing a sweater that looked like his on a girl at City College, Martin asked where she got it. "From Dieter Dengler for my birthday," she said. After years of submitting to Dieter, Martin drew the line. He came home furious, and the brothers argued. Martin gathered all his clothes from Dieter's room and was heading down the hallway when Dieter charged from the opposite direction. "This must be yours, too," Dieter said, throwing a wadded-up shirt in Martin's face. Martin dropped the clothes, and the fight was on. They grappled in the hallway, down some stairs, and through the house. Martin, who was a college wrestler, frustrated Dieter with his quickness and holds, and they fought to a draw, both left cut and bloodied.

Notwithstanding their fisticuffs, either brother would defend the other. Late one night, they were sitting in a pizza joint in San Francisco when a group of young men walked in. One of them, whom Martin recognized as a former boxer at Lincoln High School, had on a red-and-white beanie. A smiling Dieter said, "I like your hat," to which the wise guy responded, "If you want it why don't you take it?" Accepting the invitation, Dieter stood up to do so. Martin reached the guy first, and in a flash took the guy's hat off his head. The boxer swung. Martin ducked and drove for his legs, taking him down hard. One of the boxer's friends jumped forward to help, but found he had his hands full with Dieter. The fight lasted until four policemen broke it up. Dieter and Martin were placed in a paddy wagon to go to the station and be booked.

At that point, Dieter decided to fake a heart attack. He did it so convincingly that Martin thought his brother was dying until Dieter squeezed his hand. The policemen "got really scared" by Dieter's loud groans, his wild gyrations, and the spittle drooling from his mouth. They called an ambulance and began pumping Dieter's chest. By the time the paramedics arrived, the cops had forgotten all about booking anyone. Dieter was transferred to the ambulance and Martin was allowed to accompany him. When they reached the hospital emergency room, Dieter stood up, said he was feeling much better, thanked the paramedics, and, with Martin at his side, strolled out of the hospital. "If they had booked me," Dieter told his brother, "I would never become a navy pilot."

Dieter and Martin decided to join a fraternity. They both went through various initiations and humiliations, including being taken, in the middle of the night, to some surrounding hills and ordered to strip and be at school by 7:00 A.M. Dieter went through it all until one day at the fraternity house when he was doing push-ups as ordered by two frat brothers. With one of them standing on each side of him, they simultaneously jerked his arms out from under him, causing him to fall flat on his face. "More push-ups!" one of them yelled. Dieter came off the floor like an enraged bull, slugging both the frat boys. "Don't *ever* do that again," Dieter said. "I want to be in your club but don't be stupid with me." With that, Dieter dropped to the floor for more push-ups. By the time of the pinning ceremony a few weeks later, Dieter had changed his mind. Although Martin stayed for his fraternity pin, Dieter announced to the group, before walking out, "I've been watching you guys. You have no idea what life is about. You're all just out of high school. I don't want to be part of your club or be around you guys. And I don't want to pay thirty-five dollars to join."

After a year at City College, Dieter hit a stumbling block of his own making. Although he had already passed the mathematics examination required for graduation, Dieter feared he would not pass the required English exam. Having come to the United States as an adult with limited exposure to English, Dieter would always speak, write, and think best in German. Yet this exam covering English grammar and spelling was a requirement for a two-year degree. Learning that Martin was scheduled to take the English test first, Dieter asked a favor: after he filled out his answer sheet, could Martin smuggle out the test?

Martin knew all about Dieter's propensity to get what he wanted with little regard for rules, tradition, or, at times, consideration of others. Martin did not make excuses for Dieter's ways or methods, although he understood where they came from. In fact, having experienced a childhood in the poverty of postwar Germany, Martin had some similar tendencies, like splicing into a neighbor's cable for television and radio reception and being caught only when the other guy reported reception problems. Together in San Francisco, he and Dieter climbed telephone poles and "dropped wires down" in order to make free calls to Germany and elsewhere.

Indisputably, Dieter's daring and calculating ways had helped the family eat and survive in desperate times. To Martin, Dieter was still the hero of Calw. More than once Dieter had saved Martin's hide, sometimes by reputation alone. When Martin was pounced on by a gang of toughs ten miles from home, they stopped when he hollered, "My brother is Dieter!" In a real sense, Martin, even in adulthood, was continuing to try to repay his older brother for being there for him throughout the years.

So, Martin smuggled out the English test and gave it to Dieter.

Dieter went into the examination room having memorized the multiple-choice answers to each question on the standardized test. The only problem was that he was given a different test, which he of course flunked. Told that he could retake the exam until he passed it, Dieter came back the following week. When he was handed the test, he said helpfully, "This is the same one I took last week." The monitor thanked him for his honesty, and handed him another test form—the version that Dieter had memorized.

The first one called into the dean's office was Martin. Although there was no question in anyone's mind that Martin had legitimately passed the test, the monitor had reported one copy of the test missing after the session. Then, oddly enough, his brother Dieter went from "flunking to 100 percent correct," said the dean. The dean went on to say that he liked Martin, and hoped that he would tell the truth because it would be a shame for him to be kicked out of school. Martin told the truth, and went home and told Dieter to do the same. When it was his turn before the dean, Dieter was given a choice: withdraw voluntarily, or be expelled for cheating. Dieter took the out he was offered. His official record noted: "Honorable Dismissal Granted."

Dieter enrolled the following semester at College of San Mateo, twenty miles south of San Francisco. The only two-year college in the area that offered a degree in aeronautics—emphasizing ground school fundamentals but no actual flying—San Mateo "kind of saved" Dieter as a student. He earned three A's and three B's during his first semester, in spring 1962, in courses that included mechanical drawing and elementary aeronautics. After another semester he was named the Aeronautics Student of the Year. Along the way, he even passed the required English examination—without cheating.

To be nearer to the new school, Dieter left San Francisco and lived in his van, sleeping on a raised platform he had built in the back and had covered with a thin pad and sleeping bag. He lashed his surfboard and skis to the roof. The commercial van was windowless but had ample ventilation from a three-foot hole in its side. The furnishings were sparse; the walls were unfinished steel; and there was an old carpet remnant on the floor. Most of his clothes he kept folded in his old air force duffel bag. A wire hanger holding a shirt or two was usually hooked to the ceiling. Dieter sometimes found friends who let him park in front of their residences and gave him bathroom privileges, but often he pulled into the school parking lot for the night. In the morning he used the gym facilities for showering and shaving. He was a vagabond on wheels, and to all who met him in those early-1960s, pre-hippie days in the Bay Area, Dieter, "full of life and overflowing with exuberance," epitomized the term *free spirit*.

When it came to the opposite sex, Dieter was a charmer with an unquenchable appetite. His handsome visage, winning smile, and engaging manner were part of the package, and there was also his beguiling foreign-correspondent accent, which his buddies thought allowed Dieter to suggest things to women that would have earned them a slap in the face. Once, Dieter conducted his own neighborhood sex survey. It began with a conversation in the school cafeteria—Dieter and some buddies were discussing a class assignment in sociology having to do with what percentage of married women would engage in extramarital sex. Twenty percent was the agreed-upon number. Dieter estimated that the average suburban neighborhood had ten to twelve homes per block, so two married women per block would swing. Dieter said he would test the theory. The next day, he reported to his friends that 20 percent was indeed correct. Dieter had selected a block at random, knocked on front doors, introduced himself to the woman of the house, and thereafter stated his amorous intentions. He got halfway down the block before striking gold, and did not doubt he would have had similar statistical success on the other half of the block. His classmates had no doubt, either.

There was no shortage of girls at school willing to date Dieter, and he could at times be selective. He especially liked it when a girl's father was "a doctor or lawyer or banker." Girls who had money, Dieter discovered, often bought presents for a guy living hand-to-mouth out of his van. Whenever necessary, he was happy to supply them with an appropriate occasion, like his birthday. In those days, Dieter had a birthday "maybe once a week."

One friend that Dieter made at College of San Mateo was Mike Grimes, also an aeronautics major who planned to become a navy pilot. It didn't take long for Grimes to realize that Dieter had no income but "survived on his charm." Dieter was a "people magnet"—not just with women but with men, too. "You couldn't help but like him and want to be around him. Everything was always fun with Dieter." Invitations to parental homes for dinner abounded, and Dieter accepted them all, eating heartily, entertaining family members, and happily taking as many leftovers as were offered. When Grimes brought Dieter home he was a big hit with Grimes's mother and teenage sister. "You can bring that boy home anytime," his mother said.

Sometimes Grimes, at close range, could see just how well Dieter scored. One morning, Dieter approached Grimes and said he had two girls ready to party and needed another guy. "We should be studying," Grimes protested. "We have a physics final at two o'clock." Dieter said they could make it work. Grab some six-packs—the girls had given him beer money, Dieter said—and drive the van out to the shore at Coyote Point, and be back in time for the test. Against his better judgment, Grimes agreed. By one o'clock, they were dropping off the girls and hightailing it back for the test. The two Romeos, feeling no pain after drinking beers and having nothing to eat, entered the physics room fifteen minutes late. Everyone was quietly taking the test. Midway up the stadium-seating steps, Dieter tripped and came crashing down, sprawled out in front of the class. For some reason, the instructor did not kick him out. The next day, Dieter and Grimes arrived at the physics lab as the teacher posted the test scores. Grimes got 94, and Dieter 98. Grimes was not surprised. He knew Dieter was a serious student who studied and did the assignments because he wanted his degree so that he could become a navy pilot. Indeed, he was the star student in the aeronautics department, whose chairman, George Van Vliet, had been a pilot in World War II and took under his wing this motivated German immigrant who always earned the top grade in any aeronautics course. Still, Grimes recognized that much of Dieter's success came from an abundance of charm and ingenuity.

One morning Grimes was riding with Dieter after leaving the Black Egg, a blue-collar bar in San Mateo known for a ghoulish betting pool: patrons wagered on when the next person would leap off the Golden Gate Bridge, the winner being whoever came closest. The bar was also known for its breakfast special: a pickled egg, shoestring potatoes, bacon rinds, and a short draft beer—all for 99 cents. Suddenly, Dieter pulled over to the curb. "My Volksy is not running so good," he said. "You stay here, Mike." Dieter got out and went back to the engine compartment. After some banging noises, Dieter came back around. Grimes noticed for the first time that they had parked behind a VW bug. Dieter popped open that car's engine compartment; took off the distributor cap; and pulled the plugs, points, condenser, and rotor. He replaced them with the corresponding parts from his van. Down went the lid. Then, Dieter went back to his engine and quickly installed the clandestine parts. On the road again, Dieter said matter-of-factly, "Volksy running good now."

In the summer of 1962, after living in his van for a semester, Dieter was referred by the college housing office to a family in Hillsborough looking for a local college student to exchange yard work and other chores for room and board. Donna and Jim Love, a couple in their mid-thirties, had four rambunctious sons spaced a year apart ranging from six to nine years of age. They had just purchased a large estate that had once been owned by a son of William Randolph Hearst. They wanted a male college student willing to work around the place, as well as supervise sporting and other outdoor activities for their gaggle of boys. Jim Love, an executive with a San Francisco stock brokerage firm, saw in Dieter "lots of spirit, enthusiasm and smarts." The Love property—only a mile from College of San Mateo—was extensive, with many mature trees, and Dieter climbed every one of them to the top. He also built a sturdy tree house in a huge oak, hauling up the required tools and materials by rope. The boys marveled at Dieter's daring and dexterity; he could swing around on ropes in trees just like Tarzan. Such feats endeared him to the boys, and made Dieter seem larger than life. He could also run circles around the boys with a soccer ball on the large field at the back of the property, but when they moved to the basketball court, Dieter had to be taught that getting the ball into the hoop was more important than nonstop dribbling. Dieter's room was off the kitchen and had its own bathroom and windows that looked out onto the wooded property. He helped barbecue steaks, sausages, and burgers—a treat for him after the scarcity of food when he was growing up—and then helped the boys with their nightly chores of doing the dishes and cleaning up the kitchen.

Dieter made a new circle of friends in Hillsborough when he "popped his head over the fence" during a neighbor's pool party, and was invited to join in. The partygoers included Jeffrey "Scooter" Ryan and Cliff Hoffman. Ryan, a future lawyer, considered Dieter "gregarious and innovative." Hoffman, a sun-bleached swimming coach with lots of girlfriends of his own, saw Dieter as "a nice icebreaker—you could throw him into any situation and see what happened." Dieter was appreciated by his new friends for being clever with anything mechanical. And there was this bonus: anyone locked out of a house or car could go to Dieter for help, as he could "break anything open."

Dieter received his associate of arts degree in January 1963. Soon thereafter, he crossed the bay to Alameda Naval Air Station and applied for the NAVCAD program, which did not take applicants older than twenty-five. He found the written test so difficult that he thought he had flunked. Three weeks later, he was informed that he had passed, and was scheduled for a physical examination. After meeting all the physical requirements, including 20/20 uncorrected vision, he signed his navy enlistment papers on April 12, 1963—only one month before the birthday that would have barred him from the program. He entered the navy with the rank of naval aviation cadet—not yet an officer but above an enlisted man. Once he completed officer candidate school as well as basic and advanced flight training—usually done in eighteen months—he would receive a commission and be assigned to active duty as a naval aviator. If he washed out of the program at any point prior to becoming an officer and a pilot, he would be sent to the fleet as an enlisted man.

Ordered to report to Pensacola Naval Air Station, Dieter was informed that aviation cadets were not allowed to bring private cars to the base. But he had no intention of parting with his home on wheels. He loaded the van and hit the road for Florida. With no time to fix a bad transmission, he had only two working gears: second and third. The cross-country trip took ten days.

In a parking lot outside the main gate at Pensacola, Dieter located an officer's car by the telltale blue sticker on the left front bumper. He pulled over so his van was blocking the vehicle, then got out and dropped from sight.

A few minutes later, an old VW van pulled up to the main gate at the naval air station that served as the primary training base for all navy pilots. The armed U.S. Marine at the gate spotted the officer's blue sticker on the front bumper, snapped to attention, and saluted smartly. The van with a surfboard and skis strapped on top proceeded slowly through the gate.

Dieter Dengler was in the navy now, and closer than ever to flying.

3

TRAINING FOR FLIGHT

Once you have tasted flight, you will forever walk the earth
with your eyes turned skyward, for there you have been,
and there you will long to return.

—LEONARDO DA VINCI

Dieter checked into the Pensacola Pre-Flight Regiment as new cadets were
arriving loaded down with golf bags, tennis rackets, hunting rifles, radios,
and other personal property, most of which "screaming and yelling" U.S.
marines, who were to be their drill instructors, ordered boxed up and
shipped home. Dieter sailed past the scene with only his toothbrush, duly
impressing the marines, who had no way of knowing that he had left everything else inside the vehicle he was not supposed to have on base.

Every week thirty to forty cadets arrived to begin training. The new class
was assigned to the indoctrination battalion for the first two weeks. From
his military experience, Dieter recognized the regimens and routines that
followed as a way to weed out those individuals who were found to be un-
suited for the military or to "get guys to quit" who weren't highly motivated.

One morning Dieter's class was ordered to run to the beach—the cadets ran or marched everywhere—and shovel sand into empty garbage cans, which they hauled back to the barracks. They were ordered to spread the sand throughout the barracks. When they finished, a drill instructor (DI) informed them there would be an inspection in an hour and "not one grain of sand" was to be found. When the DI left, there was a collective groan. Then everyone went to work cleaning up the sand, sweeping with brooms as well as bare hands, wiping surfaces down with wet rags and swabbing the deck.

The exercise brought back painful memories for Dieter. In the two years since his discharge from the air force, he had relished his freedom and independence. Now, he was again a military peon carrying out punitive and capricious orders. But he could take it because he knew that soon it would end and he would be learning to fly. There was "no hardship hard enough" to keep him from staying the course to realize that dream.

For the first two weeks they went through rigorous physical drills and testing. After that, Dieter's class—minus several cadets who did not make it through indoctrination—moved to Second Battalion, where they were assigned to four-man rooms and different instructors for the final fourteen weeks of pre-flight training. From then on they attended classes six days a week. Much of the curriculum had to do with military history, traditions, and etiquette, although there were also challenging academic courses, such as trigonometry.

Outside the classroom, there were sessions in trampoline, wrestling, rope climbing, swimming, and running. To graduate from pre-flight, cadets were required to pass water-survival tests. They had to demonstrate acceptable form in the sidestroke, breaststroke, and crawl in one of three outdoor Olympic-size pools, called training tanks by the instructors. Also, they had to tread water for thirty minutes without touching the side of the pool, jump off a twenty-foot tower and swim the length of the pool underwater, and swim laps wearing a flight suit and shoes. Dieter had taken his first swimming lessons at age six, and by age ten had progressed to the next level, which included river and lake swims. In Germany, everyone at age fourteen went through a final level of swimming instruction involving making water rescues and administering first aid. By his mid-teens, Dieter had become an excellent swimmer.

Pre-flight cadets had to post a qualifying time over an obstacle course that wound through a wooded area and included ropes to be climbed, walls, barriers, water and mud holes, balance beams, and other impediments to overcome while running in the heat and humidity of the Gulf coast. With his natural endurance and agility, Dieter had no problem completing the obstacle course in the required time.

No one made it through pre-flight without successfully escaping from the Dilbert Dunker, a water-crash simulator named after a cartoon character who appeared in posters and training pamphlets during World War II: a hapless aviator who never did anything right. The purpose of the apparatus was to train personnel to get out of a plane after ditching at sea. One by one the cadets climbed a tower and were strapped into a cage that sledded down a twenty-five-foot ramp and plunged into a pool. After hitting the water, the cage sank and flipped upside down. The cadet had to get out of the restraint harness, exit the cage, and then swim to the surface and give a thumbs-up signal. Safety swimmers with scuba gear were underwater to assist if the cadet couldn't get free or panicked. In that case, the cadet would have to take repeated rides until he made it out without assistance. The simulated crash underwater was "all fun" to Dieter. He escaped on his first attempt, and thereafter took several more rides just for enjoyment.

Ordered one afternoon to report to the instructors' office at the front of the barracks, Dieter by then knew the drill. A cadet was to stand at attention before the closed door, rap hard on the wall three times, request permission to enter, and stay at attention until granted permission. Dieter did everything as he had been trained, right up to knocking with such gusto that his fist went through the wall. He was sent to the top sergeant, a marine who looked as if he had single-handedly won a few major firefights in his day. He looked up at Dieter, his eyes narrowing. "Made a hole in my wall, did ya?" The sergeant started to smile, then stopped. "Kinda guy we need more of around here."

Not long after that, during marching practice, Dieter was asked to lead the battalion with one slight variation: he was to count cadence—"Left, two, three, four"—in German. With that, Dieter led the cadets across the parade field, barking out commands. "*Links, zwei, drei, vier.*" Instructors and officers within earshot—many of them veterans of World War II—

stopped whatever they were doing, and turned toward the bizarre scene of naval cadets being drilled like German storm troopers. Dieter soon had a new role as cadence counter, and the performance of the pre-flight class that drilled in German was repeated many times, including on weekends when admirals and other senior officers in their dress whites were in the viewing stands, hooting with delight.

Halfway through pre-flight, Dieter's class had not yet been allowed to leave the base. One Sunday afternoon when the cadets were given a couple of hours to write letters home and attend to other personal matters, Dieter slipped out to his van, changed into civilian clothes, and drove out the main gate. He headed to Pensacola beach, put on swim trunks, grabbed a towel and a cold six-pack he had picked up, and headed across the sandy beach. He staked out a spot close to the water, spread out the towel, and opened a beer, all without realizing that sunning twenty feet away was one of the instructors, with his wife. The DI looked up, and their eyes met. Dieter tried to turn away, but it was too late.

Dieter was summoned not long after returning to base. Although the DI had said nothing at the beach, he reported Dieter's unauthorized absence and beach excursion. Now, standing at attention before some of the same officers and instructors who had been so pleased with his unique skills as a cadence caller, Dieter was in trouble. He admitted everything, including having an unauthorized vehicle on base. After enduring much yelling in his face, Dieter was informed that "anyone else would be kicked out" for the same infractions. However, owing to his exemplary record so far and the overall goodwill he had built up, he would be allowed to finish with his class, under strict conditions. Although the class would soon be allowed time off base on weekends, he would be restricted to base for the rest of pre-flight. Also, he was to perform extra duties. A chastened Dieter promised to obey the new rules. One more slipup in his last eight weeks of pre-flight, he was warned, would result in his expulsion from the NAVCAD program and his assignment to the fleet as an enlisted sailor.

While other cadets were catching rays at the beach or dancing with the local women who flocked to Pensacola's clubs and bars on weekend nights to meet future naval officers, Dieter marched around the sprawling base with his rifle at his shoulder. He would be ordered to dig a hole by hand, take his gun apart, toss the parts into the hole, and bury them. The next day, he had to dig up the parts, clean and oil them, and reassemble his rifle for inspection.

When their sixteen weeks of pre-flight ended, Dieter's class lined up on the parade grounds before the viewing stands. Those with four-year college degrees were awarded their commissions as new ensigns, but Dieter and the other NAVCAD cadets would not become officers until they completed flight training. After the ceremonies, however, they all headed to the same place: Saufley Field, a naval auxiliary air station ten miles north of Pensacola, which since its opening in 1940 had provided primary flight training to all student naval aviators.

For more than a decade the first plane flown by would-be naval aviators was the T-34 Mentor, a propeller-driven, single-engine military trainer produced by Beechcraft beginning in 1953. Its two-seat tandem cockpit held a student pilot and a flight instructor, usually with the student in front and the instructor in back. Each had his own controls and instruments. With a top speed of only 160 miles per hour at full power,* the T-34 was known for its stability in flight and its aerobatic capabilities.

The late-summer Florida morning was already heating up when Dieter met his flight instructor on the tarmac at Saufley Field. The flight line was filled with parked T-34s painted in white with NAVY in blue letters on the fuselage. Not bothering with pleasantries, the instructor launched into his first-flight familiarity spiel that he had no doubt delivered hundreds of times. They circled the T-34 for a pre-flight check, which concluded with a warning on the dangers of walking into a spinning propeller, an encounter which, Dieter was advised, inevitably resulted in dismemberment or death or both. On that note, Dieter went first up the narrow walkway at the root of the wing alongside the fuselage, stepped onto the front seat, and sat down. The instructor leaned in, pointed out various controls and instruments, then made sure Dieter was strapped in.

The instructor issued a final admonishment. If Dieter became airsick on his inaugural flight and vomited in the cockpit, he would receive a "down"

---

* For continuity and clarity, speeds are given in miles per hour. The U.S. Navy uses knots: nautical miles per hour. One knot is equal to 1.15 miles per hour.

on his record. If a student received three downs during primary flight training he would wash out. Considering that primary lasted for months—ample time to get more downs for any of a multitude of reasons, including not doing a flight maneuver correctly or failing to answer an instructor's question correctly—receiving a down on one's first flight was not the best way to start out. Dieter was not particularly worried, because by then he had flown commercially a few times and had never felt any queasiness in the air.

The flight in the T-34 that day was unlike anything Dieter could have imagined. Rather than enjoy the view of the surrounding countryside or appreciate his first flight in a navy plane, he went from being pushed down into his seat by positive g-forces that made him several times heavier than his normal weight to being pulled against the harness in the opposite direction by negative g-forces. As the instructor whipped the plane into gravity-defying spins and loops, it was all "shockingly uncomfortable." With no time to enjoy anything, Dieter became dizzy and disoriented. He felt his stomach flip-flop and knew his breakfast was about to take flight, too.

Remembering the warning of his instructor, Dieter looked desperately around the cockpit for a receptacle but saw nothing that would work. He reached down and clawed at the laces of one of his flight boots. He got the boot off just in time, and retched into it again and again.

After landing, Dieter put the boot back on, laced it up, and climbed out of the cockpit. Leaving the rear seat, the instructor headed up to the front of the cockpit and stuck his head inside the open canopy. Catching the familiar scent of vomit, he searched the cockpit for incriminating evidence, but much to his frustration found nothing.

Dieter Dengler was on his way to becoming a navy pilot.

✪ ✪ ✪

Eight weeks later, after soloing in six hours and learning to fly the T-34—and "loving every minute of it"—Dieter was sent to Whiting Field in Milton, Florida, twenty miles northeast of Pensacola, for additional training.

While almost anyone can learn how to fly with enough instruction, the navy wanted student aviators who learned quickly and were soon ready to move on to the next stage. In fact, a student who failed to progress rapidly—

in the classroom or in the cockpit—was soon dropped from flight training.

Whiting, doubtless the only airfield in the world named after a former submariner—Kenneth Whiting, a 1908 graduate of the Naval Academy who was later taught to fly by Orville Wright—was where naval flight students learned formation flying and acrobatic maneuvers in the T-28 Trojan, a propeller-driven, single-engine trainer built by North American Aviation. Like the T-34, it was a stable aircraft and relatively easy to fly, but the T-28 had more power and speed, equaling the performance of a World War II fighter.

It was in the T-28 that students first flew by instruments only, while wearing a dark canvas hood that blocked any view of the outside world, as the instructor sat in front ready to take over if necessary. In this setting, students were taught to "believe the instruments, not their senses," as they practiced making precise turns, climbs, and descents. A pilot can develop temporary spatial disorientation due to misleading information sent to the brain by sensory organs like the inner ear—a state that occurs most often in limited visibility—and think the plane is doing something it is not, such as turning or climbing when in fact it is in level flight. Many pilots, suffering from vertigo, crash only because they are confused as to which way is up or down. It is essential for pilots to realize that under certain conditions— such as rain, fog, clouds, or nighttime—the senses that serve them well on the ground can be wrong in flight. They must learn to trust their instruments. For naval aviators, who often operate in adverse conditions over a shapeless swath of ocean that blends into the sky without any visible horizon while they are trying to locate and land on an aircraft carrier bobbing in a heaving sea, learning to fly their instruments is vital.

Another category of flight instrumentation taught at Whiting was how to navigate using radio beacons. Student aviators were taught tactical air navigation, or TACAN, a system used by military aircraft that is many times more accurate and powerful than the VOR system used in civilian aviation. With a range of up to 120 miles at an altitude of 10,000 feet, TACAN provided distance and bearing from a ground station or a ship at sea. Navy pilots are quick to point out that they have to be skilled at radio navigation because, unlike their counterparts in the air force, they cannot follow the railroad tracks home.

After three months at Whiting, Dieter, who never again became airsick after that first flight, returned to Saufley Field for carrier qualifications in T-28s. Before attempting the real thing at sea, the students spent weeks landing on an outlying runway painted with white lines to resemble the shape of an aircraft carrier's flight deck. The runway was wired with the optical landing system (OLS) used to give information about the glide path to pilots in the final phase of landing on a carrier. Here they practiced approaching the simulated deck at the correct glide slope, air speed, and line-up. The OLS had a concave mirror in which a bright orange light—the meatball, in navy jargon—was visible to the pilot about to land. On either side of the mirror was a horizontal line of green lights. The location of the orange ball indicated the position of the aircraft on its final approach; if the ball appeared above the line of green lights, then the plane was too high; and if the ball appeared below the lights, the plane was too low. The idea was to line up the orange ball with the green lights. In addition to "calling the ball" to determine whether they were on the correct glide path—and learning to react instantly and make necessary adjustments in speed, altitude, or line-up—pilots were taught to follow the directions of a landing signal officer (LSO) on the ground. The LSOs were experienced carrier pilots specially trained to provide landing guidance to the pilot by hand-held radio (they had used colored paddles for many years), advising of power requirements and position relative to the glide path and the flight deck. A moment before touching down—and only if the LSO decided that the aircraft was in position to make a simulated carrier landing—the student pilot was given the "cut" order both verbally and with flashing green lights. The pilot pulled back on the throttle, which was manipulated by his left hand while the right stayed on the control stick. As soon as the tires hit the pavement, the flaps were returned to the takeoff position, full power was added, and the plane took off again. If the LSO determined at the last second that the aircraft was not in proper position for a landing, he activated two vertical rows of flashing red lights on either side of the meatball to indicate a "wave-off" and gave the same order by radio. In that case the pilot would add power, regain altitude, and go around to try again. For eight days the students made endless touch-and-goes—the first two days with an instructor in the plane and the rest while flying solo—all with their plane's steel tailhook in the up position because there were no cables stretched across the runway like those on the flight deck of an aircraft carrier.

The day arrived that all naval aviators in training looked forward to with a mixture of excitement and anxiety: their first carrier landing. The thrill came from knowing that this was what set navy pilots apart; and the apprehension came not only from the potential danger—one mistake could send them crashing into the sea—but also from the realization that if they failed to pass carrier qualifications, they would not earn their naval aviator wings. In most cases, fear of failure trumped fear of death.

In a flight of four T-28s, Dieter and three other student aviators departed from Saufley. They flew solo, sans instructors, on the most important day of their training. They headed in formation for a rendezvous at sea with USS *Lexington* (CVS-16), an aircraft carrier with a storied record. Launched in 1942, *Lexington* had been reported sunk by the Japanese no fewer than four times. Each time, it returned to fight again. Tokyo Rose called the ship— the only U.S. carrier painted blue rather than in camouflage colors—"The Blue Ghost." Now operating out of Pensacola, *Lexington* had a new mission: serving as the aviation training carrier in the Gulf of Mexico to qualify new pilots and maintain the proficiency of active and reserve aviators.

Soon after the planes crossed the coast, the carrier's wake came into view—a long, whitish line on a big blue canvas. Then, the pilots saw what looked like a postage stamp from the air but was *Lexington* steaming westward into the prevailing trade winds. Air-traffic controllers aboard *Lexington* radioed clearance for the T-28s to enter the landing pattern and make their first approaches. Procedures that the students had memorized in classrooms and practiced on the painted runway seemed different now as they flew the downwind leg, parallel to the ship but in the opposite direction, and then began a long turn on final approach, aiming for the ship's squared-off stern. Even when they drew closer, the aircraft carrier looked absurdly small in the immense sea.

Their first two approaches were touch-and-goes with tailhooks still retracted. At touchdown they went to full power and zoomed off the angled deck that jutted from the port side. They soon realized that calling the ball on the OLS and following the instructions of the LSO, both of which were strategically positioned on the aft port corner of the flight deck so their signals were visible even when the nose of the aircraft obscured the pilot's view straight ahead, were the same as what they had so painstakingly practiced. After everyone made two passes, the LSO radioed the pilots to lower their tailhooks for an arrested landing, commonly called a trap or a recovery.

The arresting cable system on an aircraft carrier is an essential component of naval aviation, allowing planes to land in a short distance aboard a ship at sea. As utilized by the early naval aviator Eugene Ely for the first shipboard landing of a plane in 1911 (aboard the cruiser *Pennsylvania*), the rudimentary system consisted of pulleys and sandbags for deadweights. The recovery system had been mechanized and modernized over the years. A plane's tailhook—all carrier planes have one, which folds up under the fuselage when not in use—catches one of four cables stretched across the flight deck. The force of the plane's forward motion is transferred through the cable to the arresting-gear engine below deck. As the cable unwinds, the huge, hydraulic engine is designed to facilitate a smooth, controlled stop of the plane. But generations of navy pilots may dispute that the stop is smooth and controlled, given that a screeching halt from speeds greater than 100 miles per hour in two seconds is so abrupt that they're thrown against their seat harnesses in a "violent collision" that sounds and feels "like a high-speed automobile accident."

After four traps on *Lexington*—each time they were quickly positioned for a deck launch off the bow—the students headed back to Saufley, exhausted but exhilarated. They were not yet fully qualified for carrier flight operations, however. Not until advanced flight training at their next base would they be shot off the flight deck by a catapult.

As primary flight training came to an end, there was a "big choice" for Dieter and the other students in his class: which types of aircraft to request for advanced flight training and for eventually flying in an active-duty squadron. They were given three choices: jets; multiengine aircraft that were mostly land-based patrol planes; and A-1 Skyraiders, the last single-engine propeller-driven aircraft still in use on carriers. Each student was given a form to fill out listing his first, second, and third choices.

Notwithstanding the choices given the students, the navy used two main criteria in making these assignments. First and foremost came the needs of the service, which changed weekly. One week there might be no openings for jets, which a sizable number of students in any class wanted to fly; the following week, when the next class received assignments, there could be a dozen jet openings. Also, students received—or did not receive—their requested assignments on the basis of their class ranking. Even the top students faced uncertainty about the selection process: at the time they listed their choices, they did not know the number of pilots needed in each program that week or even their own class ranking. If the top student in the class requested jets and there was at least one opening, he would get it. But if the same student requested jets in a week when there weren't any openings, he would be assigned to multiengines, a disappointment for anyone who saw himself as the fleet's next hot jet jockey. An added twist was that a student would end up in A-1 Skyraiders, which took just three new pilots every few weeks because the program was winding down (no new A-1s had been built since 1957), only if he listed them as his first choice. Balancing the popularity of jets and the limited A-1 openings was the fact that some naval flight students listed multiengines as their first choice. These students included some who already knew they would not relish flying off carriers in all types of weather, and others anticipating a career after the navy in which having multiengine experience could help them land a job as a commercial airline pilot.

As for Dieter, he wanted only the A-1 Skyraider. With a big engine spinning a huge propeller, it had the deep, throaty sound of the World War II plane that had swooped low over his house in the Black Forest. At Pensacola, he had watched Skyraiders taking off and landing, often with open canopies right out of the goggles-and-scarf era.

It was not just in Dieter's imagination that the A-1 seemed like a throwback. Designed during the last year of World War II, the Skyraider had entered service in 1946 as the optimum carrier-based attack bomber, designed to outperform the enemy's best propeller-driven fighters while carrying to target a bomb load greater than that of the four-engine B-17 Flying Fortress. The Skyraider was the creation of the aircraft designer Ed Heinemann, who during his illustrious career at Douglas Aircraft designed more than twenty combat aircraft for the navy, including many that became legends, such as the SBD Dauntless dive-bomber. Heinemann, a self-taught engineer, described his approach to aircraft design as rather straightforward, explaining that he took the most powerful engine available and built a plane around it. In the Skyraider, Heinemann outdid himself, using the largest radial engine ever put in a single-engine U.S. military aircraft that went into production. The Skyraider had the same 2,700-horsepower Wright R-3350 engine that powered larger multiengine aircraft such as the B-29 Super-fortress, C-119 Flying Boxcar, and DC-7. The A-1's power and stability allowed it to carry aloft a payload greater than its own weight. After missing the war for which it was designed, the Skyraider saw action in Korea. During that campaign, a squadron aboard the aircraft carrier *Princeton* took up the challenge that a Skyraider could "carry everything but the kitchen sink." Under one wing a kitchen sink was attached to a 1,000-pound bomb, and both were dropped on the enemy near Pyongyang in August 1952.

There was a trade-off with the A-1: along with its ability to carry great loads for long distances, there was its lack of speed. With a normal cruising speed of 180 miles per hour, the A-1 was a slow mover in the supersonic age, when jets routinely operated at more than twice that speed. In homage to an earlier era, the A-1 was dubbed the "Spad" after a famous biplane of World War I. Being a holdover from another time and place was part of the plane's charm, contributing to tradition and nostalgia—not only for Dieter but for the other pilots who signed up to fly Spads and the crews who maintained them. A "typically cocky Spad jockey" possessed an abundance of "style and derring-do," and became accustomed to landing at a new base, shutting down the roaring engine that drove a fourteen-foot propeller and smelled of burning oil, only to have gawkers who saw "sleek jets every day and couldn't care less" come over and stare at the A-1 asking endless questions. "Hell, everyone drives a Ford," one Spad pilot remarked, "but how many Model T's do you see on the road?"

After turning in their list of aircraft choices, the students were told they would receive their assignments when they reported to Corpus Christi Naval Air Station, located on the Gulf coast of Texas some 700 miles from Pensacola.

Dieter heard scuttlebutt that the limited Spad assignments were "first come, first served" in Texas, and that one would have a better chance by being early on the scene, before all the available slots were filled. However, no one could leave until their order to proceed to Corpus Christi came through, so the opportunities for a head start were not good. Dieter, though, was dating the daughter of the Saufley base commander, and she told him one night that his class would receive their orders in two days at exactly 3:00 A.M. Dieter planned his getaway.

When the lights came on in the barracks at three o'clock, Dieter was fully clothed under a sheet. As soon as he had his orders in hand and while others were milling about discussing their travel plans to Texas, he hurried out the back to a waiting bicycle. The NAVCAD cadets were still not allowed to have cars on the base, and Dieter had already learned that lesson. He biked to a nearby car dealer's lot. Dieter had sold his VW van, along with his surfboard, and had saved enough of his monthly pay to buy a used Porsche Speedster. The dealer had agreed to let Dieter keep the car on the lot for a while. The old bathtub coupe, with a ski rack on the back, was already fueled and packed with his belongings. Dieter slipped behind the wheel and "made one beeline" to Texas.

When he arrived, Dieter scrambled to be first to check in. He was surprised to find himself in line behind a classmate who also wanted Spads. It turned out that the other guy was also dating the base commander's daughter, and a day or so earlier had bought his airline ticket to Corpus Christi. As luck had it, they were both assigned to Spads, and had the same young woman to thank.

Dieter and the other students in his Skyraider class went through several weeks of A-1 ground school, learning about the instruments, engine, emergency procedures, flight characteristics, fuel loads, and even how to start the plane. Then, they went to the flight line.

The A-1 Skyraider was not like the forgiving, less-powerful trainers they had been flying. Big and powerful, the Spad had to be flown with a sure hand. With throttle, mixture, rudder, aerodynamic, and torque characteristics to monitor, the pilot had his hands full with an airplane that could be unforgiving if he made an error in judgment. The problems could begin as early as ignition-on, as the Spad's engine was known for difficult starts. Pushing the starter button, the pilot turned the engine through four complete rotations of the four-bladed propeller. Then, on a thumbs-up from the crew chief, he flipped the magneto switch to turn on the ignition, waited one second, pressed the primer button for a richer fuel mixture, and as the engine caught adjusted the mixture. If this process was done too quickly, the engine would backfire and possibly damage the fuel induction system. Too big a backfire would require shutting the plane down until the engine could be inspected. If the pilot eased the throttle forward too slowly, the engine would die and have to be restarted, usually with an auxiliary power unit to save its battery. Even when everything went right with the start-up, a hallmark of the Spad was the smoke clouds pouring from the engine cowling like an old locomotive chugging uphill.

Unlike their first flights in T-34s and T-28s, newly assigned Spad pilots were on their own from the beginning, as there was only a single seat in the cockpit. The instructors, however, did not let them go far. In fact, their first ride in the plane was called a "taxi and abort." They rolled down the runway until they got up to takeoff speed—with the plane's tail in the air but the main landing gear on the ground—before aborting the takeoff. Unless they had a foot down on the right rudder pedal when they were at full power, the plane would veer to the left, owing to the torque caused by the propeller, which spun counterclockwise and sent back a strong prop wash against the tail and rudder. On the runway, the plane would go off only into the dirt infield. The problem was that the Spad would do the same thing in the air, a dangerous tendency that could lead to a 180-degree snap roll to the left and possible loss of control. The flight instructors began by showing the students how and when to use right rudder to avert sudden and disastrous turns to the left.

Even taxiing an A-1 was tricky. Unlike the trainers the students had flown, which sat parallel to the ground on tricycle landing gear, the Skyraider was a "tail dragger" with a main gear under each wing and a smaller wheel under the tail. The tail-down, nose-up attitude meant that a pilot could not see what was in front of him while he was on the ground, even though the plane had a bubble canopy—first designed during World War II— to provide better all-around visibility in the air. The only way to see ahead while on the ground was for the pilot to steer in S patterns and look out to each side as he went down the taxiway.

Once Dieter showed he could handle the taxi-and-abort exercise, he took off in a flight of three other Skyraiders, two flown by students and one by an instructor. Cautioned at first not to go higher than 500 feet because other aircraft were approaching the field at 1,000 feet, the Spads flew low over a drawbridge, then headed out over the Gulf. The instructor had them climb to 8,000 feet and level off. When they were forty miles south of Corpus Christi, the instructor told one student to begin orbiting, and took the others with him farther south. Every twenty miles he left another student orbiting at 8,000 feet.

In the air, Dieter felt at home in the Skyraider. The layout of the cockpit instruments—similar to that in many World War II aircraft—was basic and made the instruments easy to read. The stick and throttle both felt solid and reliable; and the aircraft was responsive, with a big engine under the hood. As Dieter orbited, awaiting further directions, he had an idea that he was going to have some fun flying a Spad. He couldn't wait to have his first dogfight with another student.

The instructor had a different experience in mind.

One at a time, as the instructor observed from nearby, each student was told to lower his landing gear and flaps as if for landing. The students were directed to hold their altitude and pull slowly back on the throttle until they were descending at 700 feet per minute. Then, they were to take their feet off both rudder pedals and place them flat on the floor. "Now jam the throttle all the way forward to the stop." Amid the thunderous roar of the supercharged engine, the plane snap-rolled to the left and in a second was inverted. With plenty of altitude there was no problem dropping the nose, regaining speed, and pulling up into level flight. But that was the point: it took altitude and time. Back at the base, the instructor analyzed the exercise aloud, explaining that if they were on final approach to a carrier—with wheels and flaps down and descending toward the flight deck—and were suddenly waved off and went to full throttle without adding hard right rudder, the same thing would happen. Only then, with insufficient altitude to recover, they would snap-roll inverted into the ocean. And so went the vital lesson of "the right leg thing." A Spad pilot soon developed muscles that made his right leg bigger and stronger than his left leg.

By his third month of advanced flight training, Dieter was practicing aerial bombing at a military range situated on a deserted section of Padre Island—the world's longest barrier island, stretching for 130 miles off the southern coast of Texas. His Skyraider carried nonexplosive Mark 76 practice bombs, weighing twenty-five pounds apiece and loaded with a smoke cartridge to mark the point of impact. While it was usually impossible for a pilot to see his own hits or misses, his bombing accuracy was scored by a range observer on the ground. The technique being practiced was one the Skyraider had been designed to perform: dive-bombing, in which the plane made a nearly vertical dive at the target and released its bombs on target at high speed. Used during World War II, the technique allowed the pilot to place bombs accurately without a complicated, precision bombsight while limiting exposure to antiaircraft fire, which was generally more effective against horizontal bomb runs.

One morning when Dieter reached Padre Island, it was obscured by scattered clouds. Nevertheless, he rolled his plane into a dive and waited to break out of the clouds—and waited. He was soon in a screaming dive. When he broke through the overcast, he was much too low. He dropped his bomb and yanked back hard on the stick to bring the plane out of the steep dive, pulling five g's as he did.

"That was scary—I barely made it," Dieter admitted later to a fellow flight student, Doug Haines, twenty-four, a recent graduate of Iowa State University. Naval ROTC graduates like Haines—already commissioned officers—were trained separately from NAVCAD students at Pensacola, and Haines and Dieter had not met before Corpus Christi. Hearing about Dieter's nearly fatal dive through the clouds, Haines considered it "pure undisciplined behavior" because they had been warned not to dive through an overcast—and the former ROTC platoon leader decided that the guy with the strange-sounding name and accent had a broad streak of the daredevil. Still, from what Haines had seen in training, Dieter gave every indication of being a "good navy pilot," which to Haines meant he had to be "pretty sharp."

The final test for students in advanced flight training was a round of carrier qualifications on *Lexington* in the type of aircraft they would fly when they were assigned to a squadron. By then, Dieter and Haines each had about 100 hours in a Skyraider. After four touch-and-goes, they were cleared for six arrested landings. This time after each trap they were positioned in line with a steam catapult—their plane's landing gear bridled to the shuttle that ran on a track nearly to the end of the ramp—and launched

Dieter with his squadron mates from VA-145 in admiral's stateroom aboard *Ranger*, July 22, 1966.

Dieter, right, meeting the Spad pilot
Lieutenant Colonel Eugene Deatrick,
who saw him at the river in southern
Laos and called in a rescue helicopter.

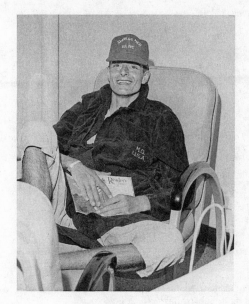

U.S. Navy.

Dieter on the mend at
San Diego Naval Hospital.

U.S. Navy.

Dieter in his tropical
whites after returning
from Vietnam.

U.S. Navy.

Dieter with his fiancée, Marina Adamich, August 1966. At right, public affairs officer Gaylord "Hap" Hill.

U.S. Navy.

At the San Diego press conference, September 13, 1966, Dieter introduces his mother, Maria, and his brother Klaus, from Calw, West Germany.

Dieter with Ed Sullivan prior to appearing on Sullivan's
television show, September 18, 1966. Hap Hill at right.

Family photograph.

Dorcas Haines and Duane Martin, college students in
Boulder, Colorado, shortly before their wedding in 1960.

A-1 Skyraider crossing over the ramp of flight deck for arrested landing.

USS *Ranger* (CVA-61) during WestPac cruise, 1966.

off the flight deck. With throttles pushed forward to the maximum revolutions per minute, seven-ton Spads were fired into the air from zero to more than 100 miles per hour within 300 feet in 2.5 seconds, an experience akin to the "the fastest roller-coaster ride . . . times ten."

Dieter and Haines passed their carrier qualifications, and each had his coveted naval aviator wings of gold pinned on at a ceremony on August 14, 1964. At the same time—having made it through the NAVCAD program—Dieter was commissioned a new ensign, the lowest officer ranking in the navy.

A month later, the two classmates from Corpus Christi happened to be assigned adjacent lockers at Lemoore Naval Air Station in the heart of California's San Joaquin Valley, where they joined VA-122, the A-1 Skyraider training squadron that provided replacement pilots and enlisted maintenance personnel to the Pacific fleet as needed. The VA-122 squadron was known as the west coast RAG squadron, for Replacement Air Group.

One Monday morning not long afterward, following a weekend liberty in San Francisco, Dieter was at his locker getting ready to fly. He said he had something to show Haines. Unzipping the front of his flight suit, Dieter revealed that he was wearing a pair of women's strawberry-print panties. As Haines stared, aghast, wondering if the panties were a kind of trophy, Dieter explained nonchalantly that he had not had any clean underwear with him over the weekend and had helped himself to "some of hers." By then, Haines was of the opinion that Dieter was "167 degrees off from conventional." Of course, Haines was married—"stable and steady"—and Dieter was racing around in his Porsche with a different beautiful woman every weekend "like the wild man he was." As Haines came to hear more stories about Dieter's hardscrabble upbringing in postwar Germany, he began to understand why "Dieter's mind didn't work quite like most people's minds."

In mid-January 1965, Dieter, Haines, and a group of other pilots from the Skyraider RAG squadron were loaded onto a navy bus and driven south to North Island Naval Air Station in San Diego for a six-day survival, evasion, resistance, and escape (SERE) course designed to teach aviators how to live off the land and avoid capture, as well as what was expected of them if they ever became prisoners of war.

The course began in a classroom, with instructors focusing on real-world applications of the Code of Conduct for the Armed Forces of the United States. The pilots learned the code's six articles, which they would be expected to honor as prisoners of war no matter how uncertain or hostile the environment, and while resisting their captor's efforts to exploit them.

ARTICLE I

I am an American, fighting in the forces which guard my country and our way of life. I am prepared to give my life in their defense.

ARTICLE II

I will never surrender of my own free will. If in command I will never surrender those under my command while they still have the means to resist.

ARTICLE III

If I am captured I will continue to resist by all means available. I will make every effort to escape and aid others to escape. I will accept neither parole nor special favors from the enemy.

ARTICLE IV

If I become a prisoner of war, I will keep my faith with my fellow prisoners. I will give no information nor take part in any action which might be harmful to my comrades. If I am senior I will take command. If not, I will obey the lawful orders of those appointed over me and will back them up in every way.

ARTICLE V

When questioned, should I become a prisoner of war, I am required to give my name, rank, service number, and date of birth. I will evade answering further questions to the utmost of my ability. I will make no oral or written statements disloyal to my country and its allies or harmful to their cause.

ARTICLE VI

I will never forget that I am an American, responsible for my actions, and dedicated to the principles which made my country free. I will trust in my God and in the United States of America.

The SERE instructors—mostly navy chiefs and senior petty officers—were equal parts guide, mentor, psychologist, and tormentor. All were highly skilled and well trained, and considered it their personal duty to teach every naval aviator how to survive behind enemy lines during wartime conditions. They proudly wore the SERE uniform patch—a knife slashing through barbed wire in enemy territory—and embraced the program's motto: "We train the best for the worst." The tenets of the course were based on the experiences of surviving U.S. POWs in World War II and Korea.

For a field exercise called "Sea Survival," the pilots were taken to nearby Coronado beach. They were fitted with parachute harnesses and the survival gear they would most likely have with them after bailing out of an airplane, and were taken by boat in small groups to a platform in the bay. Each man jumped into the ocean, and was dragged by the boat to simulate being dragged across the water by a parachute. The pilot freed himself from the parachute harness, inflated his raft, and signaled for rescue. Eventually a helicopter swooped in, dropped a line with a rescue harness, and hauled the pilots up one by one, depositing them ashore. After being shown how to "go hunting for seafood," which consisted mostly of scraping mussels off rocks, they spent a long night on the beach.

In the morning they were loaded onto another bus. An hour and a half later they reached the Navy Remote Training Site at Warner Springs in the foothills of Palomar Mountain northwest of San Diego. For two days they camped out and learned wilderness survival skills, such as emergency first aid, land navigation, camouflage techniques, constructing a shelter using parachute material, procuring and purifying water, building fires with a variety of starting tools and techniques, communication protocols, ground-to-air signaling using parachute panels and smoke flares, and making improvised tools. With the instructors they hiked through tall grass, brush, cactus, and dense groves of pine and fir trees. They were shown how to trap and field-dress rabbits and other small game, which they cooked over an open fire. As the pilots were not being provided with food other than a few potatoes to throw into a pot of boiling water at the end of the day, most were willing to sample the variety of edible plants pointed out to them, but fewer were hungry or daring enough to bite into the lizards, snakes, and insects that were recommended as good sources of protein.

At the end of three days the pilots were "pretty miserable." Unaware of the next ordeal they were about to face, they were relieved when they were loaded onto a waiting bus. They hardly had time to settle into the hard seats before the bus stopped at the top of a bluff, and they were ordered out.

The "survival and evasion" portion of SERE was to conclude with another test. The pilots were directed to head downhill through what looked like a couple of miles of chaparral scrubland dotted with bushes and trees. If they reached the end of the course without being captured they would be rewarded with a sandwich and carton of milk, which sounded very good. The instructors who had been with them the last few days departed on the bus.

On their own to try to evade capture, the men took off running. They had entered the last phase of SERE, "resistance and escape." One by one they were captured by trainers posing as enemy soldiers, complete with a red star on their caps. Rooted out from under bushes, inside shallow burrows, and behind trees, the pilots were taken to a set of low-slung buildings surrounded by guard towers and razor-topped fences. With atypical institutional humor, the navy had called this mock POW camp "Freedom Village."

Among those shepherded into the main compound, Ensign Tom Dixon, twenty-two, of Syracuse, New York, a recent flight school graduate and Spad pilot who had been in the RAG squadron only a few days and didn't know many of the other guys, was surprised to see one pilot sitting off by himself having a sandwich and a carton of milk. Grinning like the Cheshire cat, the fellow left no doubt that he was thoroughly enjoying his private picnic.

As the rest of the pilots were being gathered up like "lumps of coal,"

Dixon thought it inconceivable that anyone could have gone undetected through an area with so few places to hide while being hunted by expert trainers who had to know every square foot of their own course.

"Who's that?" Dixon asked one of his fellow POWs.

"Dieter Dengler. He made it down without getting caught."

After his repast, Dieter slipped away for a few minutes without anyone seeing him, before joining the other pilots. Ordered to strip to their skivvies and socks, they were made to crawl on their stomachs under rolls of barbed wire while being sprayed down with high-pressure hoses. By the time they made it through that ordeal and got their dark green flight suits back on, they were soaked, and freezing to the bone. Not long afterward, each man was locked in a small, dark box—"one size too small for everyone"—and left to fight the demons of claustrophobia.

When it was time for interrogations, the exhausted pilots were taken one by one to a special room located a short distance outside the main compound. The rules allowed for the pilots to be slapped with an open hand and verbally abused by the guards, some of whom had distinct sadistic leanings. When it was Dieter's turn to be questioned under a blinding spotlight, he found himself facing several guards. He was asked to identify his unit and the type of aircraft he flew. When he refused to provide the information, a guard slapped him on the face. After this drill was repeated several times, all but one guard left the room. When that guard turned his back, Dieter pulled out from his sock a short length of pipe he had found in an unlocked workshop near where he had been left earlier to eat his sandwich. Using the shop's grinder, he had quickly made a sharp end on the pipe, turning it into an improvised shiv. He now sprang forward, grabbing the guard from behind and placing the pipe next to his head.

"I've got a knife at your throat," Dieter said.

Under the rules of the mock POW camp, any sharp instrument pulled on a guard by a prisoner was construed to be a deadly weapon. The guard would be considered dead or incapacitated—as in most war games—and would stand aside for the prisoner to continue with any plan he had for escape.

"Okay," said the guard. "What do you want me to do?"

"Take off your uniform."

When Dieter stepped outside in the dark, he was dressed like a guard. He headed for the building where he knew the camp food was prepared. In the back he found what he was looking for: the garbage cans. He picked over the leftovers, finding apple cores, old pieces of bread, and chunks of hamburger, then hid in the bushes and ate with abandon. Scrounging for food was something he had done most of his life, and he didn't see any reason to stop now, especially since food was being used as a reward here. When he got too cold, he turned himself in.

When the POW exercise ended the next day, Dieter was ready to make his third escape in twelve hours. The first to escape multiple times from the navy's simulated POW camp at Warner Springs, he was also the only SERE graduate to gain weight during the rigorous program. Asked by the trainers—as well as his fellow pilots—how and why he had been able to excel in the survival course, Dieter told about growing up in Germany during tough times when he had to do "such things to stay alive." By the end of SERE, Dieter had "gained three pounds," while everyone else lost weight. Dieter credited this to his eating "everything the guards threw away."

Another Spad pilot who went through SERE at the same time, Ensign Dave Maples, twenty-four, of Nashville, Tennessee, considered Dieter "in a class all by himself" when it came to escaping and in the process "exasperating" the guards. His fellow pilots "loved his successes," and everyone was "astounded and amazed at how well he did."

As word of his SERE escapes spread, Dieter, although so junior he had not yet flown a single mission with the fleet or even been assigned to a regular squadron, began to "make his name" among navy pilots.

In a letter of January 28, 1965, to the RAG squadron's commanding officer with a copy to Dieter's personnel file, Captain L. W. Metzger, commander of the Fleet Airborne Training Unit that included SERE, commended the young pilot for his "exemplary conduct and motivation." Further, "he expertly manufactured and cunningly utilized potential weapons to effect two different, ingenious and successful escapes from confinement . . . and had completed plans and was ready to attempt a third escape" when the exercise ended. "Ensign Dengler is to be commended for his out-standing conduct during training. His persistent and successful efforts to escape directly contributed to the high morale of his fellow students. The ingenuity and foresight displayed by this officer exemplifies true American spirit and ideals."

4

THE SWORDSMEN

Ensign Walt "Bummy" Bumgarner, twenty-four, of Orinda, California, the newest pilot in VA-145, a Skyraider squadron based at Alameda Naval Air Station in California, had his hands full as he tried to stay on the tail of a wildly gyrating Spad over the eastern slope of the Sierra Nevada.

The two pilots had recently graduated from advanced flight training at Corpus Christi a few months apart. They were violating a navy policy then in effect that prohibited practice dogfights—as aerial combat between two aircraft first became known in the skies over France during World War I— because such maneuvers were deemed "too dangerous."

Two months earlier and only days after joining the squadron, Bumgarner, a graduate of Diablo Valley Community College who received his commission through the NAVCAD program, had learned there was navy *policy* and there was navy *flying*. One of the squadron's senior pilots, Commander Donald E. Sparks, thirty-seven, of Royal, Nebraska, a veteran of two Korean combat tours aboard the carrier *Princeton* (CVA-37) and formerly a flight instructor at Pensacola, made it a point to test the flying skills of the new guys, known as nuggets in navy parlance. He had challenged Bumgarner to a game of "tail chase," with Sparks flying lead and the nugget trying to stay on his tail, thereby simulating aerial combat. It did not turn out as Sparks planned: the senior aviator was unable to shake Bumgarner, who stayed within fifty feet of Sparks's tail throughout various turns, rolls, and dives. Sparks finally radioed, "Okay, you take the lead and see how you like it." The stocky Bumgarner, who had displayed an innate confidence since his first flight in a Spad when he flew between the open spans of a drawbridge like a 1920s barnstormer, keyed his radio mike and said, "I'll get rid of you in thirty seconds, sir." As soon as Sparks got on his tail, Bumgarner pushed the stick all the way to the left and held it until he was pulling six g's, then stomped down on the right rudder pedal. The Spad went into a snap roll and kept going—spinning faster and faster until it was rolling 300 degrees a second, twice as fast as its normal roll rate. Then he went hard right, pulling six g's the other way, and came up right behind Sparks. "Get on my wing," Sparks said sternly. "We're heading back."

Now, Bumgarner was on the tail of a fellow nugget, who was desperately trying to lose him. The other pilot dived for the deck and Bumgarner followed, confident he could do with his airplane whatever this fellow did. They had started at 12,000 feet, and usually the guys in the squadron broke off play-fighting at 5,000 feet for safety's sake, but the pilot in front did not pull up. As Bumgarner drew steadily closer all he could see out the front of his canopy was the big-ass tail of the Spad he was chasing. Then, in a nanosecond the guy pulled off and was gone. The only thing then filling Bummy's field of vision was the ground. Pulling out of the dive at an altitude of only 200 feet, he realized he had chased the guy into a gorge surrounded by jagged, low-slung mountaintops. Coming close to "buying the farm," Bumgarner realized: *That hotshot was ready to wipe me off the side of a mountain rather than have me beat him.*

The hotshot who did not like to lose was Dieter Dengler.

The A-1 Skyraider squadron that was to become VA-145 began in 1949 as a group of weekend warriors at Dallas Naval Air Station in Texas. Originally designated VA-702 and named the Rustlers, the reserve squadron was activated in 1950 for service in Korea. Redesignated VA-145 during its second Korean tour, the squadron changed its nickname to Swordsmen and adopted a gung-ho slogan: "Live by the sword, die by the Swordsmen." Ironically, the first navy pilot to die in the next war would be a Swordsman.

In the summer of 1964, as events unfolded in the waters off Southeast Asia that would lead to full-blown U.S. military involvement in Vietnam, VA-145 was deployed aboard the carrier *Constellation* (CVA-64) in the South China Sea.

Late on the afternoon of August 2, 1964, the destroyer *Maddox* (DD-731), steaming in the Gulf of Tonkin gathering electronic intelligence outside the twelve-mile territorial line claimed by North Vietnam, was approached in international waters by three North Vietnamese torpedo boats. What happened next would be the subject of conflicting reports: *Maddox* claimed to have opened fire with its guns only after evading a torpedo attack, but a top-secret report by the National Security Agency declassified in 2005 states that *Maddox* fired the first shots—"three rounds to warn off the communist boats," which then returned fire. The U.S. ship was hit with a single machine-gun bullet that caused minor damage. A flight of F-8U Crusaders from *Ticonderoga*—already airborne—quickly showed up to assist *Maddox*. The planes attacked the retreating torpedo boats, leaving one dead in the water and two damaged.

Constellation, meanwhile, was at anchor off Green Island in the port of Hong Kong. That same evening of August 2 found many VA-145 pilots partying at the Eagle's Nest Bar at the top of the Hong Kong Hilton. About 9:00 P.M., someone walked in and informed the group that all leave and liberty had been canceled and everyone was to report to the ship. It took another day to gather up all the ship's crewmen and air wing personnel. *Constellation* got under way at 8:00 A.M. on August 4 to rejoin *Ticonderoga* in the South China Sea.

Later that same day *Maddox*, now in the company of another destroyer, *Turner Joy* (DD-951), was back on patrol in the Gulf of Tonkin in gusty winds and choppy seas. That night at 8:41 P.M. sonar and radar contacts were reported, possibly signaling another attack by North Vietnamese naval forces.

Launching at midnight when *Constellation* came within range in the South China Sea east of Hainan Island—where Chinese MiG fighters were known to be based—were four VA-145 Skyraiders led by Commander Harold

"Hal" Griffith, a seasoned aviator. Normally, the squadron's commanding officer (CO) would lead such a high-stakes mission, but it had fallen by default to Griffith, the squadron's executive officer (XO), or second in command. Upon the scheduled rotation of VA-145's commanding officer to his next assignment, the previous XO, Commander Harold T. Gower, had been due to "fleet up" to CO. However, Gower experienced "some problems" during night carrier landing qualifications and thereafter turned in his wings, an ignoble end for any navy pilot but one which everyone knew could happen given the nerve-racking nature of the work. As a result, the same month Griffith had joined the squadron—January 1964—he was swiftly promoted to XO to replace Gower. Griffith had then expected he would become the next CO, but the bureau of personnel decided to bring in a more senior officer to take over. The new CO, Commander Melvin Blixt, had only recently reported aboard, and assumed command of VA-145 in Hong Kong just a couple of days earlier. Since Blixt had so little time in the squadron, Griffith was given the mission.

Griffith, thirty-eight, of Port Jefferson, New York, had joined the navy in 1943 at age seventeen. Instead of going to sea with the fleet in wartime, he was sent to Colgate University as a NAVCAD cadet. In January 1945 he entered flight training, during which one of his instructors was the famous baseball player and Marine Corps fighter pilot Ted Williams. By the time Griffith received his commission and wings, the war he had hoped to help win was over. He was among a large contingent of reserve pilots no longer needed who were released from active service. Called back to duty during Korea, Griffith was assigned to an east coast squadron, but he never saw action in what became known by navy pilots as the "west coast war," as the west coast squadrons were the only ones deployed to the combat zone. After Korea, Griffith went to night school at the University of Maryland and earned his BS degree. He was then allowed to transfer from the reserves to regular navy, so he was at last on track to make the navy his career. Before VA-145, he had served as operations officer and then XO of VA-25, a Skyraider squadron aboard the carrier *Midway* (CVA-41). After missing the last two wars, Griffith was to lead the first missions in the new war.

Forming up in the dark, the Spads flew southwest across the moonlit sea until they cleared Hainan, thereby avoiding Chinese airspace. They then turned north into the Gulf of Tonkin. Each was loaded with LAU-3 wing pods that fired nineteen high-explosive rockets individually, sequentially, or simultaneously, and full ammunition (200 rounds each) for their four 20 mm cannons.

As they neared the position of the two destroyers, Griffith switched to the radio frequency for *Maddox*, the flagship of Captain John J. Herrick, commander of the two-ship task force operating in the gulf, and checked in with the ship's air controller. For the next two hours the Skyraiders circled into and out of a thin cloud layer between 3,000 and 4,000 feet, waiting to be directed by ship radar or sonar to "water targets," but they never were.

For two hours preceding the arrival of Griffith's flight, the destroyers had reported countless surface contacts on radar and sonar. There were also urgent reports of torpedoes in the water, causing the destroyers to take "wild evasive maneuvers," which themselves caused sonar reports as sound waves reflected off the turbulence of the ships' own propellers. *Turner Joy* had fired 300 rounds at elusive targets, but *Maddox* had not fired a single round; *Maddox*'s gunnery officer was unconvinced there were any targets. Jets from *Ticonderoga*, arriving well before Griffith's Spads, had been vectored repeatedly to reported surface contacts, and each time dropped flares and searched the ocean for torpedo boats. "No boats," the *Ticonderoga* flight leader, Commander James Stockdale (a future POW, admiral, and vice presidential candidate), reported upon returning to the aircraft carrier, "no boat wakes, no ricochets off boats, no boat gunfire, no torpedo wakes—nothing but black sea and American firepower." At 11:35 P.M., the reported contacts stopped. Stockdale's jets, low on fuel, left as Griffith's Spads arrived.

For the two hours they orbited above, Griffith, like Stockdale, saw only the U.S. ships. The reported North Vietnamese attack this far out in the gulf struck Griffith as odd. After nightfall, the two destroyers had moved from twenty or so miles off North Vietnam's coast to some sixty miles into the gulf. A torpedo boat capable of thirty to forty miles per hour would take two hours to reach the U.S. ships, and equal time to return to shore. Why would such boats risk it, given the presence of carrier-based airpower that could blow them out of the water? Coming that far out, in Griffith's opinion, would have been foolish. The daytime attack on *Maddox* two days earlier—verified visually by the U.S. pilots from *Ticonderoga* and confirmed by the minor damage to *Maddox* caused by enemy gunfire—had taken place closer to shore. And if the torpedo boats did venture this far out to engage U.S. warships this night, why had the planes found no sign of them?

Unbeknownst to Griffith, Captain Herrick, aboard *Maddox*, was also having misgivings about what had happened that night. Shortly before 12:30 A.M., Herrick, after reviewing the communications log and radar and sonar data, wired Admiral U. S. Grant Sharp Jr., commander-in-chief of the Pacific Fleet, Pearl Harbor, stating: "ENTIRE ACTION LEAVES MANY DOUBTS . . . NEVER POSITIVELY IDENTIFIED A [ENEMY] BOAT AS SUCH." Herrick recommended aerial reconnaissance in daylight and a "COMPLETE EVALUATION BEFORE ANY FURTHER ACTION." Sharp immediately called the Pentagon, and relayed his own concerns to Admiral Thomas Moorer, chairman of the Joint Chiefs of Staff, and Robert S. McNamara, Secretary of Defense. Sharp, the top admiral in the Pacific, surmised that "over-eager sonar [and radar] operators" and "freak weather" could have caused false contacts, and emphasized the absence of visual confirmation of any hostile activity against U.S. forces in the gulf on the night of August 4.

As Griffith led his flight back, he had everyone drop the full rocket pods into the water, which planes carrying unused bombs and rockets routinely did before coming back aboard ship to prevent accidental explosions. About then, Griffith realized they had entered an electrical weather phenomenon known as Saint Elmo's fire, which he had heard about but had never experienced. This static-electric phenomenon, named after the patron saint of sailors, lit up the leading edges and tips of their wings, canopies, and spinning props in a bright blue and violet glow. Eerily, the planes looked as if they were on fire.

Back in his stateroom aboard *Constellation*, Griffith hit the rack at 3:00 A.M. Jolted awake an hour later, he was summoned to the ship's Air Intelligence Center, where he learned that Operation Pierce Arrow, a retaliatory air strike against North Vietnam, had been ordered by President Johnson hours after the reported August 4 attacks on the two destroyers. Coming fully awake over a cup of strong coffee, Griffith broke out charts of North Vietnam's craggy coastline and helped plan a coordinated assault on torpedo-boat bases near the coastal city of Hon Gai, eighty miles east of Hanoi.

Standing before the pilots in the ready room, Griffith, the Skyraiders strike leader, said they had been given the green light to attack any North Vietnamese torpedo boats that were in port or at sea. As they headed for the flight deck to launch, Griffith worried about the lack of intelligence concerning the air defenses they would encounter over North Vietnam. And he could not shake off the feeling that higher-ups in Washington were using what he knew to be a "non-incident" in the Gulf of Tonkin as an "excuse to go to war." It occurred to him that this might have something to do with the current presidential election campaign, in which the Republican candidate, Barry Goldwater, was forcefully criticizing President Johnson for being soft on defense. Other pilots had their own troubling thoughts. Griffith learned that several *Constellation* A-4 pilots refused to participate in the strike because they "did not want to fly into a war," and turned in their wings. It was one thing if a carrier pilot had a close call landing at night or in bad weather and lost his nerve, but Griffith and the other pilots did not respect individuals trained at great expense and effort by the navy who refused to fly because someone would be shooting at them. The dissident pilots were "quietly removed" from the ship the following week.

Griffith's flight of four VA-145 Skyraiders launched after sunrise. Because they were slower, had a longer range, and could stay airborne much longer than jets—which usually required in-flight refueling to stay in the air longer than a couple of hours—Spads were most often first off and last to land, usually after six or seven hours in the air. Today was no exception: the jets were scheduled to launch later, and everything was coordinated so that they all arrived over the targets at the same time. As the ordnance crews did not have time to haul up 250-pound bombs and bigger rockets from the storage magazine and rearm the planes, the Spads were loaded with the same type of ordnance they had carried the day before: rocket pods containing smaller rockets that Griffith considered "practically useless," and for their four cannons—"very powerful weapons"—20 mm armor-piercing ammo mixed with tracer rounds that burned brightly to light up the trajectory so the shooter could adjust his aim.

When they arrived off the coast of Hon Gai two hours later, Griffith's flight orbited over the gulf. He raised the incoming flight of jets on his radio, and talked them in. The plan had been to make a coordinated assault, but the A-4s didn't wait to join up with the Spads and headed straight for the targets.

Thundering inland with his own flight, Griffith led the first of several rocket-and-cannon runs on torpedo boats outside Hon Gai harbor that were firing at the attacking planes. They left several boats burning.

The sky was dotted with black mushroom-shaped clouds as anti-aircraft artillery (AAA) ringing the harbor joined the torpedo boats in firing at the planes. To Griffith, it "looked like World War II," and it seemed as if the enemy gunners had been expecting them. Only later would he learn that President Johnson had announced the retaliatory strikes on national television while the aircraft were "airborne and heading for the North Vietnamese coast." Griffith heard pinging and knew his plane was taking shrapnel hits, but nothing stopped working, so he kept going. One advantage of the Spad was its thick armor plate around the cockpit and engine cowling; another was its self-sealing internal fuel tank—protecting pilot and plane alike. Jets were not so well protected; a piece of metal in the intake or fuel tank could mean disaster for a jet.

Over the din of battle came a distress call from one of the A-4s.

"*Four Eleven*, I'm hit." Then: "Can't control it. I'm ejecting."

Unfortunately, there was nothing to be done for a downed pilot that day, as there were no helicopters in the area or other provisions for rescue. Anyone going down was on his own, and this was what happened when the A-4 pilot, Lieutenant Everett Alvarez, Jr., twenty-seven, of Santa Clara, California—whose plane was hit on its second sweep across Hon Gai harbor—parachuted safely and was captured. Released from the infamous Hanoi Hilton eight and a half years later, Alvarez was the longest-held American POW of the war.

VA-145 pilot Lieutenant (j.g.) Richard C. Sather, twenty-six, of Pomona, California, was not so lucky that day. He was in a second wave of attacking Spads, and his plane was the last in his flight to dive on five North Vietnamese torpedo boats near Loc Chao estuary and Hong Me Island. The flight was led by the VA-145 operations officer, Commander Samuel Catterlin, thirty-eight, of Van Nuys, California, who had cautioned his pilots before they launched that there was "no target out here worth dying for." The other planes made it, but Sather did not. His Skyraider was seen to "go straight in" and make a huge splash in the water two miles offshore. No parachute was observed and no emergency radio beeper heard. Sather was declared missing, then KIA; his remains were recovered by the North Vietnamese but were not returned to the United States for twenty-one years.

With Al Alvarez the first American POW and Dick Sather the first navy pilot killed over North Vietnam, a new generation's war had begun.

That same day, President Johnson sent a message to Congress about the Gulf of Tonkin incidents, asking for a joint resolution to give him authorization for the future use of military force in Southeast Asia without a formal declaration of war by Congress. The resolution passed both houses by a nearly unanimous vote. The incident of August 4, 1964, in the gulf involving the two destroyers was, according to the CIA's deputy director at that time, Ray Cline, "just what Johnson was looking for." Marking the start of a rapid escalation, Secretary of Defense Robert McNamara immediately announced the reinforcement of U.S. ground, air, and naval forces in Southeast Asia.

✪ ✪ ✪

"Where's Vietnam?" Dieter Dengler asked over beers with his squadron buddies during happy hour at the Alameda Naval Air Station Officers Club.

"Over by Hong Kong," someone chimed in.

"Is that where they have good camera deals?" Dieter asked.

"Cameras, stereos, you name it. And the women . . ."

It was the summer of 1965, and VA-145 had a new CO, Hal Griffith, who relieved Mel Blixt in August. The Swordsmen were training for a December deployment to the western Pacific—WestPac in navy lingo—aboard the carrier *Ranger* (CVA-61).

Dieter had joined VA-145 in February 1965 when the Swordsmen returned from the *Constellation* cruise. Following him to his new assignment had been an officer fitness report covering his four months in the RAG squadron. "Ensign Dengler has completed training as a Fleet Replacement Pilot. He is an above average aviator. He is eager and enthusiastic about everything he does. He has an excellent military bearing and is well liked by his fellow officers."

The new pilots in VA-145 may have been excited about camera and stereo deals and exotic ports of call, but they had no idea what was awaiting them in Southeast Asia. Griffith and the senior officers knew they were preparing the squadron for war, although even they weren't sure what kind of war. They had all heard the popular domino theory: that if one nation fell to communism in Indochina, others would follow. Most of the pilots believed that U.S. intervention was needed in the region to stop the spread of communism. For the new pilots like Dieter, however, it wasn't just about patriotism, but also an opportunity to be part of something exciting after all their training and preparation. Soon, it would be about staying alive.

What was to be a sustained air war over North Vietnam by carrier-based aircraft began in March 1965. Operation Rolling Thunder, which would continue with few interruptions until November 1968, was intended to halt North Vietnam's support of communist forces in South Vietnam by destroying its air defenses and industrial infrastructure. After only a few months there were already complaints from navy and air force pilots about the rules of engagement (ROEs) drawn up by politicians to indicate which targets could be hit and which were off-limits. From what Griffith was hearing, the overriding rule seemed to be that American pilots "couldn't shoot anyone unless they shot first." What the hell kind of war is that? If the other guy is a good shot, you're dead. Under such rules, the United States would "still be fighting World War II."

Of VA-145's twenty pilots, half were junior officers (ensigns and lieutenants junior grade) with limited flying experience. In the opinion of the squadron's new CO, the only way to improve stick-and-throttle skills was to spend the requisite hours in the air. During the week, they worked on bombing, gunnery, formation flying, and navigation. Then came the weekends. "I don't care if you get liquor in Mexico, lobster in Boston, and see your girlfriend in Seattle," Griffith told his pilots. "I don't want to see any planes sitting on the flight line on weekends." For many pilots, including Dieter, this would be the best flying summer of their lives.

The squadron regularly flew to the Marine Corps Air Station at Yuma, Arizona, for weapons training. Because the intense heat radiating off the desert surface could cause a tricky uplift for aircraft, they practiced early in the morning—starting around five o'clock. With "everyone wanting to do better than his comrades," Dieter was awarded an E for excellence in dive-bombing. Learning that "bombing is quite an art," the pilots were taught to roll in over the target from 6,500 feet at about 230 miles per hour. They practiced various angles of attack; at thirty degrees they would release their bombs at 2,500 feet, by which point they would have accelerated to nearly 375 miles per hour. A fifty-degree dive resulted in a speed of 400 miles per hour and necessitated a release point of 3,500 feet. During the pullout, they would be pressed into their seats by powerful g forces—the steeper their dive, the faster their speed, the greater the g's, and the bigger the swoop. The accuracy of aerial bombing was determined by how closely the pilots observed the benchmarks they were taught regarding altitude, prevailing wind, angle of attack, and release point. As the VA-145 pilots were to soon learn, however, practice bombing was not the same as combat operations over the jungles of Southeast Asia, where there were no bull's-eyes laid out on a flat, desert floor.

By noon, the pilots were usually lying around the pool at the air station's officers club—such facilities were known worldwide as O clubs—drinking cold beers, getting tanned, and "planning for the evening." A nighttime or weekend jaunt might include a visit to Winterhaven, Yuma's neighbor to the north, located on the California side of the Colorado River, or dropping down to "find women and drink beer" in the Mexico border town of San Luis.

On their way back to Alameda from one stay in Yuma, four VA-145 planes diverted for a flyover of the Las Vegas Strip. Dropping down and lowering their flaps to reduce their speed, the formation overflew the high-rise casino hotel where the annual Tailhook Association convention for naval aviators was being held. Pushing open their canopies, Dieter and the other pilots—including Ensign Norm "Lizard" Lessard, twenty-three, of Shrewsbury, Massachusetts—dropped hundreds of "Spads forever" leaflets. This was the slogan of all "Spad drivers," and one the VA-145 guys announced "loud and clear" whenever they entered a bar en masse, espe-

cially when "jet jocks" were around. Dieter, Lizard, and the other Swordsmen knew that jets were the future—and if they stayed in the navy they
would one day fly jets—but they were proud of the old-time prop planes
they had volunteered to fly, and were unwilling to "give up the good old
Spad days easily."

The primary mission of carrier-based Skyraider squadrons—indeed, of
all navy attack (VA) squadrons—was to drop nuclear bombs in the event of
World War III. As created in 1960, the Single Integrated Operational Plan
(SIOP) was an ultrasecret U.S. plan for a massive nuclear strike—with retaliatory as well as preemptive options in the event the United States decided to hit first—on military and urban-industrial targets in the Soviet
Union, China, and countries allied with them. An all-out nuclear strike,
launched in retaliation to a strike by the Soviet Union, would have delivered 1,700 nuclear weapons by missiles and planes, and a preemptive strike
nearly twice that number. VA-145 practiced diligently for its role in such a
cataclysmic undertaking, and to a man the Spad pilots understood that
they would probably not survive a SIOP mission. Once they deployed
aboard a carrier in the Pacific, each pilot would be assigned three targets,
known only to him and a few senior officers. Each pilot was responsible for
developing a detailed plan for attacking his targets, and having an escape
route. The plans were kept under lock and key except when a pilot would
be called in to brief one or two senior officers, who would direct any
changes necessary to improve the plan. In the event a nuclear strike was
ordered by Washington, D.C., a pilot would be handed orders that directed
him to hit one of his targets. It was a mission he would fly without a wingman or with other aircraft. Each plane could carry one nuclear weapon on
a centerline bomb rack. If all of VA-145's twelve Spads made it to their targets, they would drop a dozen nuclear bombs, all larger than those dropped
on Hiroshima and Nagasaki to end World War II.

One typical nuke practice run began for Dieter with a full day of planning at Alameda, poring over charts to prepare a flight plan he would carry
out without navigational aids such as TACAN, as no electronic devices could
be used during the real thing, a restriction meant to keep the enemy from
homing in on the signals and shooting down the plane. When he took off
early the next morning, he headed out over the Pacific. When he was about 75

miles off the coast, he turned around and dropped down to fifty feet to simulate approaching an enemy coastline under the range of radar. His ingress point back to land was Point Reyes on the rugged coast north of San Francisco. When he hit landfall, which navy pilots call feet dry, as opposed to feet wet—being over the ocean—Dieter climbed to only 100 feet off the ground, still under radar range. He would maintain this low altitude for the duration of the five to seven-hour flight, which would end with his dropping a practice bomb on a range near Fallon Naval Air Station in western Nevada. Looking out the cockpit and navigating solely by visual references, Dieter marked his progress on a plotting board that showed rivers, mountains, railroad tracks, bridges, and roads. Once he cleared the coastal hills and forests, he crossed the flat San Joaquin Valley and headed east for the Sierra, avoiding large cities and towns but undoubtedly shaking the rafters of some rural outposts along the way. With so little altitude, Dieter had to be vigilant as he terrain-hopped—climbing to get over each hilltop and mountain, then diving into the next valley. The pilots all thought flying low was great fun and joked about the flights they called sand-blowers being good practice for a career as a crop duster.

Commercial crop dusters, of course, sometimes die because they are flying so low and have such a slim margin for error. That's what happened to one of the more experienced pilots in VA-145: Lieutenant James Thigpin, a veteran of the *Constellation* cruise who had taken part in the Gulf of Tonkin retaliatory strike at Hon Gai with Hal Griffith. On a sand-blower mission in the spring of 1965, Thigpin was crossing the central valley east of Fresno when he "did something wrong" in switching over from his belly tank to his main fuel tank, causing the engine to stop. Without enough altitude or time to make an emergency landing, he crashed and was killed instantly. The fatal incident involving a popular and capable pilot was "very sobering" for everyone, including Lieutenant (j.g.) Daniel "Farky" Farkas, twenty-five, of South Bend, Indiana, who joined VA-145 on the day Thigpin crashed. Griffith made the accident a lesson for his pilots: Jim Thigpin was a "damn good pilot," but he had made a mistake and "you can't make mistakes when you are flying that low."

When Dieter was half a mile from his target in the Nevada desert, he pushed the throttle forward and brought the nose up to forty-five degrees.

With his finger on the release button on the stick, he waited, as he had been trained to do, until he was pulling 4 g's, which he could read on the cockpit g-meter if he wanted to but knew by feel alone now. Then, at about 1,500 feet, he released the twenty-five-pound practice bomb loaded with a white-smoke charge. The maneuver—known as loft bombing—threw the bomb upward before it fell to earth, giving the pilot added time to get away before detonation. Dieter banked left 135 degrees into a "half Cuban eight," allowing the nose to drop forty-five degrees before pulling to level flight at nearly maximum speed and heading in the opposite direction. The maneuver was a quick way to reverse course while picking up speed, but if a slowpoke Spad was trying to outrace a nuclear blast, it would be hopeless. With the practice run over, he climbed to a higher altitude for the flight back. At that point, a famished Dieter opened his box lunch and dug in.

Through all the training and "lots of demanding flights," Dieter became "a capable pilot . . . not one we worried about," according to Lieutenant Clarence "Skip" Armstrong, thirty, of West View, Pennsylvania. An experienced multiengine pilot who had recently transitioned to Skyraiders, Armstrong would be promoted to lieutenant commander a few days before VA-145 left for Southeast Asia. Years later, he would be CO of his own squadron, then of a carrier air wing, before taking command in 1980 of the aircraft carrier *Forrestal* (CVA-59). Although not an Annapolis graduate, Armstrong would be the only member of VA-145 from the *Ranger* cruise to make flag rank, and would retire as a rear admiral. During the months leading up to VA-145's deployment to WestPac, Armstrong saw Dieter—"a mix of ideal military and bit of a wild guy"—and the other nuggets working hard and getting better.

The best pilot in VA-145 was widely acknowledged to be Lieutenant (j.g.) Malcolm "Spook" Johns, twenty-eight, of Detroit, Michigan. Johns had decided to become a navy pilot at age eight, after seeing a newsreel of an F-6 Hellcat crash-landing on a carrier deck during World War II and hitting the ship's island, which split open the plane's fuselage, and the pilot "unbuckling and getting out like it was another day at the office." A veteran of two earlier cruises, Johns, who had joined the navy in 1960, was due to get out in the fall of 1965 but voluntarily extended the length of his service to go on the *Ranger* cruise even though he had been passed over twice for promotion to lieutenant for reasons other than his flying abilities, such as being a "square peg in a round hole" when it came to military discipline. Although he would proudly state, "I'm in the military but the military isn't in me," he decided to stick around for two reasons. First, he was an only child, and his squadron mates had become like "a band of brothers." Second, one of his fondest dreams was to shoot down a MiG fighter in a dogfight. After what had happened that summer over North Vietnam, when a North Vietnamese MiG-17—a subsonic jet capable of more than 700 miles per hour, nearly three times the top speed of a Skyraider—had made the mistake of flying low in front of two Spads from the carrier *Midway* (CVA-41) and was raked by their 20 mm cannons and went down burning in a farm field, Spook hoped that the *Ranger* cruise might give him a chance to make his dream come true.

A self-described "wild man," Johns thought the Spad was great, but it drove him crazy that some of the senior guys flew the airplane "like a bunch of old ladies." In fact, when the previous CO, Mel Blixt, was checking him out to be a section leader, Spook engaged in aerobatics that resulted in his plane going into a violent spin. Observing from a distance, Blixt was aghast at what he considered reckless flying, and refused to let Spook lead his own section. Thereafter, Spook began calling Blixt "Cashmere," as in cashmere sweater, because Blixt "sweated everything." The name stuck.

With the wild streak they both possessed, it was not surprising that Spook and Dieter became buddies, although Spook, as the older, more experienced pilot, was the leader while Dieter tried to keep up like an eager little brother. They partied together in their free time, and tangled more than once in the air. On one night mission soon after he joined the squadron, Dieter was flying wingman for Cashmere, who had dropped down to 500 feet over the San Joaquin Valley on a practice run to "find Soviet T-34 tanks disguised as '58 Buicks." Because Dieter had not yet logged many night hours, the cautious Blixt advised him to stay above and behind Blixt's plane at 3,000 feet. Lurking above them at 6,000 feet was Spook, who spotted a faint illumination atop Dieter's fuselage coming from a running light. Spook decided to give Dieter a little scare, although in retrospect it "wasn't the greatest idea in the world." Spook flipped off his running lights and swooped down on his unsuspecting prey. Coming in from behind and below, Spook pulled up in front of Dieter with fifty feet separating the planes, knowing the kind of turmoil his plane's powerful prop wash would cause. This was called giving someone a hot nose or a thumping, and most pilots engaged in such play, although usually in daylight. Dieter, who had been cruising along with an open canopy, enjoying the night air, was startled by the roar of another plane coming out of nowhere and then suddenly finding himself in severe turbulence. As he pulled off, Spook flicked on his lights so Dieter could see who it was. Seconds later, tracer rounds lit up the night sky, and their bright trajectories passed close enough to Spook's plane to scare the hell out of him. Dieter had drawn his .38 revolver—every navy pilot carried a handgun in a shoulder holster as part of his survival gear—and fired out of his open canopy. Later, the thought would cross Spook's mind, *What if Dieter had hit me?*, but the fact was he did not. No harm, no foul, and Cashmere never found out.

Some of VA-145's training in 1965 was conducted with other squadrons from Carrier Air Wing 14, a separate unit of aircraft, pilots, and maintenance personnel—1,500 officers and enlisted men—that would deploy aboard *Ranger* for the WestPac cruise. When they were added to *Ranger*'s 3,500-man crew—known as ship's company—the carrier would leave for overseas with a full complement of 5,000 officers and men, and more than 100 aircraft.

During a weeklong stay at Fallon as the air wing's squadrons worked on the large-scale coordinated attacks they would be conducting over Southeast Asia, Dieter thought more seriously about going to war. He decided that if he went down behind enemy lines he would "not be captured," but would "shoot it out with them." He had a favorite High Standard .22 semiautomatic pistol from his air force shooting days. The gun looked like a Colt .45, complete with a ten-round clip that slipped into the handgrip. He was a skilled shot with it but realized that if he fired it in the jungle, the sound could bring unwanted company. He found a gunsmith on the base, and worked with him making different detachable silencers for the gun. Keeping "the best one," Dieter packed it away along with 250 rounds of soft-nosed ammunition.

Both in Fallon and in Alameda, Dieter spent lots of off-duty time with Lessard as they became buddies. They had met during flight training at

Corpus Christi. Lizard's first impression was that Dieter was "a wild guy who loved to chase girls." Of course, other Swordsmen said the same thing about Lizard. But although he was just as wild as Dieter and a self-described bad boy at many officers clubs, Lizard would "wear out eventually but Dieter would not." Lessard's course in life changed when he met Sharon Smith, the gorgeous daughter of a career navy officer. When she walked into the Alameda O club with her mother early one evening, it was love at first sight. Lizard immediately "started sobering up" because he thought she might be the real deal for him. They married six months later—that enchanted summer of 1965. The wedding ceremony was aboard *Ranger* and the reception at the nearby Hunters Point O club. The father of the bride, a navy captain who had recently served as executive officer of *Ranger*, invited all the brass—mid-grade to senior officers, including a few admirals—and Lizard had "all the hooligans to invite." Not surprisingly, it turned into a raucous affair. The VA-145 pilots knew they were soon going to war and had "better have fun now," as no one knew what the future held. Before it was over, a stationary bar at the club had been torn off its mounts and dragged outside so the thirsty in various states of dress could be served drinks without going inside; several Swordsmen had done the twist on the hood of Sharon's father's prized 1956 T-bird; one of the pilots was stopped by a highway patrolman while driving erratically across the Bay Bridge sans pants; and VA-145 was banned from the Hunters Point O club for the duration of their stay. This ban wasn't a big deal, because they all agreed there were too many black shoes at Hunters Point—non-aviator naval officers wore black shoes and aviators wore brown shoes. They always had more fun at the Alameda O club—a club which they considered their own at the air station, and which was always filled with fellow pilots.

As the squadron faced going to war and the inevitable death of some of their own, Dieter came up with a plan for financial gain. Finding a life insurance policy that did not have a war exclusion, he met with an agent to get an estimate. Approaching several of the other bachelors in the squadron, he found four who agreed to go in with him. The deal was this: each man would have a $1 million policy insuring his life for six months, starting January 15, 1966. The other four would be his beneficiaries. The combined premium would be $9,000—or $1,800 per man. If one of the five died, the other four would split $1 million. Willing to join Dieter in the plan were Walt Bumgarner, Gary Hopps, John Tunnell, and one of the few Annapolis graduates in the squadron, Dave Maples. "Why not?" Bummy told Dieter. "We've little to lose and a lot to gain." However, a couple of the senior officers' wives heard about the plan and thought it "ghoulish," and the squadron's executive officer put the "kibosh on it."

Although navy pilots tend to spend their free time with their squadron mates, particularly when they are away from home, that is not always the case. At Fallon, Spook, Lizard, and Dieter were soon joined by a fun-loving VF-143 pilot from their air wing: Lieutenant Wayne Bennett, twenty-six, of Akron, Ohio. Bennett flew the hottest fighter in the fleet: the $2.4 million swept-wing, twin-engine F-4 Phantom II.

A jet interceptor built by McDonnell Aircraft with a top speed of 1,472 miles per hour, the Phantom was a tandem two-seater. In the navy's configuration, the pilot sat in front, and in the backseat was a radar intercept officer (RIO) responsible for monitoring various onboard systems, including an impressive array of missiles—both heat-seeking and radar-controlled for air-to-surface and air-to-air combat. One thing the F-4 Phantom lacked—much to the chagrin of the hotshot pilots who flew this supersonic war bird—was a gun of any type. The prevailing theory was that modern air-to-air combat against enemy aircraft would not be like the dogfights of the two world wars. Rather, a sophisticated high-speed missile-platform like the Phantom would blow an adversary out of the sky from miles away, without ever getting close enough to use guns. But as for the pilots who flew the F-4s, according to Bennett, "we didn't believe dogfights were going to be obsolete." While he was training with the F-4 RAG squadron before joining VF-143, Bennett heard for the first time during a briefing that practice dogfights were prohibited by navy policy; specifically, they were considered "too violent" for the sensitive and sophisticated air-intercept radar system the F-4 carried. He looked in absolute disbelief at the guy sitting next to him: "Who are they kidding?" Rules or no rules, Bennett and the other Phantom pilots found opportunities to mix it up in the sky with their F-4s. But without any instruction in the tactics of maneuvering individually to attack or evade an adversary at close quarters, Bennett worried about how they would stack up against a MiG if they ever found themselves in a real dogfight.[*]

One weekend Bennett climbed into Spook's new International Scout and tagged along with some Swordsmen for an excursion into the desert. Spook folded down the Scout's top, giving it the look of a World War II German staff car, which the pilots "liked just fine." They loaded up on cases of beer, stacked coolers with ice, and brought along their sidearms to take potshots at the jack rabbits. Even with four-wheel drive, it was rough going when they left the road and headed out over the rugged terrain filled with sand dunes and tumbleweed. Spook was a good driver and kept them out of trouble, but for most of the afternoon Dieter kept asking to drive. Spook kept saying no.

"You'll get us stuck, Dieter."

"Come on, Spook, let me drive." Dieter went on pleading, in his lilting German accent that was getting more beery all the time, until Spook relented.

Letting Dieter take the wheel, Spook instructed him like a teenager being given the wheel for the first time, warning him not to go over the top of a dune or they might get stuck at the center of the frame with no traction.

It took no more than five minutes before they were stuck atop a high sand dune. Spook got out and circled the vehicle. With all four wheels in the air, the Scout squatted on its belly like a beached whale. Scowling, he came around to the driver's side, where Dieter still sat, smiling impishly.

"Goddamn it, Dieter. No wonder Rommel lost North Africa."

The pilots used their bare hands to dig the Scout off the hot dune.

---

* The navy concluded that inadequate training in air combat maneuvering (ACM) was responsible for too many aircraft losses in the air war over North Vietnam. As a result, the U.S. Navy Fighter Weapons School, known as TOPGUN, was established in California in early 1969, with aviators from frontline combat units selected to attend the elite course, which emphasized aerial dogfighting at close quarters. Upon graduation, these pilots returned to their fleet units to teach fellow squadron mates the ACM tactics they had learned. Beginning in 1970, the navy's kill-to-loss ratio against North Vietnamese MiGs quadrupled, with naval pilots shooting down 13 enemy planes for one of their own losses. (Incidentally, scenes for the popular 1986 movie *Top Gun* were filmed aboard the aircraft carrier *Ranger*.)

✪ ✪ ✪

Shortly before VA-145's deployment, Dieter was promoted to lieutenant, junior grade. He also announced his engagement.

Considering his deserved reputation as an inveterate ladies man, his engagement came as a shock to some of his squadron mates. During flight school, Dieter had enjoyed countless liaisons and had broken more than a few hearts along the way from Pensacola to Corpus Christi. Later, he was known to rendezvous with a cast of young women at various bases—enthusiastic playmates like Rita, an Italian beauty who looked like a "young Elizabeth Taylor." Separately—none of the women seemed to know about the others—they accepted Dieter's invitations to meet him in places like the Alameda O Club, or Fallon and Yuma when he flew there for training with his squadron.

However, Dieter's brother Martin and his closest friends knew all about Dieter and Marina Adamich: how they had met when they were students at San Mateo Junior College, and how he had fallen head over heels for the petite, blue-eyed platinum blond who was as smart as she was beautiful. Since then, Marina had been "in one category and all the other women in another." Dieter had, in spite of the geographic distance between them during his training and later assignments, "never stopped pursuing" Marina. He marveled at her combination of looks and intelligence, and he had long told his family and closest friends that he hoped one day to make her his wife and mother of his children. The daughter of a commander in the royal Yugoslav navy, she was a science-major graduate of the College of Notre Dame in Belmont, California, and at age twenty-three was working as a chemistry research assistant at Stanford University. When Dieter asked her to marry him when he returned from Vietnam, she said yes. Following a German custom for an engaged couple, they exchanged matching gold wedding bands to be worn on the right hand until their wedding day, when each would switch the ring to the left hand.

On the morning of December 10, 1965, Marina waited on the balcony of her apartment in Telegraph Hill with a signal mirror Dieter had given her. Soon, the big ship came into sight as it pulled away from Pier Three at Alameda Naval Air Station and was nudged by tugboats into San Francisco Bay.

At 9:29 A.M., the aircraft carrier *Ranger* passed under the Bay Bridge.

Marina saw the signal then, coming from the carrier's flight deck, the perimeter of which was lined with hundreds of sailors in dress blues.

Dieter, using his own signal mirror, was telling her good-bye.

Marina signaled back, hoping she was catching the sun's reflection in her mirror. She kept signaling, and so did Dieter, as the ship steamed slowly past the hilly city by the bay, and slipped under the Golden Gate Bridge— heading, like other ships before it, for a war on the far side of the Pacific.

✪ ✪ ✪

Five hours later, two Spads circled lazily overhead.

They had been launched from *Ranger*, now nearly 100 miles off the coast and steaming on a northwesterly course. With no specific orders, the two VA-145 pilots decided to take a last look at the San Francisco Bay Area.

When it was time to head back, one of the planes dropped low over the bay dotted with sailboats as they approached the Golden Gate Bridge.

"I've wanted to do this for years," Spook Johns radioed to his wingman.

"You're really going to do it, aren't you?" said David "Mapes" Maples, the Nashville native and 1963 graduate of Annapolis, who had recently been promoted to lieutenant, junior grade. He had already decided that he was *not* going to fly under the famous span, no matter what Spook did.

Spook aimed for mid-span. As he cleared the undercarriage of the big orange bridge, people on the walkway waved. He rolled the Spad victoriously.

"What can they do to me, Mapes? Send me to Vietnam?"

5

GRAY EAGLE GOES TO WAR

As one of the U.S. Navy's mightiest warships steamed across the world's largest ocean carrying the planes and pilots of Carrier Air Wing 14, Dieter worked on his plans for survival, evasion, and escape in enemy territory.

After taking inventory of his standard survival kit, he added beef jerky, dried pepperoni, sugared nuts, and some other high-protein food. He visited an air wing physician and got extra medical supplies, including salt pills to prevent dehydration, pep pills for energy, and tablets to ward off the effects of malaria.

Understanding that the steamy jungle would be a breeding ground for malaria-carrying mosquitoes, Dieter decided he needed some extra protection. He asked for a poncho, but was told none was available. He also could not get a big mosquito net. So he went to the ship's parachute-rigging shop, and talked one of the riggers into working with him. Two sheets of green nylon "about a foot longer" than Dieter were sewed together with a zipper at the top. The rigger fashioned armholes for sleeves, which ended in mittens. Snipping out a large circular hole near the top, he stitched mosquito netting over the opening. Using it as a sleeping bag, Dieter could zip himself completely inside at night—or if he was on foot he could wear it as a poncho by turning it over and putting his head and arms inside. He folded up the garment tightly, and duct-taped it inside the back of a survival vest of his own design. Inside the vest he had shroud cutters for freeing himself from a tangled parachute, medical soap for cleansing wounds, an extra fishing line and hooks, a flint and steel for starting fires, a big-bladed knife, and his small signal mirror.

Dieter next turned to customizing the Swiss climbing boots he had recently purchased, convinced they were what he needed to traverse long distances over difficult terrain. With a knife he sliced into the front of each sole, and peeled back the flap. Inside one he placed an extra navy ID card he had been given days earlier after falsely reporting losing his. Inside the other he placed the Geneva Convention card, which active-duty military personnel carried, stipulating humane treatment for prisoners of war under a 1949 treaty. Then he glued the soles back together. Next, he sliced open the leather tongue of each boot. Each was stitched back together on the parachute rigger's sewing machine with a folded $100 bill inside. Dieter figured the money could come in handy if he was ever in a position to buy his way out of trouble.

If he went down in enemy territory and was stopped and questioned by communist forces, his plan was to pass himself off as a German citizen working in Indochina. To that end, he carried the old German passport he had used for entry to the United States eight years earlier, his birth certificate, and papers identifying him—at age eighteen—as a machinist from Calw. He tucked into his gear a cheap plastic wallet containing two pictures: one of his mother, looking like the German matron she was, and the other of himself on a motorcycle bearing a European license plate.

He also had a set of civilian clothes: a light blue shirt, tan trousers, and a lightweight green jacket. As he would be wearing his own Swiss boots rather than regulation flight boots, he would be able to do a quick change to civilian attire. His plan to establish a false identity included changing the name on some of his gear, such as the navigation bag with all his maps. Should he crash, he planned to leave them behind so the bad guys would be searching for a U.S. pilot named Wilson, while Dieter Dengler, a German civilian who rode motorcycles, was allowed to go on his way. If the ruse failed, he would cut open the soles of his boots and show his navy ID so as to be afforded POW status, which was preferable to being shot as a spy.

Dieter decided some target practice was in order, too. However, there were not many places to shoot a gun on a ship without drawing undue attention.

Dan "Farky" Farkas opened the door to the corner stateroom he shared with Dieter on the 03 level one deck below *Ranger*'s flight deck—Farkas had pulled rank by virtue of his slightly senior date of commissioning to get the desirable top bunk. As Farkas entered, he heard muffled thuds and was shocked to see Dieter sitting in his bunk shooting his .22 pistol at a wooden chock set up inside an open wall safe, which each stateroom had for safekeeping of valuables. Each muted pop was followed by a thud as the slug embedded itself in the wood, or a clang as it reverberated inside the steel safe.

"Dieter, are you nuts? If you miss—"

"I never miss." Dieter held up the gun to show the silencer. "It works."

Farky had to admit that from a few feet away there was little sound.

As Dieter's roommate, Farkas was a captive audience and heard most of Dieter's strategies for survival, but since Farkas "wasn't into getting shot down" he didn't always pay attention. Dieter went on at length about a lot of scenarios, including passing himself off as a German missionary because "they wouldn't kill a minister." When Farkas asked if he had a Bible, Dieter produced a pocket-size one in German. Farkas did think Dieter's "gear for survival was perfect," and picked up a few tips for his own.

For Lieutenant (j.g.) Dennis "Denny" Enstam, twenty-six, of Kensington, Connecticut, Dieter's extensive preparation during their Pacific crossing was amusing as well as amazing to observe. An experienced pilot and a veteran of the *Constellation* cruise, Enstam had heard plenty of pilots talking about what they would do if they went down over enemy territory. But Dieter, whom Enstam had come to know as "independent, stubborn, and very innovative," wasn't just "talking or playing"; he was dead serious, spending "many hours a day making equipment to take with him and packing his bags."

✪ ✪ ✪

Shortly after 5:00 P.M. on January 9, 1965, *Ranger*'s sea and anchor detail threw the first mooring line to the Leyte pier at Cubi Point Naval Air Station, Subic Bay, Philippines, site of one of the largest U.S. Navy bases in the Pacific. Within twenty minutes the carrier was secured to the pier by a dozen lines to starboard, and the officer of the deck (OOD) had shifted his watch from the bridge to the quarterdeck, where a temporary gangway was swung into place by a crane connecting the ship to the pier. Only officers were allowed to pass over the quarterdeck. At another location on the ship's starboard side, a brow was swung into place to be used by enlisted crewmen for coming and going.

First off the brow were a chief petty officer and ninety-one enlisted men in his charge who would serve on temporary shore patrol duty that night to help police the few thousand *Ranger* sailors polishing their shoes and changing into dress whites to descend at sunset on Olongapo, a city whose myriad bars offering cheap beer, welcoming hostesses, and knockoff rock bands that performed all the popular hits of the day made it a favorite liberty port.

First to board via the quarterdeck, minutes after the carrier's arrival, was Rear Admiral Maurice "Mickey" Weisner, forty-eight, of Nashville, Tennessee, commander of Carrier Division One, who would fly his flag in *Ranger* and assume tactical command of the carrier, its air wing, and various escorts. Weisner could be excused for being overly eager: he was one of the navy's newest admirals; the two silver stars on his collar were only five weeks old. Also, this was to be his first sea duty in nearly four years, after being stuck behind a succession of desks in Washington, D.C. A 1941 graduate of Annapolis, he had soon found himself in the midst of the war in the Pacific; he was assistant navigator of the aircraft carrier *Wasp* (CV-7) when it was hit by three Japanese torpedoes and sunk in the fall of 1942. He subsequently entered flight training and returned to the Pacific as a patrol-bomber pilot. He was awarded the Distinguished Flying Cross for sinking a Japanese destroyer escort in the Battle of the Philippines in 1944.

Ranger (CVA-61), launched in 1956 at Newport News, Virginia, was one of four supercarriers of the *Forrestal* class, and the first U.S. aircraft carrier built from the keel up with an angled flight deck, which allowed concurrent launch and recovery operations. This class of supercarriers (80,000 tons fully loaded), with a flight deck longer than three football fields placed end to end, was more than twice the tonnage of the biggest World War II carriers (*Essex* class), and provided the navy with fast-strike seagoing platforms for large air wings of 100 or more planes. The angled flight deck, invented in the early 1950s by the British navy, improved flight operations and provided pilots with an added margin of safety. The runway was canted at an angle portside across the ship's deck to point out over the water, so that if an aircraft missed the arresting cables, the pilot only needed to increase engine power to maximum to get airborne again. The pilots were not in danger, as those on older carriers had been, of crashing into fueled, armed planes parked forward on the flight deck. Such fiery chaos fouled the deck, halted flight operations, and knocked a carrier out of action. The new carriers were more forgiving and efficient: planes caught one of the arresting-gear cables on the angled deck and stopped—or missed all the cables and took off down the angled deck to go around for another attempt. (The angled-deck design is used in today's *Nimitz*-class nuclear-powered carriers, which have grown to 100,000 tons, and also in the next generation of supercarriers currently being built.)

Ranger was considered a choice command for an aviation captain—only designated naval aviators command aircraft carriers—with hopes of one day becoming an admiral. A ship's CO, known colloquially as the skipper and the old man, was responsible for keeping his ship and crew in fighting shape. In the chain of command, *Ranger*'s CO reported to Rear Admiral Weisner, who answered to a more senior admiral in command of Task Force 77, the main striking arm of the U.S. Seventh Fleet, consisting of three to five carriers supported by cruisers and destroyers.

Ranger's skipper was Captain Leo B. McCuddin, forty-eight, of Reno, Nevada. A 1939 graduate of the University of Nevada, he had been studying law at the University of Arizona in Tucson when he received an appointment as an naval aviation cadet in the spring of 1941. He was commissioned an ensign upon graduation from flight training four months after the attack on Pearl Harbor. An F6F Hellcat ace who shot down six Japanese aircraft over Formosa and the Philippines, scored a direct hit on a

Japanese battleship with a 1,000-pound bomb, and blew up a Japanese destroyer with eight five-inch rockets in the Battle of the Philippine Sea, McCuddin was awarded the Navy Cross, the Silver Star, the Distinguished Flying Cross, and twelve Air Medals. After the war, the navy sent him back to law school. He graduated from Georgetown University Law School, then served two years as a lawyer on the judge advocate general's staff before returning to sea. His previous assignments included combat service in Korea, stints on four carriers, command of a fighter squadron, and command of a carrier air group.

When he assumed command of *Ranger* in February 1965, taking over from an unpopular captain who had "managed by fear" and "misused and abused" officers and enlisted men alike, McCuddin found the ship's morale "in the tank." Over the next ten months—five of them spent at San Francisco's Hunters Point shipyard as *Ranger* underwent an extensive overhaul—about half of the 3,500-man crew departed and were replaced by new personnel. The transition aided McCuddin in putting his own stamp on the ship, and making it clear to all hands—from experienced division officers down to the lowest apprentice sailors—that a "new guy was in charge" and things were going to be different. A big part of that difference was showing that it was possible to have fun while working hard, something McCuddin excelled at in his own life. First came the faux leopard-skin cover for the captain's thronelike chair on the bridge, showing all hands that their new captain had a sense of humor. It also did not escape notice that the new captain drove an MG roadster, which he kept parked near *Ranger*'s pier. (Before the ship left for WestPac, the sports car would be hoisted aboard by crane and kept under wraps at one end of the hanger deck.) Before long, his "famous red MG" had a reputation for "winning many races" against the San Francisco police. McCuddin engaged in regular monologues over the ship's 1MC general announcing system, which transmitted to all internal spaces as well as topside areas—congratulating a new father or handing out kudos to a division or department, often followed with the delivery of a cake. In his chatty talks he emphasized communication with family, and reminded everyone how important it was to set up allotments that would be sent home each payday so that spouses and kids had enough to live on or for the bachelors to save. He also announced that all crew members could visit the bridge—all they had to do was check in with the boatswain's mate of the watch. A lot of young sailors took him up on the offer, particularly those who worked many decks below in the engineering spaces that in the tropics could reach temperatures of 120 degrees. Thanks to a suggestion made by Lieutenant (j.g.) John Moore, twenty-six, of Catskill, New York, a collector of classical music, and enthusiastically endorsed by the new skipper, a musical theme was recorded to be played over the ship's speakers whenever *Ranger* left the dock and when it came alongside other ships at sea: the cavalry charge finale of Rossini's "William Tell Overture," which had been used for *The Lone Ranger* on radio and television. Then came the idea of having a woman join the crew,* which, in Mc-Cuddin's view, "really caught on" and resulted in "lots of ideas from the crew on how to have some fun with her." *She* was actually a life-size department store mannequin—a gift to the crew from McCuddin's wife, Billie, and other officers' wives. Arriving in early December, prior to *Ranger's* departure, the mannequin was named in a shipwide contest held during the Pacific crossing. The winning name: Kuddles McKudden. Officially enlisted in the navy by the ship's career information team, Kuddles soon had her own ID card, liberty card, and overnight pass. New outfits and costume jewelry were sent to the bridge by officers and sailors after shopping trips. During long periods at sea, Kuddles would be written to forlornly "like Dear Abby." Many of the helpful responses, signed Kuddles, were written by the CO. After a faux leopard stole matching the skipper's chair was delivered, Kuddles often was photographed with it draped over her shoulders. Pictured in *Navy News Magazine* wearing the leopard stole over a black cocktail dress, she stood beside McCuddin in his leopard chair, which had slung over one arm a western-style holster holding his .357 Magnum with custom wood grip. An avid hunter and fisherman, Mc-Cuddin often took potshots off the outside flying bridge a few paces from his chair. The caption read: "The same leopard? Miss Kuddles McKudden

---

* Women were excluded from serving aboard U.S. navy combat ships until 1994, when the navy assigned the first large group of female crew members (sixty-three) to the aircraft carrier *Eisenhower* (CVN-69).

Kuddles on the bridge with *Ranger*'s commanding officer, Captain Leo McCuddin. *U.S. Navy.*

and *Ranger* Commanding Officer, Captain Leo B. McCuddin, discuss this possibility on the ship's navigation bridge during a lull in the day's operations. . . . The crew knows that all is well when Kuddles is on the bridge." The article concluded: "In short, Miss Kuddles has been the biggest morale factor to this ship since the advent of the motion picture." And so the legend of Kuddles grew. Most important—given the Herculean task before them—was the perceptible "unexcelled morale" on *Ranger*, observed during shakedown sea trials off the California coast and operational readiness inspections. The crews of supply ships that came alongside *Ranger* for underway replenishments were shocked to see a dolled-up woman perched on the carrier's flying bridge, and then to hear a female voice (taped by a USO entertainer) over the loudspeaker: "Ahoy on *Sacramento*. Stand by for shot lines!"

Dockside at Leyte pier, *Ranger* commenced taking on fuel for the air wing's planes. More than one type was required because the jets and propeller planes did not use the same fuel. After that, a barge came alongside and pumped for hours to fill the carrier's bunkers with the heavy fuel oil for the eight Babcock and Wilcox boilers; these boilers provided steam to four turbines that each ran a shaft to propel the ship (top speed, thirty-four knots, or forty miles per hour) and provided electrical power throughout the ship.

A large ammunition barge tied up to the carrier's port side and a crane lifted pallets of bombs and rockets onto a lowered elevator at the end of the angled deck. *Ranger* had four such aircraft elevators—open platforms, each the size of a tract house—used for moving planes and ammunition to and from the hangar deck to the flight deck. Aviation Ordnancemen loaded the munitions onto handcarts and rolled them into the hangar bay, where they were pushed onto smaller elevators and sent many decks below for storage.

Fresh produce and other stores were brought to the dock in large trucks, unloaded, placed on a conveyor belt, then sent up to a lowered aircraft elevator on the starboard side. Sailors lifted the boxes and crates and placed them on raised aluminum rollers that snaked through the hangar deck into other compartments. Along the meandering line, men stood by pushing the supplies forward until they reached their destination.

With everyone working long hours, preparations for getting under way were completed in three days. A rotating three-section duty schedule for the 3,500 officers and men who made up ship's company (permanent crew), along with the 1,500 air wing personnel now aboard, allowed two-thirds of the men to go ashore every night while the other third stayed aboard with the duty. Like all navy ships, *Ranger* was tightly compartmentalized for watertight integrity, although most hatches between spaces remained open unless the crew was called to battle stations. The ship's company had its own berthing quarters and work spaces, as did the air wing. There was little mixing between the two groups; the crew's main job was to keep the ship operating, and the air wing was responsible for the planes and pilots.

For the next month *Ranger* would be at sea continuously, and would receive all supplies by underway replenishment—known as unrep—a method of transferring fuel, munitions, and stores from one ship to another at sea. First developed by the U.S. Navy in the late 1930s, the technique was used extensively during World War II, and gave ships increased range and striking capability without the need to put into port for supplies. *Ranger*, with its large storage capacity, would unrep its own escorts—usually two destroyers—with fuel oil and stores in between rendezvous with tankers and supply ships.

As the crew continued to make *Ranger* ready for departure, many of the air wing's pilots attended a one-day jungle environment survival training program (JEST) at Cubi Point naval air station. In addition to highly trained navy instructors, the school was staffed with a contingent of Negritos, an ethnic group native to the Philippine jungles. During World War II, Negritos were greatly feared by the Japanese—doubtless the Negritos' custom of leaving the heads of their enemies impaled on stakes marking their territorial boundaries caused much trepidation among the occupiers. Skills taught to the pilots at JEST included making utensils out of bamboo, boiling rice inside bamboo, and finding food and medicinal plants in the jungle. Samples of food prepared by the natives—including bats, ants, and snails—were served. Unlike some pilots who were more finicky, Dieter tried everything. His attention was piqued by the vivid description of what a pilot downed in the jungles of Southeast Asia would face: he could expect to be surrounded on the ground by an experienced and determined enemy who was being bombed round the clock. A U.S. pilot could not expect the enemy to show compassion or forgiveness; rather, he would be hunted down like an animal. To survive, the pilots were told, they would have to utilize animal instincts.

Early on the morning of January 12—after a civilian bar pilot came aboard to take the carrier out the narrow channel into the bay that led to the South China Sea—*Ranger* cast off all lines and swung away from the pier with the assistance of two tugboats. On the bridge the bar pilot "had the conn," meaning he was responsible for the movement of the ship. As such, he gave orders to the helmsman, who steers the ship. The bar pilot is entrusted to keep the ship on course to conform to the depth and shape of the channel. The bar pilot's responsibility for *Ranger* would be brief, lasting less than thirty minutes until the carrier reached open waters; then he would leave the bridge, climb down a rope ladder thrown over the side of the ship, and step onto the deck of a tugboat alongside.

As the bar pilot gave orders at the conn, McCuddin sat impassively in his chair. A ship's captain has ultimate responsibility for his vessel and crew no matter who has the conn, so the skipper could have overruled any orders if he believed *Ranger* to be in jeopardy. Personnelman Third Class Stewart

Hunter, twenty-three, of Ontario, California—the 1JV phone talker on the bridge who passed along the orders of the captain to other sections of the ship via the sound-powered phone circuit—could see that the skipper was keeping a "very close watch" on everything. The civilian pilot also appeared to be taking in everything: the dolled-up mannequin, the captain's leopard chair, the holstered handgun—all unusual sights on the bridge of a navy ship.

"What's the gun for, captain?" asked the bar pilot, apparently more comfortable inquiring about the firearm than the other trappings.

McCuddin, without any trace of a smile, growled, "Pirates."

The pilot left the bridge soon thereafter, and McCuddin had the conn. Seven hundred miles to the west lay the coast of Vietnam.

JANUARY 16, 1966

"*Gray Eagle*, this is *Overpass Nine Zero One*. Thirty miles out."

"*Nine Zero One*," responded air-traffic control. "Proceed to marshal."

Radio call signs had been assigned to *Ranger*—aka *Gray Eagle*—and the air wing's squadrons. The reconnaissance squadron—RVAH-9 Hoot Owls—was *Overpass*, and the three-digit side numbers on its RA-5C Vigilantes all began with the number nine. In that way air-traffic controllers aboard *Ranger* knew what type of aircraft they were directing—important information, given the varying speeds, weights, and flight characteristics. The call signs were classified, as it would have been useful to the enemy to know what types of aircraft were coming their way.

Ranger had arrived a day earlier at Dixie Station, a designated point in the South China Sea 100 miles off the coast of South Vietnam. From here, for two days, the carrier's planes had been flying air support for friendly ground forces engaging enemy guerrillas in the south, missions that afforded pilots a decent chance of ditching or bailing out without being taken prisoner. The navy kept one carrier at Dixie Station: often the latest carrier to arrive in WestPac, with the air-support missions serving as a warm-up for the more intense bombing runs over North Vietnam, where there were no friendlies on the ground.

The ship's air-traffic controllers worked in Air Ops, located in a darkened twenty-by-thirty-foot compartment one deck below the flight deck. Along the walls were several Plexiglas status boards, and behind them enlisted men with headphones wrote on the boards with grease pencils. Since they stood behind the transparent boards, which were read by people on the opposite side, they wrote every number and letter backward. The heart of Air Ops was a line of radar screens giving off a greenish glow. At the radar consoles sat enlisted air-traffic controllers—mostly chiefs or first-class petty officers. Their function in directing and controlling aircraft was one of the few instances in the navy of enlisted personnel giving orders to officers—orders that were to be promptly obeyed. The only other lighting in the room came from low-wattage bulbs illuminating the status boards. The noise level was low, with no idle chatter when controllers were working aircraft. The "scopes and radios emitted a low hum," and the air in the room—kept cold by air conditioning for the benefit of the electronics—had an "electric ozone smell" mixed with the stench of stale tobacco, as nearly everyone in the room smoked.

The Vigilante was setting up for a nighttime trap, which usually meant a straight-in approach. (Daytime approaches, by contrast, were flown in a left-hand racetrack pattern that circled the moving ship.) When the Vigilante reached its assigned orbit holding pattern, known as marshal, the pilot checked in again. An assigned altitude had been given to him before he left the ship. Other planes lining up to land had their assigned altitudes; planes were separated by increments of 1,000 feet to avoid collisions. Each was given a precise time to arrive over the carrier, called charlie time, which gave spacing to the landing planes. It was up to a pilot to enter the approach lane and start his glide slope in order to arrive on time.

When it was time for the Vigilante, the pilot, Lieutenant Commander Charles Schoonover, thirty-four, of Indianapolis, Indiana, a 1954 graduate of Annapolis, radioed: "*Nine Zero One*, pushing over." The Vigilante began descending toward the ship at 700 feet per minute as its landing gear, tailhook, and wing flaps were lowered.

The experienced Schoonover was flying one of the largest, fastest, and most complex planes in the navy. In the backseat of the tandem-seat, twin-engine Vigilante was someone at the opposite end of the experience scale:

Ensign Hal T. Hollingsworth, twenty-three, of Grace, Idaho. Hollingsworth was enclosed inside a rear section of the cockpit with only a small window on either side, but his view of the outside was less important than the world of screens and electronic systems he monitored as the reconnaissance attack navigator (RAN). Both positions had ejection seats, which could be fired separately; the pilot could also fire both together.

The Vigilante, in service for five years, had been built as the navy's main carrier-based strategic bomber for delivery of nuclear weapons to targets inside the Soviet Union and China. Strategic bombing—as opposed to shorter-range tactical bombing, which might target a bridge or railroad tracks—called for a knockout punch to a distant target for the purpose of destroying an enemy's capacity to wage war. The supersonic Vigilante was agile and fast, with a top speed of 1,320 miles per hour; but the design of the bomb bay in conjunction with the requirement on long-distance missions to carry two disposable fuel tanks in the same space led to problems. Also, this aircraft arrived at a time when the navy was emphasizing submarine-launched ballistic missiles in place of strategic bombers. As a result, the Vigilante was soon switched to an unarmed reconnaissance role, and loaded with airborne radar, infrared scanners, electronic intelligence systems, and sophisticated camera packs—all operated from the backseat position while the pilot was busy with the stick and throttle in the front seat. He was *very* busy, especially during recoveries, as the Vigilante's fast approach speed of 140 miles per hour—to prevent stalling—and its weight (it was more than twice as heavy as an A-1 Skyraider) made landing aboard the deck of a carrier challenging for even the most skillful pilot, and flat-out dangerous for an inexperienced or unwary pilot.

Air-traffic control informed Schoonover when radar showed him three-quarters of a mile from the ship, and added: "Call the ball."

"*Nine Zero One*, no ball. State, thirty-five hundred," said Schoonover, advising the controllers that he did not yet have in sight the orange meatball on the optical landing system (OLS) that would indicate the position of the Vigilante on final approach, and that he had 3,500 pounds of fuel remaining—enough to make several more landing attempts if his first approach had to be aborted.

The Vigilante now came under the control of the landing safety officer (LSO) standing on a platform at the aft port corner of the flight deck. Monitoring the plane's glide slope as it approached the carrier, the LSO—who was able to speak to the pilot by a handheld telephone over the ship's radio frequency—could order corrections, depending on whether the plane was high or low or not lined up on the imaginary centerline of the deck. The LSO made the call as to whether the plane was good to land. If he decided no-go, he would "pickle the trigger" in his right hand, activating two vertical rows of flashing red lights on either side of the meatball to order a wave-off. The plane would then have to pass over the ship, climb to 600 feet, and go around for another try.

The LSO saw why the Vigilante pilot did not see the ball. "You're low."

Schoonover reacted by adding power and intercepting the glide path. He then reported, "*Nine Zero One*, ball."

Observing on the LSO platform that night was Walt "Bummy" Bumgarner, in training as an LSO for VA-145—a position of trust and responsibility usually reserved for the best pilots in each squadron. (A measure of Schoonover's expertise was that he was his squadron's LSO, qualified to wave in Vigilantes.) The Spad pilot had never even seen a Vigilante trap on deck—although this was not unusual, given that there were only six on *Ranger*.

The distinct, high-pitched whine of the twin jet engines grew louder as the Vigilante closed on the ship's stern in the dark. It was an ominous sound that veterans of carrier operations associated with something difficult and potentially disastrous. For a Vigilante to land on a flight deck, especially at night or in inclement weather, always seemed an impractical feat.

The outline of the Vigilante with its fifty-three-foot wingspan—lit by the plane's "bright and steady" lights—hung briefly in the air like a great albatross. In the last few seconds the big jet drifted about ten feet above the glide path, and when it came over the ramp above the ship's fantail it was "high and fast."

"Bolter!" the LSO told Schoonover.

Schoonover did not respond.

Waiting nearby under the wing of a parked plane was Aviation Jet Mechanic Third Class Lawrence Petersen, twenty-one, of Mastic, New

York. Petersen was the plane captain for the Vigilante; this meant he was responsible for inspecting the plane, checking fluid levels (such as oil and hydraulic), ensuring that needed repairs had been made, and signing off on the plane's airworthiness before the pilot got into the cockpit. Keeping a Vigilante airworthy was not an easy feat. Although its engines were reliable, many of its electronics and other flight systems were state-of-the-air, and a "nightmare" to keep going. A Vigilante on average required 300 maintenance hours for every hour of flying, by far the highest maintenance ratio of any airplane in the navy. Draped over Petersen's shoulders were the heavy chains that he would use to tie down the Vigilante once it taxied to its parking space on deck.

Petersen already had a bad feeling because the night was as dark as he had ever seen, with "no moon at all and just pitch black." And with the carrier rolling in swells, the flight deck was always in motion; up, down, and sideways. It just seemed like a bad night to be flying, and he would be glad when the Vigilante was back on deck. Schoonover and Hollingsworth were returning from a photo-reconnaissance mission over South Vietnam, which with the Vigilante's sophisticated cameras and radar could be done by day or night.

With an eye trained from watching hundreds of carrier recoveries, Petersen saw that the Vigilante was high and long, and would miss all four cables stretched across the deck. It seemed that Schoonover came to the same realization at that moment, and dived for the deck. The sound of the Vigilante "just dropping out of the air" to the deck—a thunderous clang of "steel hitting steel"—would be something Petersen would never forget.

The instant the Vigilante's wheels hit the deck, Schoonover pushed the throttle forward to full power—standard procedure for jets, as it was the only way they would have the speed to regain flight in case of a bolter, when the tailhook does not snag an arresting wire and the plane has to take off again.

It all happened right in front of Petersen—the Vigilante slamming into the deck, the right landing-gear tire blowing, the landing gear itself collapsing, the strut of the landing gear pushing up into the inlet of the right engine, the "sucking of metal parts" directly into the engine as full power was applied, and then, almost instantly, the engine exploding with the force of a bomb.

As the Vigilante streaked down the deck at full power, Bumgarner on the LSO platform observed its right engine consumed in a ball of fire.

At the end of the angled deck, the Vigilante went airborne.

Everyone on the flight deck could see that only the left engine was working and the right one was ablaze. At that point, the pilot could have lit off the good engine's afterburner, which would have injected additional fuel into the turbine and provided added thrust for climbing. When an afterburner is lit, a fiery cone is emitted from the jet's exhaust, with a thunderous concussive boom known to break nearby windows. The afterburner on the crippled Vigilante's left engine was never lit. The plane "failed to climb" and settled into a slow descent that took it below the level of the flight deck, seventy feet off the surface of the water.

The LSO now gave one order and one order only: "Eject, eject!" There was ample time for Schoonover and Hollingsworth to punch out. The explosive-packed ejection seats on the Vigilante were known as zero-zero seats, meaning that they could be used on the deck (zero altitude) while the plane was standing still (zero speed), since the seats would throw a pilot far enough into the sky for his parachute to deploy. But the men in the Vigilante did not eject.

Across the flight deck boomed the dreaded announcement, amplified over outside speakers: "Airplane in the water! Airplane in the water!"

Floating light-and-smoke signals were thrown overboard to mark the location for *Ranger*'s rescue helicopter—always circling in the air nearby during flight operations—and the destroyer following a mile behind the carrier in what was called the plane-guard position, ready to respond in the event of a plane down or man blown overboard during flight operations.

The LSO platform had a mounted spotlight, which was turned on.

Everyone looked for some sign of the Vigilante.

Petersen dropped the tie-down chains meant for *Nine Zero One* and ran to the port side of the flight deck. He jumped down into the catwalk, a narrow walkway that ran along the outer edge of the flight deck. He knew Schoonover to be a senior pilot and a "nice guy," but it was Hollingsworth— the officer in charge of the enlisted plane captains—whom he knew best. Three weeks earlier, when *Ranger* had stopped at Pearl Harbor en route to

WestPac, Petersen ran into Hollingsworth on Christmas Day at Waikiki Beach. "Let's have a beer," the affable young officer said, "and talk about our families." That's what they had done.

Bumgarner and the others on the LSO platform soon spotted the Vigilante in the water off the port side of the ship. The plane was settling in the water, nose high. Both canopies were closed. One of the men on the LSO platform thought he glimpsed a flight helmet inside the front cockpit.

Petersen thought that if he jumped from the catwalk he could have landed on top of the plane. "Blow the seats!" he screamed, knowing the ejection seats worked underwater. "Blow 'em!"

Bumgarner and the others could see the destroyer and helicopter circling in the area of the floating signal lights—a mile away! The LSO tried to phone the air boss, then the bridge, then Air Ops, to report the plane in the water close abeam so rescuers could be dispatched. All the circuits were busy, and he could not get through. The men on the platform yelled and waved, hoping to get the attention of the air boss sitting in Primary Flight at the rear of the island superstructure overlooking and supervising all flight deck activities, or the personnel on the bridge at the front of the island, but there was so much commotion that no one noticed them.

For perhaps a minute, though the time seemed excruciatingly longer, the spotlight held the image of the Vigilante sinking until the men on the flight deck lost sight of it in the dark sea as the carrier hurried away from the downed plane.

In a daze, Petersen crossed the flight deck, picked up the chains he had dropped, and went below to his squadron's berthing compartment. He did not speak to anyone about the incident, and no one spoke to him. For years he would relive that night countless times, until three decades later he was hospitalized with post-traumatic stress disorder. As part of his recovery, he began talking about the accident, although to this day it still troubles him.

Schoonover and Hollingsworth, an investigation found, had probably been rendered unconscious when the right engine exploded after the collapsed landing-gear strut pierced the engine inlet. The two naval aviators surely went to the bottom of the sea strapped in their seats in the cockpit.

Ranger, operating off Vietnam for only two days, had already lost two aviators. Schoonover and Hollingsworth would not be the last.

✪ ✪ ✪

VA-145 divided its 18 pilots into two-man sections—each with a flight leader and a wingman, the latter being responsible for staying close to the leader. In most cases a newer pilot was wingman to a more senior flight leader.

Dieter found himself wingman to Lieutenant Commander J. K. "Ken" Hassett, thirty-four, of Dennis, Massachusetts, who as operations officer was the third-highest officer in VA-145 and responsible for the squadron's flight schedule and other administrative duties. Hassett had graduated from a maritime academy and had applied for flight training after several years at sea as a merchant marine and naval officer; he was "all military in appearance and attitude." A career officer who was "methodical and a paperwork guy," Hassett made it clear that he did not approve of the "loose cannons" in the squadron. The ringleader of the over-the-top contingent was Spook; and as for Dieter, he seemed to always be in trouble with Hassett, at first for infractions like letting his hair grow too long (Dieter abhorred haircuts), or failing to fill out or file routine paperwork in a timely manner. Before long, tension escalated in the air, too, between flight leader and wingman.

Dieter came to feel that things "went to hell" nearly every time he flew with Hassett. On one of their missions over South Vietnam, Dieter and Hassett were working with a U.S. Army forward air controller (FAC) on the ground who was directing by radio their attack on enemy positions. At one point, the FAC ordered Hassett to abort his attack. Hassett either did not hear the order to abort or ignored it. He continued his run from a high altitude that was safer in terms of not being struck by ground fire but less accurate when it came to hitting the target—a penchant of Hassett's that Spook soon dubbed "chicken shitting bombs." Hassett then dropped a 500-pounder that nearly landed on top of the FAC. On another flight, Dieter watched in horror as Hassett mistakenly "fired a pod of rockets" through their own formation; luckily, he missed.

Dieter also had misses. For example, on his first mission he was directed by the FAC to drop napalm—basically a "container full of gasoline mixed with gelatin." Napalm, which burned in the immediate area that it hit, was to be released as close to the target as possible in order to be effective, but Dieter—"frightened of being shot down" if he flew so low—released the cans from 1,000 feet and watched them "tumble and tumble" and miss by a country mile. Unfortunately, Spook, who regularly delivered ordnance near to the ground and could be counted on to "find some action" whenever he flew, saw Dieter's display of timidity. Back on the ship, Spook made fun of Dieter for missing everything except whatever poor sap had the bad luck to be walking underneath some small section of jungle canopy at that moment.

Although Dieter did not admit it to anyone, he was having troubling thoughts about the role he found himself in. As a boy, he had seen the terrible suffering and devastation caused by war in general, and by aerial bombardment specifically. His time in the military—first the air force and now the navy—had been about one thing: wanting to fly. The navy had given him his wings, and for that he was extremely grateful. In return, the navy had brought him here, expecting him to use his new skills to fight. That made the situation no longer just a matter of flying or even practicing to attack the enemy, which could seem so detached as to be unreal. *This was a shooting war.*

The exhilaration he so often felt when flying morphed at times into something else, particularly during night operations: Flying through a pounding monsoon at 200 miles per hour in the middle of the night, trying to find the carrier in total darkness, his only lifeline the voice of an air-traffic controller or LSO over his headset, then suddenly seeing the row of optical landing system lights that appeared out of nowhere in the blackness with no ship seemingly attached to them. Lights, just lights, to which he trusted his life. Then the "enormous bang" when his landing gear hit the flight deck, and being directed by aircraft handlers twirling lighted cones to hurriedly pull off to one side so the plane behind him wouldn't crash into him. He did so not knowing how close he might be to rolling off the deck into the sea. As he turned off his engine, and the propeller spun down, *wa-wa-wa*, and then stopped, that's when it started. His legs began to tremble mightily and "shake and shake." He pressed his hands against his trembling legs but "couldn't hold them still." Sometimes he would have to sit in the darkened cockpit for five minutes before he could crawl out.

On January 17, a FAC directed Lizard Lessard and two other VA-145 Spads to an area "to work over." Lizard's first bomb detonated in the middle of the biggest of numerous structures, and the Spads finished off with napalm strikes that set the remaining structures on fire. Seven buildings were destroyed, five damaged. The next morning, they were back at it, destroying three structures, damaging four others, and strafing a river sampan. The following afternoon they hit an area west of Saigon that was "infected with VC," destroying a large bunker and uncovering 300 yards of trenches.

After recovering all aircraft on January 19, *Ranger* turned northward and steamed hard through the night. Although their stay at Dixie Station had been planned to last a month, new orders directed the ship to proceed to Yankee Station—a designated point at the entrance to the Gulf of Tonkin—where the carrier would be in position for its aircraft to strike North Vietnam.

Spad moves forward for catapult launch. *U.S. Navy.*

Thirty-six hours later, *Ranger* rendezvoused at Yankee Station with Task Force 77, the Seventh Fleet's strike force, consisting of three other carriers—*Kitty Hawk* (CVA-63), *Hancock* (CVA-19), and *Hornet* (CVS-12)—a dozen destroyers, and two guided-missile cruisers, *Topeka* (CLG-8) and *Oklahoma City* (CLG-5), the latter being the flag ship for the commander of the Seventh Fleet, Vice Admiral John J. Hyland. Each carrier was escorted by two or three smaller ships, and together they formed a carrier division commanded by a rear admiral from the flag bridge of the carrier. In a celebratory show of force, two dozen A-4 Skyhawks from several carriers flew low over the ships in a formation shaped like the number 77, and pictures were snapped. Soon thereafter, the task force dispersed, with the carriers and their escorts separated by twenty or so miles in order to run back and forth into the wind for flight operations without interfering with another carrier. To launch and recover aircraft, a carrier required a bow-to-stern wind of thirty-five miles per hour over its flight deck; this was achieved through the ship's speed as it headed directly into the force of the prevailing wind. (The less wind, the faster the ship's own speed had to be in order to compensate.) To achieve these optimum conditions, a carrier was constantly in search of a strong breeze and room to maneuver. As the war against North Vietnam progressed, a Yankee Station carrier involved in daily flight operations would steam 10,000 to 12,000 miles monthly in an operational area that was only about 100 miles in length and breadth—a virtual small lake for an oceangoing navy.

One deck below the flight deck in squadron ready rooms where pilots changed into their flight gear and received mission briefings—or gathered when off duty just to shoot the breeze over mugs of coffee—the pilots received the "straight scoop" that in a few days they would start bombing North Vietnam after a monthlong moratorium. In the VA-145 ready room, the pilots agreed that they would be paying the price for the bombing halt. Lessard thought that the "white shirts" in Washington had accomplished nothing with the cease-fire except to give North Vietnam time to "restock and reload" and "get ready to shoot down more U.S. planes" with the latest Soviet and Chinese military hardware, including MiGs and surface-to-air missiles (SAMs) and anti-aircraft batteries (AAA). Off-duty pilots from every squadron crowded into the air intelligence offices until the space was jammed, wanting the latest information on roads, known missile sites, and anything else noteworthy. Maps and charts were pulled out, copied, cut, glued, and then marked with colored pens and pencils.

As Task Force 77 was poised to unleash its air wings against North Vietnam, VA-145 flew missions south of the demilitarized zone (DMZ) that ran along the seventeenth parallel between North and South Vietnam. The DMZ had been established in 1954 as a buffer between the communist-held state in the north and the fledging democracy in the south following the end of the French Indochina War. Although the term DMZ implied an absence of military activity along the border, nothing was farther from the truth: there was a constant flow of fighters and matériel through the DMZ from the north to the south. The mission to disrupt those communist supply lines by bombing and strafing targets of opportunity along roads and bridges was ideal for the slow, low-flying, heavily armed Spads. Their pilots could spot things in the jungle that jets—known as fast movers—zoomed past without seeing.

On one daylight bombing run near the DMZ, Dieter completed his run but did not see Hassett, so he orbited nearby and waited. Dieter kept circling even though enemy guns on the ground were "shooting like gangbusters" in his direction. Hassett finally came up on the radio. He was nearly seventy miles away—safely over the water—having left the target and his wingman "without saying a word." When they got back to the ready room, Hassett lit into Dieter, blaming him. Dieter took it for as long as he could, then said that he could not read Hassett's mind. Dieter said it was wrong of Hassett not to have radioed his intention to head back. The discussion became heated as the two pilots, who did not like each other, "had it out." When Hassett saw Dieter's clenched fists at his side, he ordered all the other pilots to clear the room and directed Ensign Robert Herrmann, thirty-three, of Brooklyn, New York, a former enlisted man who was the squadron's assistant maintenance officer, to stay as a witness. Then Hassett told Dieter, "If you want to take a swing, be my guest. I'll kick your ass, then court-martial you."

As much as he wanted to slug the guy, Dieter kept his fists at his side. He told Hassett to find another wingman. "I'm not flying with you anymore."

Back in his stateroom, a "red-faced" Dieter fumed about Hassett. He told his roomate, Dan Farkas, what had happened, adding: "I could kill that son-of-a-bitch."

Farkas, who had never seen Dieter so upset, advised him to back off with Hassett or he could end up in serious trouble. Whether around the ready room or participating in happy hours, Farky had always found Dieter "more of a jolly guy, not a fighter." Dieter had told Farky that he had fought as a kid in Germany, often over food, but didn't look for fights now.

That evening, Dieter was summoned back to the ready room, where Hassett was waiting. He said Dieter was "restricted to the ship for the rest of the cruise," meaning that whenever *Ranger* visited a port of call, Dieter would be confined to the ship. The thought occurred to Dieter that if Hassett's threat stood, he would just have to "sneak out" whenever they reached port.

Not informed of Hassett's threat to restrict Dieter to the ship was the one man who would have had to approve such a punitive measure: VA-145 CO, Hal Griffith. He knew Dieter was "not one to fall in line and follow orders" and that he was "a little reckless," and yet Griffith considered the spirited young officer a capable pilot. Also, Griffith was always being asked by officers from other squadrons about Dieter's escapes from SERE—now the stuff of navy legend—and Griffith retold the young pilot's story regularly, like a proud papa.

Word quickly spread of the heated words between Hassett and Dieter. Other junior officers made it clear they would not willingly switch sections to fly Hassett's wing. Not only was Hassett the most unpopular senior officer in VA-145, he was considered by more than a few to be the squadron's worst pilot, someone who "led with his rank rather than with his knowledge and skill."

Dieter and Hassett, with bad blood between them, were stuck with each other. While still bothered by Hassett's words and actions, Dieter knew that for his own good he had to let it go and forget the matter.

Early on January 27, off the coast of Vietnam, Dieter wrote to Marina, explaining that she might have difficulty reading the letter because he was flying with one hand and writing on his lap with the other. "Not many girl-friends will be able to say that they got a letter written over Vietnam at 6,000 feet. . . . I got the idea of writing to you just a few minutes ago when the sun came up. I have never seen anything like it. The sun is so big and so red and golden it is frightening in a way. The clouds are thick cumulus, and a warm wind is from the south. . . . The coast is only 30 miles away. We knew when the jets hit the coast because the whole sky lit up from anti-aircraft guns. . . . This morning's mission is exceptionally easy. We are protecting a seaplane which is airborne in case a pilot goes down over water. While the seaplane makes the pickup, we are here to shoot at whatever tries to stop the rescue. . . . So far no one got shot down today. We just circle and wait for somebody to call." Dieter wrote about his issues with Hassett. Then, warning her not to tell anyone, he explained some of the "rules of engagement" dictated by Washington that the pilots had to follow. They could hit only certain targets within 200 feet of a road; and many targets, even military ones, required special clearance. "If a MiG jumps me, and now we are talking about a pilot's life, I have to radio and get clearance to shoot. I could go on and on." In closing, he said he'd like to "fly this air mail letter and deliver it myself."

In his stateroom on the ship four days earlier, Dieter had written a missive of another kind to Marina—one he hoped would never be sent.

23 Jan. 1966

Dear Marina,

I am writing this in case I have to bail out. Naturally, <u>I will be back</u>. I have asked my roommate to mail this if something should happen.

Sweetheart, they may pack up all my stuff. I gave them your address, so everything will come to you. I also have some things in storage at NAS Alameda. It's all marked. Leave it there until you get bad news, then get everything. I made out a will. It's aboard Ranger.

<u>But I will be back,</u> so don't get all shook up. Please write Mother and tell her that. If I go down, I will take my time. I know the woods. So, it may be some time before you hear from me. Just don't forget that I love you and miss you. Please don't cry.

All my love,
Your Dieter

6

SHOOTDOWN

When Task Force 77 received the go-ahead to bomb North Vietnam at the end of January 1966, bad weather delayed the attack for two days. Then, at 8:30 A.M. on January 31, *Ranger* commenced combat air operations.

The resumption of the air war over North Vietnam was a continuation of a top-secret operation, Rolling Thunder, which had begun ten months earlier. The latest rules of engagement handed down by Washington identified "armed reconnaissance against moving targets" as the primary objective, with secondary targets being "bridges, truck parks and storage areas." Missing from the approved target list was any major city or port—neither Hanoi, the capital, nor Haiphong, the port through which flowed most of the Soviet-bloc weapons and matériel being used against American forces in the war, was listed.

The weather was still marginal. As dozens of warplanes from *Ranger* and *Kitty Hawk* approached North Vietnam, a heavy cloud layer blanketed the Gulf of Tonkin and the coastline.

Leading six Spads from VA-145 was Hal Griffith, the Korean combat veteran who had been in the air above the Gulf of Tonkin during the defining "non-incident" in August 1964. His wingman was Bummy Bumgarner, young and capable but thinking, *We shouldn't even be here in this weather,* because they had to keep descending to remain under the solid cloud cover. Coming in low made them vulnerable to small-arms fire as well as antiaircraft batteries, and also placed them in danger of being hit by shrapnel from their own bombs. The mission called for the Spads to attack a highway bridge and staging area.

Crossing over the coast into North Vietnam, Bumgarner was thankful to be flying the heavily-armored Skyraider that "could take hits" with its aluminum plating and added exterior steel around the cockpit and engine.

Loaded with 250-pounders left over from World War II and newer 1,000-pound bombs, the Spads rolled in fifty miles north of the DMZ over their target ten miles inland. Ten seconds behind Griffith, Bumgarner released his ordnance from 1,500 feet while in a shallow glide. As he did, he could see gun flashes on the ground and knew the bad guys were "firing back good." By the time Bumgarner finished his run, his plane had taken several hits. With a big hole in the intake pipe and "all kinds of other things wrong," the engine started running rough.

Using VA-145's call sign, *Electron*, Bumgarner radioed Griffith that he was heading out to the gulf to assess the damage. Diverting the other aircraft to alternative targets, Griffith flew out with Bumgarner and looked over his plane, finding numerous holes but "no fluid coming out."

When Bumgarner pulled the power back, the engine smoothed out.

Over the radio came word of a *Ranger* aircraft going down farther north, near the mouth of a river south of Dong Hoi, and an urgent request for assistance. Two VA-145 Spads that were closest to the location answered the call for a RESCAP, a combat air patrol to protect downed pilots and rescue forces in seaplanes or helicopters from enemy attack.

Griffith said that since Bumgarner's aircraft was flying okay now, they would start heading north and see if they could be of any assistance. As they flew parallel to the coast, they spotted smoke rising inland about five miles away.

"I'm going in closer to see what I can see," Griffith said.

The CO didn't tell Bumgarner to come with him, but as wingman Bumgarner was responsible for going wherever his flight leader went. So they headed in toward the coast, with Bumgarner behind Griffith. As they got closer, they climbed into the clouds. Griffith radioed they would hide in the overcast, then roll underneath it to get a quick look, and come back up to the clouds.

Bumgarner had clipped to a knee board attached to his thigh a map marked with information from the morning briefing, with some thirty red dots signifying known antiaircraft batteries along that section of coastline. Some of the dots were circled, which meant the batteries were radar-controlled. He knew that hiding in the clouds wouldn't provide any protection from radar-controlled guns.

Seconds later, Bumgarner lost sight of Griffith. The next thing he knew the "whole world below him was on fire" from antiaircraft shells bursting amid the puffy clouds. The sickening thuds from multiple hits to his aircraft might as well have been punches to his solar plexus. Bumgarner pushed the throttle forward to full power, and the engine began sputtering again. Without normal power, he pulled back the stick and brought the nose up forty degrees, hoping to use his airspeed to climb out of this mess. He got to about 6,000 feet, then had to drop the nose to keep the plane from stalling out and diving for the deck. He reduced power to the gasping engine.

"*Electron Lead*, engine took some hits and I'm shot up pretty bad," Bumgarner radioed. Since they were on a tactical frequency used and monitored by all the pilots on the strike that morning, Bumgarner hoped his voice didn't betray the fear he was feeling. "Might not make it back, Skipper."

Griffith responded that his plane was badly damaged, and he didn't know how much longer he could stay airborne.

Okay, he wins, thought Bumgarner, who knew he would have to go to the skipper's aid, and just hope that his own plane kept flying.

After numerous hits to his aircraft, Griffith had lost control, rolled inverted, and went into a dive. When he emerged from the clouds he was still upside down. Only "superb airmanship" enabled him to pull out of the deadly dive and roll the damaged plane upright.

When Bumgarner found Griffith, the young pilot saw that an eight-foot section of the CO's left wing was gone. Griffith was struggling to hold level flight even as he kept the stick all the way over to the right, as he had to do to prevent the plane from rolling to the left, where there was now less wing surface to provide lift. Bumgarner eyed the two 2,000-pound bombs, one under each wing. They were the heaviest bombs carried by a Skyraider. "Skipper, why don't you drop the bomb off your left rack? That might balance you out."

Griffith released the heavy bomb, lessening the imbalance.

Taking another look at Griffith's plane, Bumgarner reported that the left horizontal stabilizer was "just hanging on," with a hole in it "bigger than a basketball." He added that any G-load at all "might snap it off."

Although by then they were well out into the gulf and away from enemy shore guns, attempting to land on the carrier with a badly damaged plane was out of the question. For such an eventuality, carrier pilots were assigned at their pre-mission briefings an alternative place to land, known as a bingo field. There could at times be two or three bingo fields, in case weather, location, or other circumstances favored landing at one over another. For the carriers at Yankee Station, the Da Nang Air Base was the bingo field of choice. Da Nang had two 10,000-foot asphalt runways, and was a major base for U.S. Air Force and Marine Corps squadrons and various support personnel.

"Let's take it to Da Nang," Griffith radioed.

Da Nang was less than 100 miles away, and they made it in half an hour.

After Griffith landed, Bumgarner turned around and flew back to the ship; in retrospect, a "really stupid" decision, given the damage to his plane. But the shot-up Spad took him safely back. Upon inspection, a total of thirty-seven holes were found in the engine, wings, fuselage, and tail. Bumgarner would be given the engine intake pipe with an impressive hole in it and an eighteen-inch piece of wingtip that had to be replaced, as souvenirs of his first visit to North Vietnam.

In the VA-145 ready room to greet the returning pilots was Dieter, who as squadron duty officer that day had stayed aboard ship. Normally, Dieter hated being the duty officer because it required remaining in the ready room all day and night if necessary until the squadron's planes were finished flying. That morning, however, when it was apparent that the strike against North Vietnam was launching in spite of the adverse weather, he reveled in being "lucky to have the duty," not exactly what the guys suiting up to fly wanted to hear. It turned into a long duty day for Dieter—stuck in a room situated right below where landing aircraft first hit the flight deck. Each time one hit the deck it was "like an explosion" overhead, and by the end of the day his nerves had "just about had it." On top of that, the squadron was scheduled to send more planes out that night—one section was to drop time-delayed bombs along a highway—and Dieter would not be leaving the room until after that group returned, too. He would use some of the waiting time to write a letter to Marina, telling her he was on the schedule to fly early in the morning. With his duty that night, he wrote he might only have time to change clothes before he went on a five-hour mission over North Vietnam. He closed with: "I have your picture and I keep looking at it. I love you."

Many of the other pilots who hadn't flown that day were also in the crowded ready room, including Norm "Lizard" Lessard. They all hung on each graphic detail of what their squadron mates had gone through. Exhausted, and in flight suits stained with sweat, the returning Spad pilots filed into the room one by one and told harrowing stories about coming back with holes in their planes. Bumgarner captivated the listeners with his own story, and with the story of how the CO's plane was so shot up that it had to be flown to Da Nang. A couple of hours later, Griffith himself walked into the ready room, having made the one-hour flight to the ship in *Ranger*'s snub-nosed twin-propeller C1A carrier onboard delivery (COD) plane. Griffith looked haggard but relieved, and confessed that when his damaged plane dived out of control, inverted, through the heavy clouds, he had "thought that was the end."

Looking around the room, Lessard figured that the group could be divided into two camps: those who had flown that day and were thankful to have made it back, and those—like himself and Dieter—who had stayed aboard and were "scared shitless" about what they would encounter when it was their turn.

Although the pilots had been told that no strikes would be launched against North Vietnam unless the ceiling was at least 2,500 feet, waves of planes were launched and flown when cloud layers were far below that minimum—even as low as 500 feet—giving the pilots fewer options for their bombing runs and giving enemy gunners lower-flying and easier targets to hit. The official daily operations briefing sent to the chief of naval operations in Washington reported: "Low ceilings and nearly complete cloud cover curtailed the effectiveness of the first day's strikes and pilots report heavy and accurate AAA fire throughout most of the armed reconnaissance area."

In Lessard's opinion, which he noted in the daily journal he kept, "They caught us with our pants down when we tried to surprise them by flying in that damn weather. . . . A lot more people will get hurt before this crazy war is over."

A *Kitty Hawk* F-4 and an air force F-105 were reported down, and the fate of their pilots was unknown. One bit of good news was that the *Ranger* pilot who had been shot down—and had been the object of the RESCAP near Dong Hoi that Griffith and Bumgarner tried to reach—was successfully rescued.

The downed pilot, Lieutenant Commander Sylvester G. Chumley, thirty-one, of Clovis, New Mexico, had been leading a division of four A-4 Skyhawks from VA-55. By the time they reached their target—the Dong Hoi bridge—they were streaking underneath a solid 800-foot overcast, with little room to maneuver. These were "not sublime conditions" for launching a coordinated attack. So Chumley ordered the planes to separate, and told each pilot to make his own runs on the target. Chumley was pulling up from his fifth and last bombing run on the bridge when an antiaircraft battery nailed him. It was no doubt a direct hit on the engine, because everything stopped—the turbine, instruments, and radio. The plane tried to roll right but Chumley fought to keep it level. He made it into the overcast, but the whole time the deathly silent jet was rapidly decelerating. When he came out on top of the solid cloud cover he had no idea if he was over land or water. There was a greater likelihood of rescue if he punched out when he knew he was over the gulf—feet wet as opposed to the dreaded feet dry—but with nothing working in the plane, he had little choice. When the plane lurched to the right, out of control, and dropped earthward, he reached above his head and pulled the handle for the ejection seat. He was fired from the cockpit after the canopy blew clear, and his parachute opened normally. He was soon floating down through the clouds, without the slightest notion of what was below. He emerged from the overcast above water, but only about "two football fields" from shore. He "quietly went into the water," hoping not to attract any unwanted attention. Releasing the harness on his chute, he inflated his life vest but not his life raft. He knew that the yellow raft would be easy to spot from shore; also, he didn't want to drift in that direction. Instead, he started "swimming toward California," alternating between the breaststroke and backstroke, pulling the folded-up raft behind him. Before he went far, he saw a fishing boat leaving shore, heading his way. Like other *Ranger* pilots, Chumley had been briefed as to how downed pilots had a price on their heads, and that operators of fishing boats could expect to be paid hundreds of dollars by the North Vietnamese military if they captured a U.S. pilot. At this point, he knew he had been spotted and swam even harder. After being located by two A-4s flown by his squadron CO and wingman, who then radioed his position, Chumley heard the distinctive roar of powerful reciprocating engines. He looked up to see two Spads diving out of the clouds and wagging their wings, as in a World War II movie. They thundered toward the fishing boat closing on Chumley. One and then the other opened up with 20 mm cannon fire, raking the boat, which wheeled around and limped back toward shore. Not long afterward, a U.S. Air Force HU-16 Albatross amphibious flying boat landed close to Chumley, and he swam the remaining distance to its open hatch. As he did, a mortar round fired from shore dropped right in front of him, sending up a tall spout of water but failing to explode. He was hauled aboard the seaplane, which quickly turned for open water and took off. With only minor cuts and bruises, Chumley was delivered to Da Nang, where he spent the night before returning to the ship the following day.

It was an encouraging story in VA-145's ready room because Ken Hassett, flying with another wingman for the day because Dieter had the duty, was flight leader of the two Spads that chased away the fishing boat and provided protective cover for the downed A-4 pilot until his rescue. None of the pilots could have known there would be no such uplifting stories the next day.

Upon finishing his long day and night of duty and leaving the ready room late, Dieter went to his stateroom to get some rest. The night "seemed endless," and he got little sleep. By his count he was a veteran of nineteen missions over South Vietnam, but those flights had been "easy . . . a good way to get broken in," because he had faced mostly light small-arms fire from the ground. He knew that attacking North Vietnam with its network of radar-controlled antiaircraft guns and SAMs would be another matter. He was up before dawn for the ready-room briefing, held three hours before his scheduled 9:00 A.M. launch.

A four-plane division led by Ken Hassett included Spook Johns and his wingman, Denny Enstam, who had been so impressed earlier with Dieter's preparations for survival in the event that he was shot down. It turned out they would not be attacking North Vietnam, but only passing over its fifty-mile breadth. Their mission was deep inside Laos, where the United States had been conducting a secret war run by the Central Intelligence Agency, which the American public knew nothing about.

As early as 1955, the CIA had been orchestrating and supplying—using Air America, ostensibly a private company but in reality the CIA's own airline, which employed many former U.S. military personnel as well as Thai, Chinese, and Vietnamese—a fight against brutal Laotian communists known as the Pathet Lao, who received direct assistance from the North Vietnamese army and controlled major portions of the country. After U.S. intelligence found evidence of North Vietnam's successful efforts to expand and improve its infiltration and supply corridors into South Vietnam through the dense, remote Laotian terrain, Operation Steel Tiger, a covert aerial campaign flown by navy pilots from carriers in the gulf and marine and air force pilots based in Thailand and South Vietnam, began in April 1965. That year, it was estimated by the U.S. Defense Agency that the enemy was moving ninety tons of supplies a day through Laos and Cambodia on what the Americans came to call the Ho Chi Minh Trail, an interlocking maze of dirt and gravel roads, bicycle paths, foot trails, and river transportation systems.

Only a few miles off North Vietnam's long coastline—as long as the Oregon and California coasts combined—U.S. naval forces in the Gulf of Tonkin were poised to launch extensive search-and-rescue operations.

Pilots who went feet wet had reason to hope for a rapid and successful water rescue. However, landlocked Laos, far from any concentration of friendly forces, was an isolated and unfriendly jungle empire with some of the most primitive living conditions on earth. Local villagers, angry at the foreigners who rained death from the sky, would hunt down and attack downed U.S. pilots before handing them over to the Pathet Lao. Among pilots, it was agreed that if they were shot down over Laos and not quickly rescued, they would be on their own in the jungle—and if captured, they were as good as dead.

The mission of VA-145 that morning was a target halfway into Laos at 17 degrees 35 minutes north, and 105 degrees 14 minutes east: an intersection of Route 27 at a river crossing used by trucks heading south. No one expected to score any vehicles traveling on this gravel road—in daytime, supply vehicles were usually parked and hidden under the jungle canopy so as not to be caught in the open by U.S. planes. Supplies generally moved southward at night. The mission was to crater the highway and river crossing with 500-pound bombs left over from World War II, making the intersection impassable for a while.

Planes from VA-145 had visited Laos recently. On January 29, Lessard and Hal Griffith were launched close to 10:00 P.M. and were directed by a forward air controller (FAC) to a fifty-truck convoy heading for Cambodia on Route 923 through Laos. When they arrived, the area was already aflame from an earlier attack but "the VC were still trying to get the trucks through." The two Spads expended all their rockets and bombs, and "got a couple more trucks." On one of Lessard's bombing runs, Griffith told him later, it looked as if there were three heavy automatic weapons shooting at him "all the way down." Lessard, intent on his run, had no idea he was so popular. That experience was followed by a harrowing nighttime recovery in which a *Ranger* air-traffic controller confused the blips on his radar screen and directed Lessard toward the darkened sea until, only 100 feet off the surface, Lizard realized his plight and pulled up. That night, he updated his journal: "Like the LSO said, 'That was a close call.'" About Laos, he added, "The public in the U.S. doesn't know that we are bombing there and the government is trying to keep it quiet. Like I've been saying all along, a lot of people are going to get hurt."

After more waiting, Dieter, already in his flight suit, gathered his helmet and other gear and headed topside to check his aircraft. His plane was parked with other Spads at the far end of the flight deck above the fantail, their usual place of banishment because they leaked so much oil and grease that they could foul the deck. He checked his fuel levels—the internal tank in the fuselage held 385 gallons; and an extra gas tank that planes used to extend their range, called a drop tank, was secured under each wing and could hold 300 gallons. Filled to capacity, Spads could stay airborne for as long as ten to twelve hours, although normally their missions ranged from three to six hours, much longer than a jet's typical 1.5-hour cycle from take-off to landing. (Owing to the long duration of their flights, VA-145 pilots had taken to sitting on a rubber blow-up doughnut—the kind used to relieve hemorrhoid sufferers. These doughnuts were specially ordered by the supply officer to alleviate an occupational soreness unique to Spad pilots. The appreciative VA-145 guys came to consider the doughnuts "worth their weight in gold.") Dieter also made sure the arming wires on the bombs had been properly installed by the ordnance men so that when a bomb was released the wires stayed connected to the plane, thus being pulled out of the fuse in the nose of the falling bomb. With the wire gone, a small propeller on the bomb's nose rotated in the wind; now armed, the bomb was set to explode on contact. If a bomb fell off with the arming wire attached, it would not explode. In fact, there was a cockpit switch to release bombs with the wires attached in the event of an emergency landing, ensuring that the unspent ordnance would not explode.

Over the flight-deck loudspeaker boomed the orders from the air boss signifying the start of flight operations: "Secure loose gear. Put on flight goggles. Stand by to start all jets."

This morning the four Spads at the stern would be last to launch.

In the cockpit, Dieter buckled his shoulder harness and seat belt, and slipped on the supple leather gloves meant to provide some protection against a cockpit fire. He left the canopy in the open position, where it would remain until he was aloft. Unlike jets, which had ejection seats that would blow away the canopy before rocketing the pilot from the cockpit, the Spad had no ejection system. To bail out, the pilot blew the canopy off by activating an emergency air bottle, stood up in the seat, and jumped or rolled out, hoping he had enough altitude for his parachute to open. At lower altitudes—anything under about 1,500 feet—there could be no safe parachuting from a Spad, which is why pilots often kept the canopy open during launches and recoveries for a quick escape in the event of a ditching.

As the jets were being launched, the Spads were started up under the direction of flight-deck personnel with the usual amount of backfiring and billowing smoke as the 2,700-horsepower radial engines came to life.

Dieter checked his instruments, and everything looked good.

He switched his radio to *Gray Eagle* launch frequency. "*Electron Five Zero Four*, up and ready," he announced.

After the jets were launched, the Spads taxied forward. Dieter's plane was attached to the number three catapult, one of two cats located on the angled deck. Pushing the throttle forward to the stop with the palm of his left hand and wrapping his fingers around a grip behind the stop to keep himself from accidentally pulling back on the throttle during takeoff, he pressed his helmet back into the headrest so his neck would not be whiplashed, then with his right hand saluted the catapult officer—the universal signal that a carrier pilot is ready. Dropping his right hand back to the stick, he took a deep breath and exhaled evenly. At full power, the Spad revved up to a teeth-rattling 2,800 revolutions per minute and struggled mightily to break free of the steel bridle attached by cables to both inboard wings. The catapult officer—who was known as the shooter and wore a bright yellow vest for quick recognition—made sure the path in front of the plane was clear and everyone was ready who needed to be. Then, he crouched and froze like a statue, his forward arm pointed dramatically in the direction in which the plane was about to be dispatched. With a loud hiss and curls of steam escaping along the catapult track, the Spad was off.

Airborne in under three seconds, Dieter pulled back on the stick to bring the nose up ten degrees to begin a steady climb. He took his other hand off the throttle long enough to raise the landing gear, then reduced the power to 2,600 revolutions per minute for maximum climb. He also switched his radio to a tactical frequency, which the VA-145 pilots had been given during their briefing that morning.

Dieter happened to be piloting the first Spad launched. Once airborne, he proceeded about ten miles out to where the VA-145 planes were to rendezvous. At 2,000 feet, he set up a left orbit and waited. The others soon joined him.

The four Spads went feet dry over North Vietnam twenty minutes after takeoff. The flight regularly changed altitude and heading so as to keep radar-controlled antiaircraft weapons from locking onto the inbound flight. The skies over the gulf had been crystalline blue, but the weather deteriorated inland. It was the coastal monsoon season, and they flew through a torrential downpour that lowered the ceiling and visibility. At one point the flight dropped to "700 feet in the soup" trying to follow the terrain while keeping each other in sight. After some tense flying—their cockpit maps showed low-slung mountains of 1,500 feet or higher in the area—they broke into the clear. They regained altitude, and soon crossed Mu Gia Pass in the Annamese Cordillera range. The rugged 1,370-foot pass was the gateway to Laos, and the principal point of entry to the Ho Chi Minh Trail.

Looking down into Laos for the first time, Dieter saw a vast jungle—the "deepest green" he had ever seen—broken by an occasional outcrop of whitish, sharply chiseled cliffs. He thought the terrain looked "impenetrable." This was nothing like the tree-studded Black Forest he knew so well or the arid openness of Warner Springs, where he had displayed his escape and evasion skills.

As they continued westward, there were fewer jagged peaks and only occasional gaps in the jungle—now and then a field that looked as if it was being farmed. As the topography changed, so did the climate. Leaving behind the coastal monsoon, they entered a different season, one that was hot and dry. A strange "murky and yellow" haze hung in the air; it looked to Dieter like Los Angeles smog. He would find out later that it was caused by rice farmers who were slashing, burning, and clearing areas of woods and jungle in preparation for planting the next season's crop.

Dieter's panoramic tour was interrupted by a radio call from Hassett saying that he was experiencing radio problems, and directing the flight's next senior pilot, Spook Johns, to take over the lead. In the number two position of the four-plane formation, Dieter hoped to stay where he was and be wingman for Spook, whom he considered a "great flier." This was Spook's second combat cruise, and even though he was still a lieutenant, junior grade—having been passed over several times for promotion—that

Lieutenant (j.g.) Malcolm "Spook" Johns of VA-145 in his stateroom aboard *Ranger*. *Family photograph.*

had everything to do with his "not making career-enhancing moves" and nothing with his proficiency at flying. (During one memorable happy hour at the Alameda O club, Spook, "pretty well tuned up," grabbed the fox stole of squadron CO Mel Blixt's wife from a bar stool. Yelling "Wild animal," he threw it to the floor and jumped up and down on it.) To Dieter's displeasure, he was ordered to drop back into his regular spot behind Hassett, so that Spook's wingman, Denny Enstam, could take over the number two spot. Without keying the radio mike, Dieter swore loudly at the news. Only Spook, who happened to look over toward Dieter's plane at that moment, saw his reaction: Dieter angrily shaking his head, and pounding his fist on the glare shield above the instrument panel. The way it worked was that a wingman stayed with his flight leader. The fact that Dieter reviled Hassett, and vice versa, meant nothing.

In truth, Dieter's feelings for Hassett were only part of his frustration. Dropping back to fly Hassett's wing made Dieter number four on the upcoming bombing run, a position known as Tail End Charlie. After several planes had rolled in to drop bombs, the gunners on the ground usually had a pretty good idea where the last guy in the formation was coming from. By then, there was ample time for all the guns to be lined up accurately. Even this early in their wartime deployment, there was growing concern in the squadron about this method of dive-bombing. The prevailing theory among the higher-ups was that orderly, single-file bombing was necessary to avoid midair collisions. The senior officers had used it in Korea and were fine with it—of course, given their seniority they were now usually leading a flight over a target and the first to roll in. The junior officers "knew something was wrong" with this unimaginative approach; since they were most often the Tail End Charlies, they were especially apprehensive about being shot down as a result of such predictable tactics.

The radio snapped to life with a report of a *Kitty Hawk* pilot going down in southern Laos. Now in the lead, Spook decided, "The heck with the bombing mission"—helping rescue a downed pilot was more important. He told the others his plan: since they were only a few minutes away from their target, they would get rid of their bombs in a single run, then head south as a group to join the RESCAP.

Minutes later came another radio call from Spook: "*Five Zero Seven*, rolling in." Now that Spook had found the target, he would be the first to commence a glide-bombing attack in a west-northwest direction to drop all his 500-pounders at once: nearly two tons of explosives. Each of the other pilots was to follow four or five seconds after the guy ahead of him had rolled in.

Dieter flipped on the master arming switch, and checked his altitude: 9,000 feet. When it was his turn, the target had disappeared under his plane. In training, the pilots had practiced having the two 20 mm cannon barrels on the left wing directly on the target. He banked and yawed the plane until he had a better angle of attack. Having fallen behind the others now, he would be that much later over the target. He rolled left and kept going until he was nearly inverted. The Skyraider screamed earthward at about a fifty-degree angle, accelerating to 400 miles per hour. Throwing his head back, Dieter was peering up at the approaching ground when his plane lurched and began to shake violently.

Dieter let go of the throttle and put both hands on the stick. He tried to call out to his squadron mates, but the radio was dead—"no side tone, no click, nothing." He let the nose fall through the dive until it was pointing down at the ground. He pressed the bomb release button on the control stick, sending all his bombs away. He pulled the stick to his belly, and with the extra weight gone the aircraft leaped. As the plane swooped like a hawk on a sudden updraft, Dieter was pressed into the seat by g forces that made him five or six times heavier than his normal weight. Keeping back pressure on the stick, he let the nose come level with the horizon. Suddenly, a bright explosion "like a lightning strike" off the right wing sent the plane "tumbling through the air." Pieces of metal flew past the canopy, and the engine stopped. Fighting to regain control, Dieter instinctively carried out the emergency procedures he had learned. His hands darted over the instruments, trying to restart the engine, which coughed once. Then, nothing.

With the engine gone, Dieter knew there was no hope of his making it back to the coast. He hit the switch to blow the canopy. The boom of the air-pressure bottle going off above his left shoulder was followed by the sound of air rushing overhead with the canopy gone. He unbuckled his shoulder harness and seat belt. He wore a seat-pack parachute, and the metal release handle was secured across his chest. He pushed aside the doughnut cushion wedged between him and the rock-hard chute pack, and climbed up onto the seat. He had practiced the procedure in training and knew about staying below the powerful airstream until he was ready to jump, and then how to roll out so as not to be blown back into the plane's big tail. As the unguided Spad went through "wild gyrations," he kept being knocked back into the seat. Another nearby explosion made the plane "shiver from nose to tail." The Spad had lost altitude, and at that point Dieter decided to ride the plane down. Also, he didn't want to be swinging in a parachute over people who were shooting up at him. It was known that a Skyraider could hold up in a crash landing better than a jet, being sturdier and able to land at slower speeds and in shorter spaces. Before buckling himself back in, Dieter undid the parachute straps so as not to become entangled after the crash landing.

Dieter spotted a ridge to his right. Although he could not tell if there was any open ground suitable for a landing on the other side, he headed that way to crash-land as far away as possible from the area he had bombed—a tenet taught at SERE to give downed aviators the best chance of evading immediate capture.

As his powerless plane "wobbled" closer to the ridge, Dieter saw that he did not have enough altitude to clear it. With the windmilling propeller producing a small amount of forward energy, he tried lowering the flaps, movable devices on the rear of the wings that provide extra lift. Luckily, they still worked. With a last reach skyward, the wounded Spad flared up over the 1,500-foot ridge, clearing the densely wooded top by no more than twenty feet. Meanwhile, he tossed out his flight charts, authenticator codes, and other classified materials so they wouldn't be found inside the plane. With the Spad's glide ratio of ten feet forward for every one foot down, he knew he would have to crash-land within a few miles.

Off in the distance—about three or four miles away—Dieter saw what looked like a small clearing. It seemed an unbelievable stroke of luck. As he came closer, he began to think he might overshoot the field. Amazed that he could still steer the plane, Dieter began to swing it from side to side in order to drop lower. Passing over several huts on his left, he saw on the far side of the clearing a solid wall of trees. He would try to set down in the field short of the wooded area. His airspeed indicator showed 180 miles per hour, about sixty miles per hour faster than a normal landing, but there was little he could do to slow down. Only now did he realize that the clearing wasn't open ground after all but a field of trees that had been cut off at the height of three or four feet. The entire field—about 300 yards in length—was pockmarked with thick stumps and large felled trees. Dieter knew he had picked the wrong place to land, but his eight-ton plane had become the world's heaviest glider and there could be no change of plans now. Like it or not, he was coming down here.

Looming ahead in the center of the clearing was a single tree about 100 feet tall with only a few limbs and not a single leaf. He didn't want to hit the tree head-on, because the impact might crush the cockpit with him inside. In one of those quick decisions that pilots must make in such situations, he decided to let one of the wings take the impact. It was then he realized he hadn't dropped the external fuel tanks as he should have done when the engine died. The last thing he needed was to have the surplus fuel catch on fire. He pulled the emergency release handle, and both tanks fell away. As they still carried more than 100 gallons of fuel, the plane reacted to the lighter weight by ballooning upward—exactly what Dieter did not want now because he was already over the clearing and had to get the plane down. He pushed the stick forward with both hands and "boresighted" the nose on the lower part of the dead tree. When he was about to hit the tree, he kicked hard on the left rudder pedal. In what was to be its last controlled response, the damaged Spad obediently yawed left. The tree struck where Dieter planned: near where the wing attached to the fuselage. The tree trunk broke off, and what remained of the plane's right wing was ripped from the fuselage.

On impact, the left wing swung forward and down, and as it did the wingtip struck the ground. The entire wing snapped off the fuselage. The plane's nose dug into the earth, the windmilling prop chopping up dirt and wood chips. Dieter held the stick in a death grip as the Spad bounced into the air, careened over to the right, and then began tumbling end over end.

A tree stump ripped through the side of the cockpit, narrowly missing Dieter's right leg. As the fuselage cartwheeled five or six times on the ground, he was pushed and pulled by the force of deceleration. His helmet was wrenched off his head and flew out the open cockpit. He watched a corner of the glass windscreen start to break in slow motion. When a big piece finally broke away, it struck him on one side of his head. Then, in a surreal scene, he watched the entire tail section tumble by. Smelling oil and gas and terrified of being burned, Dieter closed his eyes and covered his face with his arms.

When the world stopped spinning and the "continuous grinding and jerking" ended, he opened his eyes. He was hanging sideways in a darkened abyss. The cockpit was filled with green foliage and a thick dust that started him coughing. The fuselage was on one side, and the metal rail for the canopy was bent inward, jamming into his side. He managed to unbuckle his shoulder harness and seat belt but found that he was still caught and couldn't get out. Then, he passed out.

When he came to, he was on his back 100 feet away.

Dazed, he looked at the wreckage. He was surprised that there was no fire. A load of aviation gas remained in the internal fuel tank, as the drop tanks were routinely used up first. He remembered turning off the gas, battery, and ignition in the last moments before the plane hit the ground. He had no recollection, however, of getting out of the plane. He was still wearing his survival vest and waist pack, and next to him were a few things he had obviously taken from the cockpit. He tested his limbs to see if they all worked; his left knee hurt, but nothing seemed to be broken.

He knew the locals would come looking for him. The sound of the crash had been thunderous, and those huts he had seen were only a short distance away. He rose to his feet, and "stumbling and falling like a drunkard" he moved as quickly as he could through the clearing toward the jungle.

When he reached the end of the clearing, he stopped. Steadying himself on weak legs, he took a last look back. A cloud of dust from the crash still swirled above the wrecked Spad that had brought him safely down to the ground.

Then, Dieter stepped into the jungle.

The three Spads circled nearby, waiting for Dieter.

When he didn't appear, Spook radioed: "*Zero Four*, check in."

Shortly after his own bombing run, Spook glimpsed Dieter starting to pull out of his run. As Spook turned in a "rendezvous circle" to meet up with the others, he lost sight of Dieter. Enstam found Spook first, and then Hassett joined up. None of them had observed any ground fire. In fact, for the first three pilots who rolled in over the target, the mission had so far been uneventful.

Spook tried again. "*Electron Five Zero Four*. Hey, check in."

Spook asked his wingman, Enstam, to climb higher, where radio reception was often clearer, and try to contact Dieter. As Spook and Hassett circled, they heard that the *Kitty Hawk* pilot had been rescued. That was doubly good news. As they were no longer needed for the RESCAP in southern Laos, they could head back to the ship as soon as Dieter showed up.

When Enstam reported from 6,000 feet that he couldn't raise Dieter, Spook decided to retrace the run over the target, looking for any sign of a plane down. He saw only smoke and dust billowing from their bombs, and what appeared to be unbroken foliage in every direction. Even with the hazy conditions, visibility was four to five miles. Still, Spook knew that the dense canopy of jungle and woods below—as high as 200 feet in places—could swallow up a plane.

"Time to get back to the ship," Hassett radioed.

"We've got a guy missing," Spook shot back.

Hassett said Dieter had probably gone back on his own.

Spook knew that could not be true. Dieter was a nugget on his first mission over Laos. It was a long way back to *Ranger*, and he would have to cross over North Vietnam. He wouldn't have tried it alone. He was either airborne in some kind of trouble—perhaps with an inoperable radio—or down. If he was down in the jungle, he might be coming up on his short-range emergency radio trying to reach them. How could they leave?

"Got our charlie time to make," said Hassett, whose troublesome radio seemed to be working just fine now.

Spook fumed. This "by-the-book jerk" was more concerned with getting back to the ship on time for their scheduled recovery than staying out here looking for one of their planes. There was no good reason to leave—finding a missing pilot always had the highest priority. They had enough fuel for at least a couple of hours. And if necessary they could refuel at Da Nang and keep looking, as there was a lot of daylight left.

Spook argued some more, and then Hassett ended it.

"I've got the lead," said Hassett. "We're going back."

Short of being guilty of insubordination, all Spook could do was follow Hassett back to the ship. Spook did not know of the recent quarrel between Hassett and Dieter, and would not learn of it for some time. However, Hassett's unwillingness to look for Dieter struck Spook not only as infuriating but also as very odd. As an experienced pilot and a senior officer, Hassett knew the primary importance placed on search and rescue. After all, they had just been ready to ignore their schedule to go to the aid of the *Kitty Hawk* pilot. And a day earlier Hassett had chased away the fishing boat when the *Ranger* A-4 pilot was rescued off North Vietnam. Spook now wondered: *Why wouldn't Hassett spend more time and effort looking for his own wingman, for God's sake?*

The three Spads made their charlie time, landing on *Ranger* 4.5 hours after takeoff. Confirming that Dieter had not returned on his own, Spook was even more disturbed by Hassett's decision.

Back aboard ship, Hassett immediately "brought up the fact" with the squadron CO Hal Griffith and others that Dieter might have "disappeared on purpose." Hassett reported that Dieter had "dropped out of formation without any communication." Even though Dieter had been Tail End Charlie on the bombing run and most vulnerable to ground fire, the senior officers agreed that it was unusual for someone to "just disappear like that." Who was to say that the "off the wall" Dieter hadn't flown to Bangkok—which, with its nightlife, cuisine, and beautiful women, was considered the jewel of Southeast Asia? Everyone knew that Dieter was prepared to live in the guise of a German civilian, and that at times he chafed under military rules and discipline.

Some who knew of the clash with Hassett and his threat to restrict Dieter to the ship for the next six or seven months wondered if that had been enough to push him over the line. His roommate, Dan Farkas, who perhaps knew Dieter's mind-set best, owing to their close quarters, didn't think Dieter would consider flying off on his own as a "good way to get out of the navy" or away from Hassett. When Farky heard about the abbreviated search for Dieter, his first thought was: *If anyone else had gone down, Hassett would have hung around longer looking for him.* He didn't see Hassett taking any risks for Dieter.

Spook heard the talk about Dieter taking off but rejected it. He felt horrible that Dieter had been abandoned without a greater effort to find him, and fretted about whether he should have disobeyed Hassett's order and continued searching. They had radioed word of Dieter's disappearance, and search-and-rescue aircraft—most probably from Thailand—would respond. But Spook had been the last to see Dieter, and knew where to start looking. With time he could have expanded his search, and maybe have found Dieter.

The other pilot who had been on the mission to Laos, Denny Enstam, soft-spoken and congenial, thought it was "fifty-fifty whether Dieter got shot down or took off." If a pilot wanted to flee, Enstam knew the best way would be to "go on a bombing run, drop down low, and disappear"—exactly what had happened with Dieter that morning. Of course, Enstam, a combat veteran of VA-145's previous deployment aboard *Constellation*, knew that an attacking aircraft could go down swiftly without being seen, and that sometimes only the pilot of a plane that was hit realized there was any small-arms fire. As for what Spook considered the shortened search for Dieter, Enstam estimated that they had looked and waited around for Dieter for fifteen or twenty minutes, and thought their departure "wasn't out of line."

Lessard harbored no suspicion that his buddy had deserted. For a navy pilot to flee in his aircraft to another country during time of war would be treason. Lessard was aware that Dieter could be "a little different sometimes," but he would have understood that such an action would have been "the end of his life" in America. He could not have returned without facing a court-martial, and he would never have found "another flying job." Lessard knew there were many things Dieter looked forward to doing, both in and out of the navy, including returning home and marrying Marina, and eventually flying for the airlines. Lizard could not imagine his buddy throwing all that away.

Dieter was not the only *Ranger* pilot who went missing under mysterious circumstances on February 1, 1966. Around 4:00 P.M., with his wingman a few feet off his right wing, Commander Hubert "Iceman" Loheed, forty-one, of Middleboro, Massachusetts, a 1948 graduate of Annapolis and commanding officer of VA-146, was attacking a barge on an intercoastal waterway north of the DMZ in North Vietnam when something went wrong. Considered a "real cool guy" by his men, Loheed had rescued an injured duck on a rural California road before *Ranger* left for WestPac, nursed it back to health, and kept it in the ready room as the squadron's mascot. Naturally, someone of a lesser rank had to clean up after the duck, but the suave Loheed regularly stood before the pilots briefing them before a mission with the duck on his shoulder. Flying A-4 Skyhawks—delta-winged, single-engine jets that were the navy's primary light bombers—Loheed and his wingman released their ordnance and pulled up into a steep climb. Suddenly, with no distress call from Loheed, his wingman, Lieutenant (j.g.) Jeff Greenwood, twenty-four, of Coral, Michigan, saw him pull up "real nose high" and roll sharply to the right. Greenwood stayed with him as they dived straight down, pulling out in cloud cover only at about 1,000 feet above the ground. He then lost sight of Loheed's plane, and a search failed to find any trace of the pilot or the aircraft. Greenwood reported that Loheed must have been "incapacitated in the cockpit" or "dead before he hit the ground" to account for his apparent failure to try to regain control of his aircraft or eject. (Loheed's remains were recovered in the wreckage of his plane in 1986.)

The assignment the next morning to look for Dieter went to his best buddy, Lizard Lessard; and his flight leader, Lieutenant Commander John Stovall, thirty-three, of Kermit, Texas (who was called "Smokey" because he always had a cigarette going). Although he held the same rank as Hassett, the easygoing, hard-drinking Stovall "wasn't uptight and stuffy like Hassett." Also, Stovall "liked Dieter and got along with him," and Lizard knew his flight leader would want them to give it their best shot in locating Dieter.

So eager was everyone in the chain of command—including *Ranger*'s skipper, Leo McCuddin—to begin a search for VA-145's missing pilot at first light over Laos that the two Spads were sent off in a special launch an hour before sunrise—some five hours before the start of *Ranger*'s regular flight operations that day.

When the Spads reached the search area an hour later, a blood-orange dawn was breaking over Laos. Starting at the river crossing, heavily cratered from the previous day's attack, the two planes began a methodical "square search pattern." They went in one direction for a minute, then turned left at timed intervals to form an ever-expanding box. Flying mostly between 500 and 1,000 feet, depending on the terrain, Stovall was in the lead with Lessard above and behind his right wing. Both pilots scanned below for any sign of an aircraft down or an emergency signal. At the same time, Stovall was responsible for keeping them high enough to clear ridges and hills, and it was Lessard's job to follow his flight leader's altitude and course changes.

About an hour later, their search pattern took them over a long wooded ridge that ran east to west. After passing over it, they soon spotted a small clearing a few miles to the north. Coming closer, they saw wreckage that was identifiable to them as an airplane. Dropping down near treetop level, they confirmed four main pieces strewn on the ground: a tail section, a denuded fuselage, a partial wing, and an intact wing. All were painted in the navy aircraft color scheme: light gull gray

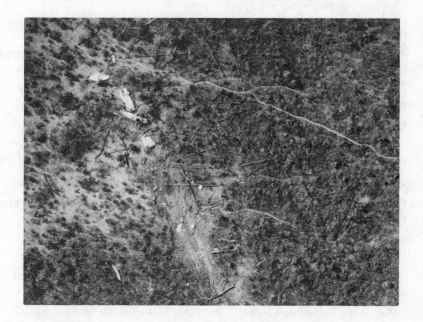

Wreckage of Dieter's Spad in Laos, February 2, 1966. *U.S Navy.*

on top and glossy white on the bottom sections. The intact wing had a white star set in a blue field with red and white stripes. On the fuselage was painted the willow-green diagonal stripe of the Swordsmen's insignia, with a lion raising a medieval sword. On the engine cowling, painted in black, were the numbers 504.

Quickly reporting the sighting, they were told that a U.S. Air Force helicopter—from a base at Nakhon Phanom in northeastern Thailand—would be en route, along with a search-and-rescue (SAR) coordinator aboard a four-engine C-54 Skymaster, equipped as a radio relay station to provide command and control for rescue missions involving multiple aircraft. Lessard and Stovall would wait to guide them to the wreckage; carrying a full complement of rockets, bombs, and ammunition for their 20 mm cannons, they would provide protective air cover.

As Lessard passed low over the wreckage, which lay at the end of a rut plainly made in the yellowish-brown soil by the careening plane, he looked for any indication that the crash had been survivable. Two things gave Lessard hope. First, the cockpit and fuselage were intact. If Dieter had been strapped in, he would have had a chance. Also, there was no sign of a fire. But if Dieter had survived, where was he now? Lessard kept hoping to see him step out of the foliage, waving skyward.

When the helicopter arrived, it was an HH-3E, nicknamed the Jolly Green Giant—a twin-engine, heavy-lift helicopter used for search and recovery as well as combat and special operations. With titanium armor plating and a high-speed rescue hoist, it was a welcome sight overhead to any downed aviator. The problem—as radioed by Stovall to the SAR units—was that there had been no sighting of the pilot and no signal from him since they had been overhead. That meant the helicopter would have to hover near the wreckage, and send down an armed crewman to look for an injured or dead pilot in the wreckage.

By then, Stovall and Lessard had been in the air for more than five hours, and they faced an hour's flight back to the ship. Arriving along with the other SAR aircraft were two air force Skyraiders, also based in Thailand. The air force flew the A-1E, a two-seat (side by side) version of the Spad with an oversize cockpit covered by a big bubble canopy. The navy pilots called these aircraft "queer Spads" because of their unusual design. When they worked SAR, the air force A-1s were code-named *Sandy*; their primary mission was to protect SAR units in hostile surroundings. This was now their show. Before departing, Lessard took another look at the broken plane in the clearing. Knowing Dieter, he was willing to bet that his friend's body was not inside the wreckage. And if there was no body, where was Dieter? The only Americans who had penetrated this deep into Laos on foot were Special Forces reconnaissance teams. It was isolated, hostile country.

Not long after Stovall and Lessard returned to the ship, *Ranger* sent out a secret radio message based on their report and an update from the SAR units after the wreckage had been searched. The message was addressed to CINCPAC—the commander in chief of all forces in the Pacific—and various naval commands in the Pacific and continental United States:

SEARCH FOR PILOT OF MISSING A1H RENEWED AT 0710H. WRECK OF
ELECTRON 504 FOUND BY RANGER A1H AT 17-42-30N/105-15-45E. WHEN
RANGER A1H LEFT SAR SCENE AT 1115H, A C-54 AND TWO A1E AND HELO
WERE OVER THE WRECK. MISSING AIRCRAFT CHECKED BY HELO CREW. NO
EVIDENCE OF BLOOD IN COCKPIT AND NO TRACE OF PILOT IN AREA. LAP
BELT AND SHOULDER HARNESS HAD BEEN RELEASED AND NOT BROKEN.
CANOPY NOT NEAR AIRCRAFT.

As for any suggestion that Dieter may have flown off to enjoy the delights of Bangkok or some other exotic milieu, the location of the crash belied any such intention. The wreckage was found eight miles north of the Route 27 intersection the Spads had bombed. Bangkok was about 400 miles in the opposite direction. In fact, had Dieter proceeded north-northwest away from the target as he was headed when he crashed, he would have arrived over Hanoi in the time it would have taken him to reach *Ranger.* No one argued that Dieter was "nuts enough" to voluntarily head in that direction or even "ditch in the boonies" of hostile Laos, practically on top of the Ho Chi Minh Trail.

Spirited talk among the pilots now centered on another aspect of Dieter's personality and reputation, and in this regard there was widespread accord. Although he had crashed in the dark heart of Laos, where once in the hands of the ruthless Pathet Lao virtually nobody made it out, his squadron mates believed that if he was still alive Dieter Dengler "could escape from anywhere."

7

WILL TO SURVIVE

Shortly after Dieter stepped into the bush, he heard what sounded like "tearing metal" coming from the direction of the crash site.

Staying in the area would help his buddies find him when they came looking—and he knew they would come, even though he had been unable to radio a distress call. But remaining in the vicinity also increased the likelihood of being captured. His best chance for evading the enemy was to get away from the wreckage, which, from the noises he heard, had probably already been found.

While dropping from the sky in his broken aircraft, Dieter had "no time for fear." He was busy with the difficult task of flying his crippled plane, and trying to get it on the ground without being killed. The crash had been over very fast, and he still had no memory of climbing from the cockpit and crawling away. He was driven now not by fear, but by a strong will to survive. It was not a new feeling for him.

He checked the small compass attached to his watchband. The obvious direction to head in was west, toward Thailand—a loyal ally of the United States in the war. But, figuring that his pursuers might anticipate his heading west, and try to cut him off before he could reach Thailand, Dieter decided to go north. If he was not rescued in a day or so, he would then turn west and walk to Thailand, since it was "so close." His evasion plan was to make it to the Mekong River, less than thirty miles away. On the other side lay Thailand. He had hiked that far in Germany, and he had learned—first from his mother and later alone—how to live off the land. He assured himself that the distance was "no sweat" and he would "walk right out of here in nothing flat." He hoped not to be stopped and questioned, and he would try to avoid contact with anyone. If questioned, he would—as he had planned—speak German and show his civilian identification.

After 200 yards he came to a creek with steep, twenty-foot banks cut by several seasons of monsoon rains. "Really, really thirsty," he slid down to the creek, only to find the water rust-colored and stagnant. Recalling warnings about deadly diseases prevalent in the jungle, he did not take a sip or even rinse his mouth. He had iodine tablets, but there was no time to stop and purify the water. He had to keeping moving. Trying to scale the bank on the other side, he sank knee-deep into powdery dirt that gave him no traction. He waded down the creek, stepping into muddy sinkholes along the way. When he came to a tree that had fallen across the creek, he was able to pull himself up the bank.

About half a mile from the crash site he stopped to get "squared away for the evasion." The heat and humidity were unlike anything he had known—he thought the temperature must be "at least 120 degrees." He had spent summers in oven-like San Antonio, Texas, but this tropical heat "had it beat all to hell." The heat and dehydration were already driving him "nearly mad," but he had to prepare for what could be a long trek if he wasn't quickly rescued.

He sat on a fallen tree in a wooded area, and rolled up his trousers to inspect his left knee, which hurt to bend. The injury was something he had "forgotten all about" in planning his escape route to Thailand, but the intense pain was coming back to remind him. The knee was black and blue and badly swollen. For added support, he wrapped it with an elastic bandage from his first aid kit. Something wet had been running down his back. He reached behind his neck, and his hand came back covered in blood. He found a shard of glass stuck behind his right ear, pulled it out, and pressed a bandage against the puncture.

He removed his survival vest and flight suit and wiped the caked blood and mud off himself as best he could. From a canvas rucksack he took out his civilian clothes, which had gotten wet in the creek but were already dry. Because of the humidity, they were not dry for long—when he put them on, they stuck to him like a second skin. He rearranged his gear, deciding what to take and what he didn't want to carry. The iodine tablets, medicine, food, fishing line, and hooks he placed in his jacket pockets. He started to shift other things from the survival vest to the rucksack when the world around him exploded with gunfire. He dived for cover.

When the firing stopped, he heard yelling.

Dieter had left his standard-issue .38 revolver on the log. After much thought he had decided not to go on missions with his modified .22 handgun. He was worried that if his German cover failed and he was caught carrying a weapon with a silencer and soft-nosed bullets, it would be considered a violation of the Geneva Convention and would jeopardize his status as a POW. Had he known then what he would later learn—that no one in deepest Laos abided by the Geneva Convention regarding the treatment of POWs—he would have brought the .22 and silencer.

His emergency radio was also on the log. He remembered what he had been told aboard ship about the handheld devices, which when activated sent out a beeper signal so a helicopter could home in on a downed aviator's location. Having learned that Jolly Green Giants would land wherever they heard an emergency beeper, the enemy had used captured radios to "bag a helicopter." Therefore, the pilots had been briefed not to let their radios fall into enemy hands because "they'll call in your buddies and then someone else will be down."

Knowing he could not outrun the enemy search party with his bum knee and convinced he would be captured "within five minutes," Dieter crawled back to the log and stuck the blade of his knife into the radio. He pushed the radio, gun, and survival vest—none of which he wanted the enemy to find—into a hole beneath the log and covered them with dirt and leaves.

With loud voices off to his right, he headed in the other direction. He slithered on his belly through the dense undergrowth, dragging his rucksack and sleeping bag with him. He had gone a short distance when he heard someone approaching. Quietly, he pulled the nylon bag over him, hoping the green material would serve to camouflage him.

A barefoot man passed five feet away. At first, Dieter glimpsed only a pair of strong, callused feet. When the man went by, Dieter looked up and saw something he did not expect. His pursuer was not dressed in a soldier's uniform. Short and with leathery skin, he wore only a loincloth. A rifle was slung over one shoulder, and he swung a machete to chop through the dense vines and branches as he went.

In a while, the shouting seemed to be moving farther away.

Dieter doubled back. His signal mirror was still in the survival vest, along with a plastic map of Laos. He wanted them both. He thought he could quickly locate the log but was unable to do so. In the meantime, the voices suddenly seemed to be circling back. To keep looking didn't seem prudent. Crouching low, he moved away, stopping every few steps to listen. When he heard nothing more than the cacophony of birds and insects, he checked his compass and turned northward again. He was determined to evade capture and stay alive, no matter what.

In a section of dense jungle, he came to a narrow path and followed it, even though the instructors at SERE had advised against traveling on trails. That may have been sound advice for downed Allied pilots trying to evade capture in occupied Europe during World War II, but Dieter quickly discovered it was not always practical in the jungle. He now faced, just two feet off either side of the trail, walls of vines as thick as his wrist and filled with thorns—obstacles that were "impossible to get through."

Somewhere off to his right he heard a girl singing. When the path meandered toward the angelic voice, Dieter backtracked and found another path to take. Eventually, he emerged from the jungle into a lightly wooded area. He came to a log fence covered with thorny vines and walked along it until he came to a cluster of bamboo. As he grabbed hold of the bamboo to hoist himself up over the fence, the ground beneath him gave way, leaving him swinging above an open pit six or seven feet deep. The hole, about ten feet wide, had been expertly covered with branches and leaves. If he hadn't taken hold of the bamboo when he did, he would have fallen in. He managed to pull himself up to the top of the fence. Looking down, he saw that the bottom of the pit was laced with sharpened bamboo spikes "staring up" at him. Had he landed in the pit, he would certainly have been killed.

On the other side of the fence was a clearing that looked deserted. Ideally, he should have circled the clearing so as not to be spotted in the open, another technique taught at SERE. But it was a long way around through dense foliage, so he moved cautiously across the grassy field. At the far end of the field he came to a picket fence. He opened a small gate and hurried into heavier foliage, ducking underneath the canopy. Stopping to get his bearings, he only then realized he was standing underneath a hut built on tree stumps about six feet off the ground. He would learn that this was common practice to keep snakes and animals from coming inside.

Dieter froze, listening for any sound from the hut. All was quiet. Hoping to find something useful, he inched his way up a wooden ladder. Inside the hut was the body of a man who had been dead for some days; at least, Dieter thought it had been a man. The lower half was gone and the "big, round eye sockets" were empty. Streams of ants and thousands of maggots were at work. The disfigured corpse made Dieter "think right away of leprosy." Afraid to touch anything, he hurried back down the ladder without searching the hut.

He soon came to a wide river. Uncertain whether leprosy was contagious, he was eager to leap right in and wash himself off, but he saw a herd of water buffalo on a nearby sandbar and wasn't sure if they would charge or not. Continuing on, he found a deep pool near the bank. He stripped down and jumped in with his bar of soap. The bath was a brief respite from the heat of the day. Quickly gathering up his clothes, he placed them and his boots inside his nylon sleeping bag to keep them dry, then eased into the river and dog-paddled to the other side, where he found a cove blocked from view. He rewrapped his injured knee, dressed, and then ate some pepperoni, which made him even thirstier. Filling up one of his boots with river water, he dropped in two iodine tablets and waited thirty minutes for the chemical reaction to be completed. Although the water still looked dirty, and smelled and tasted like iodine, his first drink "tasted wonderful" and renewed his strength.

Still heading north, Dieter entered a meadow filled with tall elephant grass. From there he went through an area of lightly wooded flatland, where he came across more clearings. Being cautious, he went the long way around. He felt safer in the cover provided by the jungle, although it was difficult to make much progress in the dense growth without a machete to clear the way.

The time was now close to 5:00 P.M., and Dieter looked for a place to spend his first night in Laos. He found a spot adjacent to a clearing, so that if a plane went over he could jump out and try to signal it. He unrolled his sleeping bag next to a log and zipped himself inside to escape the mosquitoes, which had started swarming as soon as he stopped moving. At first it was too hot in the bag and he was unable to sleep. Eventually he did fall asleep, but around 2:00 A.M. he was awakened by something crawling up his leg on the outside of the bag. It was heavy, "about 30 pounds." He kicked hard, then heard it hit the ground and scamper away. The night had turned cold, and after this interruption he was unable to get back to sleep. Monkeys whined excitedly, and night birds hooted nonstop.

Overhead, the stars were "so clear," and their illumination found its way through the roof of the jungle. He wondered if Marina and his mother had been informed yet. He imagined how surprised they would be when he showed up in Thailand. The thought occurred to him that maybe he could "lay low for a while" in Thailand before reporting to the military authorities. His $200 would probably go a long way there—he might even "take a train to Bangkok" and see the sights.

At dawn, he packed up and started out. Although he still hoped for a quick rescue, he decided to turn west toward Thailand. Already "getting familiar with the country," he followed a trail, ready to dive into the undergrowth at the first sign of anyone approaching. He came to another empty hut. Taking off his boots so as not to leave shoe prints, he scaled the ladder to a porch area. He now saw several neighboring huts, also on stilts, built on the gully of a river. They all looked deserted. Two were frames only, and appeared to have been gutted by fire.

In one corner of the hut he had entered was a hanging basket of blue orchids, cascading down like "a miniature waterfall." What looked something like potatoes were lying on the floor, and he filled his pockets. He also took an empty bottle hanging on the wall to use as a water container.

Down at the river, which looked like the same one he had crossed the day before, he washed out the bottle and filled it with river water. He dropped in iodine tablets, then washed up and pushed on.

After following another narrow trail for a couple of hundred yards, he halted when he saw the straw roof of a large hut sticking out above elephant grass taller than him. The trail appeared to be heading directly for the hut. He turned around and headed back in the direction he had come.

It was then he heard the familiar rumble of Spads overhead. The closest open area was at the river, so he ran for it. Just as he arrived, two Spads passed overhead. They were so low he could see on their sides the insignia of his squadron. *His buddies had come for him!* He watched the planes head east, getting smaller as they did. Then they turned, and appeared to be heading back. But instead of flying over him again, they turned left and climbed to a higher altitude.

As he hurried for the hut, Dieter "practically tore off" his blue shirt to get to his white T-shirt, which he ripped up one side. He grabbed a bamboo pole along the way. When he reached the elevated porch—the nearest perch—he hastily tied the white shirt on one end of the pole and waved it over his head.

Dieter soon spotted a Jolly Green Giant skimming over the jungle, "ready to do some business." The helicopter and two Spads were circling above an area about three miles to the southeast, and Dieter knew what that meant. They had found the wreckage of his plane.

If only he had his mirror, he was in the perfect spot to signal—the sun, still low in the eastern sky, was shining directly in his face. One Spad left its orbit and headed his way. He waved frantically. The Skyraider rocked its wings in the classic greeting from one pilot to another. Dieter's heart soared. "So happy," he could have yelled for joy. Then the Spad peeled off, and Dieter saw that it had been wagging its wings at an approaching C-54, which he knew to be an SAR command plane. His squadron mate had not seen him after all.

Dieter wanted to scream out, and he would have if the pilots above could somehow have heard him. It was "sickening" that rescuers were so close but had no idea he was here. Had he been able to stay near the crash site and avoid capture, they would now be pulling him out of the jungle. But he had come close to being killed or captured, and the fact that he was still alive and free meant everything.

And then, he was spotted—not by the planes but by the Laotians who were looking for him. Two natives with machetes stepped from the tall grass and looked toward Dieter, who was still waving the pole trying to signal the planes. From all the voices and commotion that immediately followed, he knew there were others behind them.

Dieter jumped down from the hut and ran for the river. Diving in, he swam to the other side. Scrambling up the steep bank, he looked back only when he was hidden in the bushes. Several men—some with rifles—were gathered on the opposite bank. One of them pointed in Dieter's direction. Someone had found a raft, and they were preparing to cross.

Dieter hurried away. As the terrain changed again, from woods to jungle, he pressed on, and no one seemed to be following him. He arrived at an elevated hut in the "middle of nowhere." The front door was open. Dieter sat underneath the hut to catch his breath. To his surprise, he heard chickens clucking. He found them inside a bamboo cage. He took a fat hen and put it in his bag to roast over a fire later. He came to a second hut a short distance away. It was so hidden by foliage that he nearly bumped into it. As he passed, he grabbed a handful of ash in the outside fire pit. Dropping embers that burned the palm of his hand, he knew someone had been here recently.

It occurred to Dieter that he was taking too many chances. He had no business approaching huts or villages. He should he traveling "deeper in the bush," even if it slowed him down. Right now, someone could be watching him without his knowing it. No sooner did that thought cross his mind than a woman dressed in black came around the corner of the nearest hut and stopped. She looked back, called out to someone, and a small child appeared. She scooped up the child in her arms and walked off.

Dieter had stepped into the foliage at the edge of the clearing to hide. He didn't think the woman had seen him—at least, she didn't act as if she had. But this was too close a call. His next thought was that he should not get caught with "stolen goods." He let the chicken go.

Now that he was determined to avoid huts and stay off trails, the going was slower and more difficult. He worked his way through the jungle, trying not to make any noise and watching for animal traps as he went. Since nearly falling into the trap the previous day, he had passed several others of various nefarious designs.

When Dieter arrived at an intersection of several trails, he checked to the left and right, and saw no one approaching. It was only twenty feet across, not far at all, he thought. Crouching low, he started to cross—

"Yute, yute, yute!"

When Dieter heard the shouted order, he knew it was meant for him. He stopped and turned slowly toward the commanding voice.

An M-1 rifle was pointed at his head.

Dieter smiled and nodded.

The man holding the rifle motioned for Dieter to come closer.

Dieter did, careful not to make any sudden moves.

The man yelled something over his shoulder, and the bush "came alive" with more Laotians in various states of dress and undress. Some obviously were local villagers, and they stood back, watching.

The man pointing the rifle wore aviator sunglasses, a U.S. Army fatigue jacket, rolled-up brown pants, and pastel-blue rubber boots like those an older woman might wear for a rainy-day stroll in Central Park. Because of the man's western if "comically" mismatched attire, Dieter wondered if he was a friendly guerrilla. Just then, the man whipped out a .38 revolver from his waistband and waved it at Dieter, yelling menacingly. Dieter was sure this was the gun he had hidden under the log. Had these guys been the ones shooting at him near the crash site? Had they been tracking him for two days? Not friendlies, he decided. Pathet Lao.

"Nicht schiessen," Dieter said calmly, asking them in German not to shoot.

Someone clobbered Dieter on the back of his head with a rifle butt, knocking him to the ground. His attacker pressed the muzzle against Dieter's neck. Dieter "waited for the bullet," but instead was dragged to an area under a nearby tree and searched.

When one of the men found the potatoes Dieter had stolen, he hit his own forehead repeatedly with the palm of his hand, wailing something over and over. Dieter expected to be hit again but was not. It would be weeks before he learned that what he had taken from the hut were not potatoes but opium balls. Had he been hungry enough to eat one, it probably would have killed him.

Motioning for Dieter to empty his rucksack, they let him keep almost everything, including the iodine tablets, his razor and blades in their dispenser, the pepperoni, and the water bottle. The leader pointed to Dieter's watch, which he unhesitantly took off and handed over with a smile, as if offering it to a friend. He didn't mind losing the timepiece as much as the compass. The man then pointed to Dieter's gold ring. That was where Dieter drew the line. He was not giving up Marina's ring. He firmly shook his head, and was kicked in the side for his refusal. The two men with rifles seemed to argue over the ring—at an impasse, they apparently settled the issue by letting Dieter keep it.

Dieter showed them his passport and other civilian identity papers. Pointing to himself, he chattered away in German. He soon realized that his cover story was not going to work when the oddly dressed leader and another man studied one of his papers upside down. Clearly, they were illiterate. No doubt they also didn't know the difference between German, English, and Swahili. What they understood, however, was that he was a white man in their jungle kingdom, and therefore the enemy. The details could be sorted out later.

They motioned for Dieter to stand up and put out his hands. When he did, a length of rope was tied in a slip knot around one wrist, which was jerked up behind his back. The rope was looped around his neck, then tied around his other arm at waist level. A length of rope remained, which one of the men always had hold of. The leader gave the rope a vicious jerk, and off they went down the trail. A villager in a loincloth was their guide, and another villager brought up the rear; both carried machetes.

Dieter ignored the pain in his injured knee, but when his legs cramped after an hour of running he collapsed. Nearly done in from the heat and excursion, he was allowed water but couldn't keep it down. When he could go no farther, the muzzle of a rifle was placed against his forehead. The man with his finger on the trigger motioned Dieter to get up. Dieter made it another mile before buckling again with cramps. The leader put down his weapons, knelt in front of Dieter, loosened the ropes, and began massaging his legs.

The two villagers, not even breathing hard, stood about ten feet away looking disgusted by this special treatment Dieter was receiving. It occurred to him that these people were in such good shape from a lifetime of hiking, climbing, and hunting in this unbearably hot, humid climate. Dieter was thankful he was not a smoker; otherwise, he would be "dead by now."

The Pathet Lao seemed in a hurry to leave the area, and Dieter figured that their haste had to do with the planes heard from time to time flying overhead, sometimes quite low—even below treetop level over clearings. Dieter was sure these unusually low passes meant they were still looking for him. Whenever a plane approached—the Laotians had "real good ears" and always heard the drone before Dieter did—the men "stopped dead in their tracks." He saw his captors quaking in fear of the planes; no doubt they had seen the damage that planes could inflict on ground targets. His captors would force Dieter to the ground and cover him with leaves, then do likewise themselves. No one moved until the planes were gone. They never crossed an open field, they never traveled when aircraft were in the area, and his captors never carried a rifle that wasn't camouflaged with branches and leaves. They even stuck branches down the back of Dieter's shirt, and camouflaged themselves in similar fashion. Dieter now understood why it was so difficult to see these guys from the air in the daytime.

Dieter began looking for opportunities to escape. The man working on his legs had placed the rifle and the .38 on the ground close by. Dieter debated with himself as to whether he should try something. He knew that to have any chance, he would have to kill them all. He decided against it for the time being, but then later chastised himself for "not having the guts" to act. After thirty minutes, he was trussed up again, jerked to his feet, and kicked to get him moving.

Dieter stumbled forward, in danger of falling with every lunging step as he struggled to keep up. For nearly seven hours—from his capture before noon until sunset—they went at double time. Their guide was changed regularly from one village to the next. Other men, many of them dressed in khaki uniforms, occasionally joined the group, until there were nine armed Laotians. Dieter worried that he had passed up his best chance for escape when he had only four natives to deal with.

They stopped for the night at a camp tucked under the jungle canopy. Already at the camp were more than a dozen armed Pathet Lao. The only one who looked like a real soldier was their leader. He wore a brown uniform, and his belt buckle had a red star. Approaching Dieter, he stood no more than a foot away and looked him up and down, apparently curious about his civilian clothes. Suddenly, he brought his hand up in a gesture like shooting a gun and made the accompanying sound. Dieter, whose nerves were on edge, flinched. Everyone laughed.

The uniformed leader wanted to see everything Dieter had with him. Dieter first showed the pictures in his wallet. The man nodded, and made a comment to someone behind him. Dieter spoke in German, pointing emphatically to himself, but that only seemed to confuse the issue. So far, Dieter had not come across even one person who could say a word in anything but the local language, so how could he expect these men to differentiate a German from an American? When Dieter got to the pepperoni, the uniformed man took a link, smelled it, and gave it back. Dieter took a bite and chewed happily. "Red Star" then grabbed it and took a big bite. He made a face, spat it out, and slapped Dieter on the side of the head. Then he helped himself to Dieter's other dried foods and medical supplies, including the first aid kit. He also took Dieter's passport and other papers, and placed them inside his small brown cap, which looked like the caps Dieter had seen Chinese soldiers wearing in photographs and movies.

Four wooden stakes were driven into the ground, and Dieter's arms and legs were tied in spread-eagle fashion. With the guerrillas silently smoking their bamboo pipes not far away, Dieter, fatigued and hungry, and with sharp rocks and sticks poking into his back, was soon asleep. He dreamed of walking through an airport to catch a flight to the Black Forest, but all the planes had been "smashed to pieces." He was convinced that the pieces would start to move around and reassemble themselves, and that his flight home would be on time. But the pieces stayed scattered on the ground, and he grew "more and more horrified." When he awoke, his heart pounding, the sun was above the horizon.

Dieter's face was a swollen mass of mosquito bites. He was barely able to open his eyes, and his body was crawling with ants. He hollered to be untied, but no one came for half an hour. When his restraints were released, his arms were numb, and he rubbed them to get the circulation going. A handful of barely cooked rice was thrown onto the ground in front of him, as if he were a farm animal. He was given his water bottle, which had been refilled. His iodine pills had been taken away, but at this point he was no longer worried about cholera or dysentery; he would "drink anything." Then he ate every kernel of rice off the ground.

As the group prepared to move out, Dieter noticed that his original escorts were gone. He was now in the company of a squad of heavily laden guerrillas with automatic weapons, bandoliers of ammunition, and hand grenades—long, thin Chinese-style grenades, usually about a dozen per man. Several Laotian women were also in the party, and each carried on her small frame a load that must have weighed fifty pounds. One native balanced a pole on his shoulder that had a large basket of rice at either end and two live chickens hanging upside down—that night's dinner, no doubt. Another native carried on a wire a small pot that contained fiery charcoal embers, which would be added to during the day. Someone else had a long-handled bamboo fan that looked like a lawn rake. Smeared over its surface was sticky sap from a plant. As the party traversed the jungle, this man would reach up with his fan and catch a flying insect or tasty bug, then drop it onto the fire to cook. Once, Dieter turned around to see a small bird being barbecued for a midday snack.

They started out through a wooded region, then followed a trail into the jungle. The terrain was flat, and the canopy of foliage shielded them from the sun's intense rays. Whenever they passed under direct sun, Dieter found the heat almost unbearable. He drank three bottles of water by midmorning. In spite of the heavy loads being borne, the pace was nearly as quick as it had been the day before. They started off as a caravan of nineteen, eight in front of Dieter and ten behind him. Almost all were barefoot, and no one made a sound on the trail. It was the most disciplined and efficient marching Dieter had ever seen, with no malingerers or complainers.

He wondered where they were taking him. As near as he could tell from glimpses of the sun through the jungle canopy, they were generally proceeding east by southeast—away from Thailand and deeper into Laos. Although he was disappointed to be moving farther away from Thailand, he was relieved that they were not going north, toward Hanoi.

They crossed over a ridge, then started down a steep mountainside. The trail was so overgrown it had to be widened with machetes. With his arms tied behind his back, Dieter had difficulty keeping his balance on the descent, and "fell most of the way down." They were only halfway down when the sun dipped below the horizon. Without discussion, they pushed on until they arrived at the valley floor, in darkness. A small village was situated near a narrow stream, and here they made camp.

Not long afterward, two of the guerrillas returned with a tall man who obviously held some position in the village. He motioned for Dieter to empty his pockets. When the tall man saw the dispenser of razor blades, he fussed with it a bit before producing a blade. In obvious disbelief, he loudly chastised Dieter's guards. Someone handed him Dieter's German passport. Obviously confused by what he was seeing, the man seemed to be demanding other identification and grew "angrier and angrier" when it wasn't forthcoming. Dieter decided that since the prospect of pulling off his fake identity with these people was dimming, it was time to show his military identification and reveal himself as a downed U.S. Navy pilot—and therefore, a prisoner of war to be treated humanely under the terms of the Geneva Convention.

Dieter took off his boots. He pointed to the razor blade the man still held and made a cutting motion. The man warily handed him the blade. Dieter sliced into the soles of both shoes just enough to remove his ID cards. They did not appear to surprise the man. He barked an order to the soldiers, who, with "dirty looks," came for Dieter as they clicked bolts on their guns. *This is to be my execution*, Dieter thought. Instead, they beat him with their rifle butts and fists, then staked him out for the night.

In the morning, two permanent guards were assigned to him. They wore matching light khaki uniforms and sandals cut from tires. They both carried backpacks filled with ammunition and hand grenades. Dieter soon dubbed one of them Thief, because he took a "simple, ten-cent comb" from Dieter's jacket and refused to give it back; and the other one Bastard, because whenever he had a chance he harassed Dieter "out of pure hatred." Although Dieter was continually "looking for a chance to get away," the two were always with him. Thief carried a U.S. carbine and an ammunition belt around his waist. Bastard had an old-style Russian automatic rifle fed by an attached drum magazine.

The next day, they passed several antiaircraft sites; the guns were well hidden under the jungle canopy. Later, in the dark, they crossed Route 12, a major thoroughfare for military supplies heading southward, before settling down about a mile away in a large cave where a group of villagers were also spending the night. Dieter was tied to a platform, and the soldiers sat at the cave's entrance smoking their pipes.

A pretty young woman with a baby in her arms sat down near Dieter, who smiled at her. She shyly smiled back. Dieter motioned, asking if he could hold the child. To the obvious surprise of others nearby, the woman came over and handed him her baby. Dieter cradled the infant lovingly, careful to support its head. The baby at that moment seemed to Dieter like his only friend. When he handed the infant back it was as if a "spell in the cave" had been broken. Other mothers came forward, offering their babies for him to hold. When the mother of an older child approached, the boy burst into tears and held onto her skirt. Dieter took off the St. Christopher medal he was wearing and hung it around the boy's neck. The boy stopped crying, and touched the shiny medal like "a newfound plaything." During those moments of positive human contact, Dieter could forget his predicament; he was "almost happy."

On Dieter's fifth and sixth days as a prisoner they continued their trek, with regular but brief stops for water and food at villages along the way. Everyone including Dieter had the opportunity to take a quick bath in a wide river that snaked through the countryside, irrigating rice paddies on either side. The guerrillas bathed with their hands held modestly over their genitals.

During one stop, everyone was gorging on bananas given by a villager. Dieter got Bastard's attention and pointed to the bananas, hoping to be given one. Bastard's answer was a burst from his automatic rifle, which sent dirt flying all around where Dieter was sitting. Certain he had been hit, Dieter was surprised to find no blood. Then, his fear replaced by anger, he started for Bastard but thought better of it.

Each night now, Dieter was being given a handful of half-cooked sticky rice formed into balls and served on a banana leaf. All his life, Dieter had hated rice, but he was learning to "like and respect" it as the main food that would keep him alive. Sometimes, he was served meat of unknown origin and bananas, both special treats. While he ate, his hands were free but his ankles were kept tied to a stake, and one of his guards remained nearby. After that, it was time for the familiar drill of being staked out spread-eagle for the night. He had learned to push away rocks and sticks jabbing into his back by moving from side to side. If the moon and stars were visible, he looked at them last before shutting his eyes. It gave him comfort to think that Marina might be looking at the sky and seeing the same view. He often awoke in the middle of the night when it turned bitterly cold, but was so exhausted he usually went back to sleep quickly. Every morning he awoke to find a mass of new insect stings and mosquito bites. He also often found leeches on him. They wiggled along on the ground until they found something warm-blooded to which they could attach themselves, dropping off only after becoming engorged with their host's blood.

Dieter was particularly repelled by the leeches; their flattened bodies could be up to an inch long. Once, noticing blood running down his ankles, he pulled up his trousers to find dozens of the slimy bloodsuckers clinging to each ankle. He tried to pull them off, but their slippery surface made it difficult to get hold of them. When he did grab one, it ended up attached to a finger. A native came to his assistance, using a flat bamboo stick to scrap each one off and fling it away. Dieter discovered that something in the chemistry of the leeches prevented blood from coagulating. Even after they came off, every place they had been attached bled until the wound was washed.

Whenever they entered a village, Dieter was tied to a post or tree and put on display. In the larger villages more than 100 men, women, and children would gather around him. Most were polite and did not say anything—they just stared at him as if he were from another planet. Occasionally, his presence provoked a different response: rocks were thrown, and people would spit at him. Each village, large or small, provided the group with water and sustenance, along with an experienced guide to take them on to the next village.

On the seventh day they stopped at a village whose name sounded to Dieter like Yamalot. A local elder, "evidently a province chief," came to see Dieter. He was carrying Dieter's military identification cards. Short and rotund, he wore a blue shirt and trousers, a light jacket, leather boots, and horn-rimmed glasses. Dieter wondered how this gentleman, who would look at home in San Francisco, had ended up deep in the jungle. Dieter's curiosity turned to surprise when the man spoke in fluent French.

"Comment ça va?" asked the province chief.

Dieter answered in French, adding how good it was to find someone he could converse with. He was already regretting, however, not having spent more time on his French lessons in middle school.

The man offered his right hand and Dieter shook it.

The province chief placed an arm around Dieter's shoulder and walked him up steps cut into a massive rock overhang where they sat down across from each other. Dieter's two guards came with them, but they were uncharacteristically subdued; even Bastard nodded deferentially to the chief. The rope around Dieter was removed, and he pointed to the burns on his neck and wrists. The chief said something to the guards, who hung their heads. Dieter took off his boots and rolled up his trousers to show his sores. A soldier summoned by the chief appeared with a case of medicines, and went to work on Dieter, cleaning his wounds and painting them with Merthiolate. Having noticed Dieter's accent, the chief asked where he was from originally.

"Deutschland," Dieter said.

The chief said he had been to Germany, and named several cities he had visited. When he mentioned Stuttgart, Dieter interrupted excitedly, saying he was from a small village near Stuttgart. The man made a point of saying that he had been to the Geneva conference several times, leading Dieter to expect he would be well versed in the international treaty regarding the treatment of prisoners of war.

Dieter began to have faith in this educated, well-traveled man. At the very least, for the first time since his capture he was in the hands of someone in charge who seemed to be a "genuinely good man." Now that his arduous journey was apparently over, Dieter hoped that things would be different and he would be well treated.

The chief said Dieter's "poor mother" must be very worried. He said he would let Dieter write a letter to her and another one to his wife to tell them he was "alive and well." When Dieter explained he wasn't married but had a fiancée he hoped to marry as soon as he returned home, the chief said he should write to her.

An old woman appeared with a small blue notebook, which she handed to the province chief. He ripped out a few pages and gave them to Dieter, along with a fountain pen from his shirt pocket. The chief encouraged him to tell his loved ones that he was "in good hands" and would be released soon.

Dieter couldn't believe his good fortune, to be under the authority of such a reasonable and intelligent man. He was glad he hadn't made a stupid attempt to escape in the jungle and been killed. When he thought of going home—to America to see Marina, and to Germany to visit his mother—his spirits rose to a level they had not reached since the crash.

Dieter wrote the letter to his mother in German, and printed the one to Marina, leaving no spaces for anyone to insert added words or phrases. There was much to say but he was careful not to write anything that could be used for military or propaganda purposes. He did not say what he had gone through or where he was—he said nothing to keep the letters from reaching home. Mainly, he wanted to get across that he was okay, and would see them again. He printed his name at the bottom of each letter: he would not write his signature, since a forger might copy it on a false confession. Dieter had picked up this precaution in his SERE training.

As he wrote at a small table, the province chief remained seated across from him. The chief kept asking more about Dieter's life in Germany, and how Dieter had ended up in the United States. Slowly, his tone changed from friendliness to agitation. "How could you fall for the American trick?" he demanded. "It was they who killed your father and leveled your towns, and now you are just about giving your life for them."

"I am a pilot," Dieter said evenly. "I have a job to do and I do it when I'm told. When I joined the navy there was no war in sight, but now there is, and I'm obligated to it."

After an hour, Dieter was finished with his letters.

Dinner that night was delicious: he had two boiled eggs, and some sugar was sprinkled on his sticky rice. As Dieter ate, the chief kept up the banter. Finally, leaning toward Dieter, he quietly said, "You will be released in two weeks but you must promise me that you'll go back to Germany."

Dieter smiled happily, saying of course he would return to Germany. He did not say how long he would stay; nor did he mention that his tour in the navy would not be finished for two years.

The chief had more good news, telling Dieter he would be kept with other Americans until his release.

Dieter was overjoyed at the prospect of seeing other Americans. "Where are they now?" he asked.

In a camp about "one and a half day's walk from here."

After a luxurious bath that night, in a hut where an old woman brought in buckets of warm water, followed by more sticky rice and further doctoring of his sores by the man with the medical bag, Dieter fell asleep. When he awoke on a thin mat, with no ropes securing him to stakes, he thought he must be dreaming. Food, tea, and water were served; then, in mid-morning, the province chief arrived in a jolly mood, shaking Dieter's hand like an old friend and offering cigarettes for the umpteenth time even though Dieter had repeatedly said he didn't smoke. Dieter's two regular guards were in the room—as they had been all night—but they remained unobtrusive.

Again the two men sat across from each other at the table. The province chief gave a lengthy discourse about the ills of America, touching on racial discord and accusing the Americans of trying to tell the Vietnamese people how to live when they couldn't solve their own problems. He knew about various antiwar demonstrations in specific cities and universities. He even commented derisively about the assassination of President Kennedy by "one of his own fellow citizens." Dieter listened but said little, feeling that he was no match for this man's grasp of American history, dates, and names. When the comments became more personal—when the chief accused U.S. pilots of intentionally bombing women and children—Dieter answered, "just short of yelling," that such claims were untrue. Then he stopped himself. He wasn't about to get into a discussion about the strict rules of engagement the pilots were following, which so limited the targets they could hit.

The province chief took from a leather attaché case a typed paper, which he put on the table in front of Dieter along with the same pen Dieter had used the previous night to write the letters home. The official said Dieter no longer had to be "ashamed of his true feelings" about the war and was now free to sign a statement denouncing the bombings.

The paper was such a dark copy that Dieter could barely make out the words, but he was able to decipher enough for him to stop reading it before he reached the halfway point. It stated disagreement with the "murderous policies" of the United States and confirmed that American pilots were attacking innocent women and children.

Shaking his head, Dieter pushed the paper across the table.

The province chief picked it up and put in front of Dieter again.

Dieter again pushed it back across the table.

"Americans are imperialists and we are peace-loving people. You have seen the villagers—did they hurt you? Has anyone hurt you here? We are all your comrades and we want to help you. The United States are the aggressors. We will help you and you can stay with us."

Dieter looked up, incredulous. "Stay with *you*? Why the hell would I want to stay here with you? I have a home and a country."

"You can come to Hanoi," the chief said, his voice rising. "You can go to China and see for yourself. You can fly for the Chinese."

"No thanks."

"Sign the paper and you will be released in ten days."

Dieter shook his head.

The province chief stood up. He went over to the guards, spoke to them quietly, and then walked off as if he had an appointment at the office.

Finally unleashed, the guards came for Dieter with a vengeance. They grabbed him, tied his hands behind his back, took him outside, threw him to the ground under a big tree, and started kicking him. At first he tried to fight back, but that only enflamed them, so he went limp. They tied his ankles together, threw the end of the rope over a limb and hauled him up until he was swinging headfirst off the ground. The thrashing started in earnest then, with rifle butts and bamboo sticks.

Dieter saw stars, then passed out. He came to when water was thrown in his face. They beat him again until he passed out, and again brought him back for more punishment. He lapsed into and out of unconsciousness. When he came to, he could make out "blurry feet and legs" kicking dirt in his face as the blows were delivered to his body. He was grabbed from behind by his hair and pulled up nearly level with a grinning guard's sweaty face. Dieter struggled to get air against the flow of blood and fluids running down his throat and pouring freely from his nose and mouth. Then he blacked out again.

When he came to he had been cut down from the tree and was lying in a fetal position on the ground in a pool of bloody mud. He wondered if he was dead, but then he felt pain and knew he wasn't. A sharp kick in the back caused him to cry out, and a bucket of water was dumped over him. He tasted blood, and told himself to swallow it all because he couldn't afford to lose any more if he ever wanted to go home.

A villager approached, leading a water buffalo. Dieter's hands were tied in front of him, and the other end of the rope was looped around the curved horns of the sedate beast. A crowd had gathered in anticipation. Someone slapped a stick on the buffalo's flank to get it moving, and it reluctantly moved. More slaps, and it went a little faster. Dieter, trotting behind, managed to keep up with the animal. The animal was halted, and Dieter's legs were tied at his ankles. More slaps to the flank, and Dieter struggled to stay upright by hopping, as in a sack race; the soldiers and spectators thought this was hilarious. Someone then knocked Dieter off his feet, and the buffalo was slapped harder. As Dieter was dragged over sharp rocks and brush that sliced his skin, he tried to protect his head by tucking it between his outstretched arms. When the spectacle was over, Dieter could barely stand. He was half-dragged back to the province chief, who wordlessly placed the confession and pen in front of Dieter.

Dieter picked up the pen and "threw it at him."

The province chief took the unsigned paper and walked away.

Shortly after sunrise the next morning, Dieter and his two guards, traveling with a dozen guerrillas, left Yamalot, heading southeast. They marched all day and late in the afternoon stopped at a village, hoping to spend the night. But the head of the village informed them that there was no extra food, and it was impossible for them to remain. They continued on toward the next village, at the top of a mountain. Climbing the steep jungle trail in total darkness, the party stayed together by having each man drape his arms over the shoulders of the person in front of him. The local guide, leading the way, seemed to know every bend of the trail with his eyes closed.

Dieter's hands, which had been kept tied behind his back all day, were freed so he could lean over the shorter Bastard.

A day or two before their arrival in Yamalot, Dieter had noticed something that had given him a "sudden surge of hope": a small built-in mirror in a tobacco box that Bastard always kept in the left breast pocket of his shirt. Dieter knew if he had a mirror and could escape he could get into the open and signal a plane overhead.

As they jostled along in the dark, Dieter's chest was pressed against Bastard's back whenever they tripped on roots or slid on the slippery footing and bumped into each other. He had no problem sliding his left hand down to Bastard's pocket that held the tobacco box. Finding the pocket buttoned, he worked on it until the button came undone. Then, he lifted everything out of the pocket. Keeping his chest against Bastard and his right arm over Bastard's shoulder, he brought his left hand back and worked fast. There were rolled cigarettes and paper money, which he dropped to the trail. Opening the box, he let the coarse tobacco fall out. He worked the mirror loose with his fingernails, and it finally came out. He slipped the mirror into his own pocket, which was half filled with rice. Needing to throw away the box but afraid it might strike a rock and make a noise, Dieter pretended to slip. He fell with a loud grunt, and flipped the box into the bushes.

It had been a close call because by then they were only twenty feet from the top of the hill, where the group stopped to rest. Bastard, reaching for a smoke, found his pocket empty. He lit a cigarette lighter and walked back on the trail, searching the ground. Dieter was afraid he would find the discarded items, but Bastard returned empty-handed and angry with himself for the loss.

Several hours after sunset they entered a village at the top of a low-slung mountain. While the other members of the party scattered throughout the village to find places to sleep, Dieter and his two guards went into an empty hut that had no walls and only a lean-to roof. Dieter's boots were taken away, and the three men climbed onto a sleeping platform with Dieter tied down in the middle. All three were soon asleep.

About midnight Dieter was awakened by a guard's foot smacking against his leg. He pushed the foot back, and the guard didn't wake up.

This happened two or three times. By then, Dieter knew that Laotians were "very heavy sleepers." He sat up slowly, and looked at the two snoring guards. Deciding that now was the time to escape, he quietly worked to untie the rope on his wrists until he was unbound. Each ankle was tethered by rope secured underneath the platform. Lying down again, he used every bit of his strength to raise both legs upward, pulling hard against the rope. As the slipknots tightened painfully around his ankles, the rope underneath finally gave way. The platform creaked with his every moment, and he covered the sounds he was making with "fake snoring." As the guards continued their heavy sleep, he slid down from the platform and took the rope off his ankles. Nearby he found his boots, and the rucksack with most of his belongings. He also grabbed a machete and tiptoed outside. He went about 200 yards before putting on his boots, then followed a trail down the mountain. At the bottom he came to a dry creek. Wanting to get off the trail, he followed the creek bed under the light of the moon. An hour later he spotted a familiar tree that had grown crookedly over the creek, and realized he had circled the base of the mountain and was back where he had started. Deciding it was a waste of energy to wander around aimlessly in the dark, he found a protected place to spread out his sleeping bag, climbed inside, and went to sleep.

He awoke at daybreak. Nearby was a karst mountain, looking like a giant camel's hump covered with moss. Its sides had sparse vegetation and were interspersed with sharp ridges and irregular rock formations. At its top was a plateau. Dieter had done some climbing in the California mountains and knew it would be a difficult ascent of perhaps 2,000 feet. But if he could make it, the top would be a perfect place for signaling aircraft with Bastard's mirror. There would be no need for him to come back down again, as a helicopter could lift him right off the plateau.

The climb was unlike anything he had done in his life. Not until he started up the rocky side of the mountain did he discover that its edges were as sharp as razors. At times it was fifty feet straight up, and he crawled upward with the toes of his boots on one thin ledge after another. Then, it would be a steep drop of thirty feet down the other side to get to the next rocky spire. The terrain was a "series of hundreds of ridges," everything was straight up or down, and descending was as difficult as climbing. As he went higher, he heard voices below yelling, *"Americali. Americali."* He figured the men would never come up here searching for him; and, hidden as he was among the rocky ridges, they would not spot him from below.

Dieter reached the top at noon; he knew the time because the sun was directly overhead. The plateau was only four by six feet and made of limestone. Somehow, through tiny cracks in the stone, orchids had sprouted. He could see for miles in every direction and it all looked "just beautiful" from above the canopy of vegetation. The sky was cloudless, and the sun beat down unmercifully. There was no place to sit that wasn't sizzling hot and razor sharp, so he took off a boot and used it for a cushion. He practiced with the mirror, catching the sun's reflection and bouncing it off a nearby ridge. Then he waited for the planes to come. It had been ten days since he was shot down. He had heard his buddies in their Spads several mornings since then. The morning launch off the carrier would already be coming over Mu Gia Pass, which he could see off in the distance. That is, the planes would be there *if* they were coming to Laos today.

The relentless heat and the lack of shade and water made the wait nearly unbearable. Dieter took off his jacket and shirt and draped his nylon bag over his head to block the sun. Several jets passed overhead, flying so high that they left contrails as they streaked toward Thailand, no doubt returning from a mission over North Vietnam. He tried to reflect the sun at them, but they were much too high. Later, two Air Force F-105s came by lower and Dieter tried signaling them. One "dipped a wing" and made a half circle. Dieter was sure he had been seen, but nothing came of it and the jets flew on.

That day, the low-flying Spads never came.

By the middle of the afternoon Dieter was severely dehydrated. Spotting a succulent plant growing on a nearby ledge, Dieter climbed over and used the machete to top it. He had seen natives on the trail harvest plenty of plants for liquid, but as soon as he sucked on the plant there was a tingling sensation in his mouth like "an injection of Novocain." When his mouth swelled shut and his cheeks went numb, he thought he would suffocate. Although his nose was tingling, too, he could still breath through his nostrils. Then, the poisonous reaction dissipated as quickly as it had occurred, and the swelling and numbness receded.

Dieter, with his head spinning and his "vision . . . off," knew he would die on the plateau if didn't get down and find water. He started down but was already so weak that he fell, landing on his back in a deep crevasse. After recovering, he had to scale thirty feet in order to resume his descent. Clinging frantically to vines to try to control his descent, he nevertheless endured a series of falls. When he came off the mountain, he stumbled toward a putrid waterhole which he had passed that morning and which seemed to be the only one in the area. Once he reached it, he collapsed in the "brownish, scum-filled water" and "drank and drank." When he heard shouting, he looked up to see a group of Pathet Lao surrounding him.

Dieter was yanked from the water. His hands were tied behind his back, and the rope was looped around his neck and ankles. When it was pulled taut, constricting his throat, he gagged. Bastard, yelling "like a madman," began beating him with a stick. When one angry soldier tried to club him with a rifle butt the gun discharged, firing a bullet into the stomach of a comrade and killing him. A third soldier shot the first one in both legs. Dieter lay on the ground, thinking he himself would soon be dead as bullets whizzed past so close he felt their heat.

When order was restored among the soldiers, Bastard went back to work on Dieter, loosening the rope around his left arm and inserting a stick. Bastard twisted the stick and Dieter cried out in pain, his screams sounding like stifled gurgles because the rope was strangling him. When Dieter felt as if his arm had been ripped off, Bastard loosened the rope and inserted a second stick in the tourniquet knot. He twisted it again and again until Dieter felt pain such as he had "never known before."

Time no longer registered for Dieter; he was aware only of pain. He was later dragged down a trail, hung upside down from a tree, and beaten until he passed out. When he came to there was a puddle of blood on the ground under him. He now tasted on his lips the honey which a guard had smeared over his face while he was unconscious. Someone had dragged over an active ant nest—"as large as a watermelon"—and positioned it under the tree. Dieter was lowered until his head dropped onto the nest of "thousands of angry black ants." Drifting into and out of consciousness, Dieter no longer felt much pain, "only numbness."

After he was lowered from the tree some hours later, he was pushed blindfolded down a trail. Helped up a ladder leading to a platform off the ground, he was pulled into a small cave. The blindfold was removed and he was lowered upright into a hole about seven feet deep and three feet across that was partially filled with water.

Through an "endless night" standing in cold water, Dieter thought a lot about his failed escape. He went over the things he had done wrong. He should not have gone up to the plateau without water. He should not have come down the same side he went up; there must have been water somewhere on the other side. He had to learn from his brief flight to freedom and not make the same mistakes again. Not caring what the guards heard or understood, Dieter mumbled aloud for anyone to hear:

"There *will* be a next time."

8

"WE'LL RUN OUT OF PILOTS"

On the evening of February 7, 1966, a secret message was sent by *Ranger* CO Leo McCuddin to the secretary of the navy (SECNAV), the commander of naval aviation in the Pacific (COMNAVAIRPAC), the commander in chief in the Pacific (CINCPAC), and the commander of the Seventh Fleet (COMSEVENTHFLT), advising them that the search for Dieter Dengler had been terminated with negative results. "Evidence of death not conclusive. Status remains MIA," the message said. McCuddin, the World War II ace who did not like giving up on a missing pilot, added, "Aircraft on Steel Tiger [Laos] missions will continue to monitor the area for signs of downed pilot."

The first step in the bureaucratic process that followed involved Lieutenant Algimantas "Doc" Balciunas, twenty-nine, of Newark, New Jersey, one of two flight surgeons assigned to *Ranger*'s air wing. Balciunas had entered the navy in 1964 upon graduation from Georgetown Medical School and following a year of internship at Los Angeles County General Hospital. During the flight surgeon program at Pensacola, Balciunas soloed in a single-engine T-34 Mentor. He was also trained to handle the array of backseat duties in an F-4 Phantom as a radar intercept officer (RIO), and as such would fly twenty-four combat missions with the VF-142

Ghostriders aboard *Ranger*. His primary duty, however, was providing medical care to the pilots and other air wing personnel.

Balciunas knew Dieter from the extended time the squadrons spent at Alameda, Yuma, and Fallon preparing for their WestPac deployment, and the nights and weekends of liberty the aviators enjoyed in those locales. He had hoisted beers in honky-tonks and O clubs with Dieter, which made it all the more difficult when Balciunas received from a corpsman a copy of Dieter's death certificate.

The typed form was considered a "rough copy" to be kept in the medical department's files until higher-ups in Washington asked for a death certificate. Even though the document was left unsigned by the two parties whose signatures would be required—McCuddin and the ship's senior medical officer—its factual declarations conveyed a finality that Balciunas hoped would prove to be unfounded:

TIME OF DEATH: FEBRUARY 1, 1966, 11:48 AM

PLACE OF DEATH: SOUTHEAST ASIA.

DISEASE OR CONDITION DIRECTLY LEADING TO DEATH: CAUSE UNKNOWN.

SUMMARY OF FACTS RELATING TO DEATH: REMAINS WERE NOT RECOVERED.

Notwithstanding the navy's need to produce such paperwork, Balciunas wasn't about to give up on Dieter. He knew that Dieter was energetic, charming, bigger than life, and a hard charger who gave the impression he "could do anything." Balciunas was convinced—as a friend, flight surgeon, and fellow aviator—that "if anyone could get out" from deep inside enemy territory, "Dieter would."

With the loss of any carrier pilot, it became the responsibility of his roommate to pack his belongings. Dan Farkas began doing so ten days after the wreckage of Dieter's plane was found, without any definitive word as to his fate. Farkas folded the uniforms and other clothes and put them in Dieter's canvas seabag, which he took to VA-145's locker room. Dieter's other possessions were placed in his metal cruise box, which was locked up in a secure storage space. Dieter had told Farkas which things he wanted sent to his mother and had given his roommate her address in Germany. The rest was to go to Marina. Farkas planned to send everything on when the ship returned to Alameda in six months.

When he finished clearing out Dieter's belongings, Farkas sat on his own bunk. He realized how empty the corner stateroom now seemed—and quiet, too, without Dieter yapping excitedly in his characteristic staccato delivery. On February 2, the day the wreckage of Dieter's aircraft was found and inspected, Farkas had written in his journal: "There was no blood [in the cockpit], and it seemed as if he walked away from the wreckage. We hope now that he's making his way to friendly people, and that he's not captured. Dieter was extremely well equipped for evasion and survival." Still, at this point Farkas didn't know how to feel, because he did not know if his roomie was dead or alive.

Six months earlier the fate of another friend of Farkas's, Ensign Joseph Bates, twenty-five, of Oklahoma City, Oklahoma, had been more certain. In the summer of 1965, Bates, a Cherokee Indian, had been on a nighttime training mission with his Spad squadron, VA-115. They had been practicing gunnery in the California desert, with the targets lit by flares dropped by parachute. When one chute failed to open and the flare fell to the ground still burning, Bates had homed in "with pilot fixation" on the bright light, probably believing the flare was airborne. He hit the ground while diving at nearly 400 miles per hour with cannons firing. There was little left of the plane or Joe Bates, whom Farkas knew to be a "squared-jawed character" who would "give you the shirt off his back." Farkas escorted the body to Oklahoma, where the pilot was to be buried and where his Cherokee widow, Linda, lived with their six-month-old son. Wearing his wool dress blues in the heat of a Southwest summer, Farkas rode the train from Twentynine Palms to Oklahoma City, unable to dispel the pitiful image of what little was left of his friend inside the casket riding in the baggage car. "Not much there," the navy undertaker had said when he signed the remains over to Farkas, explaining that the family should be strongly advised not to open the casket: "Part of a hand wrapped in a flag and a ring finger with a wedding ring."

Another squadron mate holding out hope for Dieter was his buddy Lizard Lessard. On the day Dieter went missing, Lessard noted in his journal that he was not writing to his wife, Sharon, "in the hopes that I'll have some good news." After he and Stovall found the wreckage of Dieter's plane, he again held off writing to Sharon, "hoping for good news." The next day, February 3, Lessard and Stovall, along with the skipper, Hal Griffith, and his wingman, Walt "Bummy" Bumgarner, returned to Laos and searched for hours with "still no sign of Dieter." That night, Lessard finally wrote to Sharon about "Dieter's mishap." On February 5 and 9, he wrote identical entries in his journal: "Still no word on Dieter."

On February 10, the Swordsmen lost another pilot.

Lieutenant Gary Hopps, twenty-nine, of Rochester, New York, was a barrel-chested former high school and college football player who had graduated from the University of Rochester (New York) with a degree in economics and had received his wings in 1963 through the Aviation Officer Candidate Program. He was a veteran of thirty combat missions, most of them during VA-145's previous WestPac cruise aboard *Constellation*. On the last day of his life, Hopps briefed for a mission as the third plane of a two-plane flight; this arrangement was common in case one of the other two Spads had mechanical problems and couldn't launch. However, the other two planes were good to go that afternoon on their mission to drop, along a highway near Mu Gia Pass, time-delayed bombs set to detonate in the middle of the night when troops and matériel rolled southward. But rather than unload the ordnance from his plane, it was decided to launch Hopps anyway. Hopps was carrying bombs with live fuses, so the flight leader, Ken Hassett,[*] had Hopps drop his bombs first on a "suspected truck park" in North Vietnam, which, although no vehicles could be observed under the jungle canopy from the air, had been reported as a "target of opportunity." Hopps then followed the other two planes to Mu Gia Pass. Every squadron had a plane equipped with a mounted camera, as the navy wanted film of its missions in Vietnam; that day, Hopps happened to be VA-145's cameraman. Hassett rolled in first, followed by his wingman, Lieutenant (j.g.) Tom Dixon, who had trained with Dieter and witnessed

---

[*] After Deiter went down, all the junior officers in the squadron had to take turns flying as Hassett's wingman, a universally unpopular assignment that was known as being "in the basket."

his escapes from the mock POW camp in Warner Springs. Hopps, no longer carrying bombs, followed Dixon down to film his run. Dixon released his bombs, and as he did he caught a brief flash behind him in his cockpit mirror. When Hassett and Dixon regrouped, Hopps was missing and didn't respond to their radio calls. Dixon decided to go back over the highway, and he "got down really low" for a good look. He could see only the little fins from the back of the external fuel tanks the Spads carried—they were on the ground right near where Dixon had dropped his time-delayed bombs. As he pulled up, Dixon received fire from small to medium arms on the ground. It seemed apparent what must have happened: Hopps was "hit in the head" by a bullet or otherwise killed or rendered unconscious during his camera run and his aircraft flew "straight in." Inasmuch as Hopps's fatal mission was only to take footage "so the navy," Spook Johns griped, "could do a remake of *Victory at Sea*," it struck everyone as a "waste." Two days later, VA-145's backup camera—attached to a bomb rack under one wing—"mysteriously" fell off a Spad during recovery. It bounced down the deck and went over the side. The squadron's second in command, Commander Donald Sparks, who had quietly ordered the "screws and bolts on the camera removed" so it would fall off with the first good jolt, let it be known that the next camera anyone put on a VA-145 Spad would fall off and go over the side, too. No new camera was ever installed.

"That's two pilots lost out of twenty in the squadron in ten days," Lessard wrote in his journal hours after Hopps went down. The reality hit home for everyone.

"At this rate," Farkas opined, "we'll run out of pilots."

The shootdowns of Dieter and Hopps "engendered a whole new program" for VA-145's bomb-run tactics; gone for good were the follow-the-leader attacks which made the last planes prey for enemy gunners on the ground. No one thought it coincidental that both Dieter and Hopps had been Tail End Charlies on their final missions. From then on, the Spads of VA-145 would come thundering in from different directions, crisscrossing over a target to confuse enemy gunners. In spite of earlier concerns, the new tactics did not lead to midair collisions, but surely saved lives.

On February 12, *Ranger* departed from Yankee Station after thirty-one days at sea, heading to Subic Bay for replenishment of stores, ammunition and fuel—and, most important to the crew, ten days of liberty in port.

That afternoon, with the cessation of flight operations and as the carrier steamed for the Philippines, a memorial service was held for Gary Hopps in hangar bay number one, located in the forward part of the hangar deck, where all work had come to a standstill for the solemn ceremony. Officers and enlisted men wore their dress whites, acceptable in the tropics—given the heat and humidity—for official functions. Pilots and enlisted men of VA-145 were present, along with Rear Admiral Weisner, Captain McCuddin, and the Protestant chaplain, Commander Robert Anderson. After the navy hymn was performed by the admiral's "great-sounding" seventeen-member band, led by Musician Chief Petty Officer E. O. Delight, Hopps's commanding officer, Hal Griffith, gave the eulogy.

"Gary and I both reported to VA-145 on January 10, 1964," said Griffith, his demeanor, posture, and deep voice radiating the desirable quality known as command presence. "I soon learned that he was an outstanding naval officer and pilot. Gary was a man that one could depend on to get the job done. During the Gulf of Tonkin incident in August 1964, and on missions during current operations requiring combat alertness, Gary distinguished himself repeatedly in aerial combat under enemy fire. His courage and devotion to duty were always in keeping with the highest traditions of the United States Naval Service. His dedication and loyalty to his service and country shall serve as an inspiration to each and every one of us. We have all lost an outstanding shipmate and naval officer to the cause of freedom. We'll miss him but will never forget his supreme sacrifice."

Chaplain Anderson offered prayers, read scriptures from the Old and New Testaments, and offered a brief message of consolation. When he finished, seven ramrod-straight marines in dress blues with white gloves snapped an about-face and swung their M-1s to their shoulders. Aiming their weapons out the open sliding door of the forward starboard elevator, they fired three volleys that echoed throughout the hangar bay.

As a lone bugler played taps, McCuddin presented a folded U.S. flag to Griffith. The flag would be sent home to Milton and Gladys Hopps, in

Oakland, California, along with photographs of the service for their son and a personal letter from Griffith.

Before *Ranger* arrived at Subic Bay, most of VA-145's pilots had already flown off and landed at nearby Cubi Point Naval Air Station, thereby getting a head start on drinking away the bad memories, which many Swordsmen set out to do.

A few days later, VA-145's ready room was abuzz with news of the sighting of an American POW "about 12 miles" from where Dieter crashed. The message from CINCPAC in Pearl Harbor arrived printed—as all secret dispatches in the navy were—on pink paper. Although Dieter was not named and there was "nothing firm" as to his status, the location of a Caucasian male in the hands of the Pathet Lao supplied by a "good guy" on the ground caused most Swordsmen to assume there was a "90 percent chance" it was their missing pilot. Lizard Lessard was certain it meant Dieter was alive, "running around out there somewhere."

That being the case, Lessard pulled out Dieter's list of electronics and photography equipment he planned to buy at reduced prices at the navy exchanges in Subic Bay and Japan, which *Ranger* was scheduled to visit. When Lizard had helped Farkas pack up Dieter's belongings from his stateroom, he had pocketed the list, unsure at the time what he would do with it. Now he knew: he would buy the things on Dieter's list.

When Dieter escaped, he would want to have them to take home.

9

PRISONERS OF WAR

If I am captured I will continue to resist by all means available.
I will make every effort to escape and to aid others to escape....

—ARTICLE III, CODE OF CONDUCT FOR
THE ARMED FORCES OF THE UNITED STATES

When Dieter was lifted from the hellhole in the cave, he found himself in the custody of soldiers of the North Vietnamese army. Although they proved to be equally brutal, he soon realized they were a "different breed" from the ragtag Pathet Lao.

The Vietnamese were dressed in dark-green uniforms accented with cravats made of white parachute material. Their military training was apparent; they were disciplined and precise, and their equipment was modern and in tip-top shape. The first thing they did was inspect the way Dieter had been tied up by his Laotian guards. They did not approve, and they retied the ropes more securely but less painfully. However, the more comfortable bindings came too late for Dieter's left hand and arm, which were still numb from Bastard's tourniquet torture. He would have no feeling in either for months.

The party formed up to leave. Dieter was to be escorted by four North Vietnamese regulars—who were clearly "running the show"—and three armed Laotians. He was surprised when his boots, rucksack, and sleeping bag were returned to him, although it was made clear he was not to wear the boots but to hang them around his neck. Dieter stood under guard for several minutes on an incline overlooking a field of rice paddies. Below, more than 200 young recruits performed calisthenics, led by two North Vietnamese drill instructors. Jeeps made in the Soviet Union were parked next to several wooden structures that looked like barracks. Dieter wondered how this large military training camp had been missed by navy and air force planes.

It was a beautiful morning, with crystal blue sky visible through gaps in the emerald canopy. Dieter, still in a weakened state from the beatings, soon became exhausted. Walking barefoot on the trails turned the soles of his feet into a mass of open sores. Dieter realized why his captors didn't want him to wear his boots: without footwear, he was less likely to dart off the trail into the thorn-blanketed jungle. With the North Vietnamese leading the way, the Laotians pushed and prodded him on. Thinking more about rest and getting off his feet than escape throughout a long day of hiking, Dieter was relieved when they stopped for the night at a bustling village.

The group was directed to a large hut, where a toothless old man was boiling rice in a big pot. Dieter was untied so he could eat, and the guards dropped their equipment and settled in one corner of the hut. The old man approached Dieter, pointing to his gold ring. Dieter shook his head, but the man kept making gestures as if he wanted to look at it. Dieter finally slipped the ring off and handed it to him. The old man turned so that the Vietnamese could not see him slip it on his finger, then started to walk away. Dieter called out to him, pointing to the ring and making it clear he wanted it back. Looking furtively at the soldiers, he took off the ring and gave it back to Dieter.

After the guards had received their food and were busy eating, the old man brought to Dieter a porcelain bowl heaping with steaming rice and cooked greens. With hand signals he made it clear that Dieter's choice was either "food for the ring or nothing to eat." Famished and not wanting to make a scene that would involve the soldiers, Dieter handed over the ring. He shoveled the food into his mouth with his fingers, then licked the bowl clean.

As night fell, Dieter unfolded his sleeping bag, crawled inside, and zipped it up for protection from the mosquitoes. He said a "long prayer," then dropped off to sleep and didn't wake up until morning.

After eating a bowl of rice, Dieter was taken by three soldiers to a "construction of bamboo pieces" from which diverted river water ran out like a faucet at shoulder level. His bindings were removed so he could wash. The soldiers were in no hurry, so he took advantage of the opportunity. Stripping down, he was surprised at how many cuts, sores, and bruises covered his body. He washed off the "filth and blood" as best he could without soap, which was long gone, and used small rocks to scrub his clothes, which he put back on soaking wet.

As the group prepared to leave the village, the toothless man was paid in Laotian currency by one of the soldiers. Dieter saw his ring glinting on the man's finger and pointed to it. The man shook his head and walked away, counting his money. Uncertain if he should bring the matter to the attention of the soldiers, Dieter kept quiet. He felt miserable, however, about losing his "only remaining link to home."

After a couple of hours on the trail, the party stopped at a wide river. One soldier threw a Chinese hand grenade into the water, and everyone dropped to the ground to await the explosion. After it came, ten seconds later, dozens of dead fish floated to the surface. A fire was made, and everyone—Dieter included—cooked fish impaled on long sticks. Dieter tried the special Vietnamese seasoning: red ants rubbed on the fish, which gave it a peppery taste. It was Dieter's best and most filling meal since his last visit to the officers' mess aboard ship.

Still upset about his ring, Dieter showed the soldiers the whitish mark on his finger where it had been. He gestured toward the village, trying to convey that the old man who fed them had taken his ring. The soldiers spoke among themselves, then packed up everything. Much to Dieter's surprise—as well as to the surprise of the Laotians traveling with them—the

North Vietnamese turned the group around, and they all headed back to the village, now at a much faster clip.

When they reached the village they went directly to the old man's hut. Without a word being spoken he was grabbed by two soldiers, one on each arm. A third soldier, obviously in charge, whipped out a big knife from a sheath on his belt, pressed the old man's hand down on a wooden block, and chopped off the finger with the ring. The old man screamed as blood spurted everywhere. The soldier picked up the severed finger, removed the ring, and put the ring on Dieter's correct finger.

Dieter was horrified. Had he any idea of the punishment that would be administered, he would never have reported the incident. After being badly treated himself, he hated being the reason for another man's suffering. He also understood that he could not mess around with the North Vietnamese. While they seemed honest and precise to a fault—the leader always checked his watch and marked in a little notebook the times they arrived at and departed from each village—they plainly did not value the well-being of anyone who got in the way of their assigned duties. Dieter knew that if he wasn't careful he might be "cut up to bits," too. He had already decided that if he tried to escape from the custody of the North Vietnamese, he had better be successful. He suspected that these hard-boiled jungle fighters would sooner shoot him than chase him.

On February 14, Dieter arrived at his first POW camp. It was near the village of Pa Kung. He would later learn that this was at 17 degrees 7 minutes north, and 106 degrees 14 minutes east—some eighty-five miles southeast of where he had crash-landed two weeks earlier. Dieter had been looking forward to arriving at the camp, believing that nothing could be worse than what he had already endured and wanting to share his misery with other Americans, particularly fellow pilots. He also hoped that a doctor might be present to look at his injured hand and arm.

The setting was not what he expected. He had thought that a POW camp, even one in Southeast Asia, would look more like the one in the "Steve McQueen movie" *The Great Escape*, with uniformed pilots milling about an expansive compound, hanging out their laundry to dry in the sun, tending their vegetable garden, and busily planning their next escape.

The North Vietnamese soldiers handed him over to a few half-dressed

Pathet Lao who jumped from their guard hut with weapons in hand. He was escorted to the entrance of a stockade encircled by tall bamboo fencing. At the gate, two guards watched him approach "down the sights" of their rifles. Inside the fence was a dusty yard with several huts. The hut he was taken to was made of logs and bamboo, with nothing inside other than spider nests and cobwebs. A swinging door was crisscrossed with wooden bars. Without any other openings, the interior was dark and stifling, and its rectangular shape brought to mind a coffin. After being shut inside, Dieter sat cross-legged at the door, peering out into the empty yard. The whole place seemed "dead and deserted."

After the guards went away, someone whispered, "Hello."

The voice seemed to be coming from next door.

Dieter slid over to a common wall between the huts, and answered at full volume. "Hey, anybody over there?"

The whisperer warned him to keep his voice down.

"I'm a navy pilot off the *Ranger*," Dieter said softly.

It sounded as if two people on the other side were exchanging hushed comments. Dieter put one eye up to a small hole in a section of rattan between logs. He saw part of the face of a bearded white man.

"I'm an air force helicopter pilot. Name's Duane."

It was all Dieter could do to keep from shouting for joy. It was a relief to hear English and to know that he was with another U.S. pilot.

"How many are you?" Dieter asked.

Six in all, Duane answered.

"How long you been here?"

Duane said his helicopter had been shot down five months earlier. "Two and a half years for the others. They're Air America."

Two and a half years? Dieter didn't know how that could be possible, and thought they may have lost track of time. He knew Air America was a clandestine airline run by the CIA. The CIA recruited former military pilots for big money—rumored to be as much as $100,000 a year. In fact, when Dieter was in flight training word had spread that Air America's recruiters were interviewing in a Pensacola motel.

"Did you say two and a half years?" Dieter asked.

"Shhh. Someone's coming."

The same guards who had escorted Dieter to the hut were returning, one carrying a long block of wood that he slipped through the bars of the door before entering. He pointed to Dieter's bare feet, then to what the Laotians called a foot trap, which Dieter could now see had a matching top and bottom about three feet long and a foot high. An elongated hole had been chiseled out in the middle.

At first, Dieter had no idea what the man wanted.

The guard finally grabbed one of Dieter's feet and pulled it toward the blocks. Realizing it was like a medieval foot block, Dieter yanked his foot back. A tug-of-war ensued.

"Not gonna get me in there, you bastard!"

The guard went outside, leaving another guard standing in the doorway. He picked up his carbine, which he had left leaning against the hut, and came back. Pointing his rifle at Dieter, he gestured to the foot blocks.

"Put it on," Duane said calmly. "If you don't, they'll shoot you."

The next thing Dieter knew, the muzzle of the gun was pressed against his forehead. Part of him wanted to make a stand right there, but Dieter knew it wasn't the right place or time. He nodded, and pulled the foot blocks over to show that he was complying.

The guard put down his rifle and worked both of Dieter's feet into the opening in the middle of the blocks. It was a tight fit; they had to go in sideways, one at a time, before Dieter could straighten them. The guard hammered home a wooden pin that went through the hole on the top, ran between Dieter's feet, and went into a smaller hole at the bottom. Then the guards left, "slamming the door and laughing."

Dieter stared in disbelief at his hobbled feet.

"Don't worry about it," Duane said. "You get used to it."

That was exactly what Dieter did *not* intend to do. He did not want to get used to being hog-tied or beaten. He did not want to get used to being a prisoner. If those were the alternatives, he would rather have taken his chance atop the mountain even if it meant dying. Good as it was to have Americans here, he did not intend to stick around.

"Hey, you guys," Dieter said defiantly. "It was nice knowing you, but I won't be around by tomorrow. I'm getting out tonight."

"Don't be stupid," Duane said. "You'll never make it. Lack of water will get you. You'll dehydrate." He explained that there was little water in Laos this time of year and that Dieter should wait a few months for the start of the summer monsoons, when heavy rainfall soaked the region.

Dieter knew about the pitfalls of lack of water. The last time he escaped, the Pathet Lao had simply staked out the nearest water hole and waited for him to show up. He didn't want to make that mistake again. Duane's caution reminded him of the most important lesson he had learned from his previous escape attempt: the jungle was the real prison.

When Dieter heard the guards outside, he dragged himself to the doorway and watched as the hut next door was opened. Motioning the prisoners out, a squad of guards stood aside with rifles at the ready.

The first one out Dieter recognized from the peephole. Duane had long, stringy brown hair and a full beard. He was wearing two-piece green fatigues with MARTIN sewed in block letters over one pocket, and AIR FORCE stitched above the other pocket. The first thing he did was look in Dieter's direction. Dieter waved through the bars. Duane nodded, then began a measured walk through the yard and down a slight embankment that Dieter would later learn led to the latrine.

First Lieutenant Duane Martin, twenty-six, of Denver, Colorado, flew as copilot of an HH-43 Huskie, a rescue helicopter assigned to the U.S. Air Force's Thirty-Eighth Aerospace Rescue and Recovery Squadron at Nakhon Phanom Air Base, Thailand. On September 20, 1965, Martin and his pilot, Captain Thomas F. Curtis, and their crew—Airman Third Class Arthur N. Black and Airman First Class William A. Robinson—were scrambled to pick up a downed F-105 pilot who had been located twelve miles east of the Laos border inside the North Vietnamese province of Nghe Tinh. The copter dropped into a small bowl-shaped canyon about 800 feet deep and enclosed on all sides by steep slopes. It was hovering 100 feet above the downed pilot when enemy gunners lying in ambush opened fire from two sides of the canyon. Hit in the main rotor blade, the helicopter fell straight down, landing on its side. Martin, the last one to scramble out, headed up the opposite side of the canyon and hid in dense foliage. The three men from Martin's crew, along with the F-105 pilot, were quickly rounded up by North Vietnamese troops. Martin evaded capture that day. He had an M-14 carbine and sidearm but no signal devices or emergency radio. The only food he carried was a single chocolate bar. Rather than head farther into North Vietnam, Martin, who was a seasoned Colorado Rockies outdoorsman, went west, knowing he had to cross Laos to reach Thailand. Weeks later, Martin was wandering in mountainous terrain in Laos, weak and delirious, when he was found by a Hmong family who nursed him back to health. For a week Duane was breast-fed by a young mother "just to keep him alive." Eventually, the Pathet Lao discovered his whereabouts, and he was carried on a litter "by two girls for six or seven days" until he was strong enough to walk on his own. He arrived at the prison camp on December 3, 1965.

The second prisoner out of the hut wore ragged clothes and a jacket made of small pieces of different material. He emptied out a bamboo container filled with urine, then gave a little wave to Dieter. A beard covered much of his face, but when he smiled at Dieter he showed a mouthful of bad or missing teeth. His name was Prasit Promsuwan. He was a Thai civilian working for Air America as an air freight kicker, a job that entailed pushing out of a transport plane crates and sacks of cargo dropped by parachute to friendly forces and villagers.

Two other Thai prisoners emerged from the hut. One, Prasit Thanee, had the same first name as Promsuwan, so he was referred to by his last name. At twenty-three, Thanee was the youngest of the group, and also the tallest and biggest. Since he understood Laotian, it was his job to eavesdrop whenever possible on the conversations of the guards, then pass along any important information to the other prisoners.

The third Thai—all three Thai were cargo kickers—was Phisit Intharathat, formerly a paratrooper in the Royal Thai army and a veteran of eighty jumps. He came to the door of Dieter's hut and introduced himself. To Dieter's surprise, Phisit took out from a porcelain bowl he was carrying a toothbrush and toothpaste and began brushing his teeth.

Also stepping out from the hut was To Yick Chiu, a Chinese civilian who was a native of Hong Kong and was known as Y.C. He was in his early forties, of smallish build, with graying hair and a deeply wrinkled face, and dressed in khakis. Y.C. was a radio operator for Air America. "Take it easy, man," he said softly to Dieter before heading down Latrine Hill.

The last prisoner from the adjacent hut was the third American held in the camp: Eugene "Gene" DeBruin, who had a long red beard and light skin dappled with freckles. He, too, wore a patchwork jacket. In his early thirties, DeBruin was the second eldest in a Wisconsin farm family of ten. After serving as an enlisted man in the air force, he had enrolled at the University of Montana and graduated with a bachelor's degree in forestry. After spending three summers in Alaska as a smoke jumper, he was in search of new adventures and had hired on with Air America. He was sent to Southeast Asia in August 1963 as a cargo kicker. Only a month later, he found himself parachuting not into a fire, but out of a flaming aircraft.

For the crew members Gene DeBruin, Y.C., and the three Thai, that fateful day—September 5, 1963—started out as a routine one in Air America's hush-hush air-freight delivery service over Laos. Around 7:00 A.M., the two men in the cockpit—the pilot, Joseph C. Cheney, forty-three, of Ellensburg, Washington, and the copilot, Charles G. Herrick, forty-four, of Buffalo, New York—fired up the twin engines on the C-46 Commando, a World War II–vintage transport plane with its left rear door removed. After taking off from the airport in Vientiane—the Laotian capital under the control of the pro-western Royal Lao government, engaged in a nationwide civil war with the communist Pathet Lao—and making a brief stop to pick up a cargo of rice in bundles that weighed 600 pounds each, they completed their first drop over southern Laos with "no sign or hint of enemy AAA." They went back to load up a second time and completed that cargo drop, also without incident. When they departed for their third supply mission of the day, it was nearly 4:00 P.M. Flying the same route they had taken earlier, they were heading for the drop zone when puffs of smoke from antiaircraft fire surrounded the plane. A violent explosion rocked the aircraft, and the right engine caught fire. The pilots shut down that engine and turned for home. In less than a minute the right wing was ablaze, and the order came from the cockpit for the crew to bail out. The four crewmen jumped as the two pilots fought to maintain control. Heavy flames were then seen to engulf the aircraft, which exploded "in a giant fireball," killing Cheney and Herrick instantly.

The idea that Air America crewmen had been prisoners in Laos for two and a half years had seemed preposterous to Dieter, but as soon as he saw them he "started to believe." Their clothes—old, worn, stitched haphazardly—told a story. And there was more. The years were etched on their faces, and in their sunken, haunted eyes there was a sadness that could not be hidden by their brief smiles and friendly greetings.

In the short time the men were allowed to walk around the yard before being herded back into their hut, each came over to speak briefly to Dieter. In different ways, the Air America crewmen asked the same question: *Is the war winding down? How are the Geneva peace talks going? Is there talk of prisoner exchanges?* They were obviously living on false hopes, and it pained Dieter to tell them that the war was not winding down, but escalating. More troops and ships were being sent to the combat zone, he explained, and U.S. Navy and Air Force planes at that moment were hitting North Vietnam.

Phisit, the former paratrooper, brought Dieter his own toothbrush and tube of toothpaste, explaining that the guards had received a shipment of Chinese dental supplies and there were enough to go around. He also gave Dieter a bamboo cup and a spoon made from a coconut shell.

After the guards had secured the other prisoners in their foot blocks for the night and checked on Dieter, he went to work freeing his feet. Sliding around on the floor, he found two sticks, probably left over from when the hut was built. One was long and the other short and thin. The pin that locked the foot blocks was tapered toward the bottom. He first tried driving it out by holding the smaller stick against the pin at the bottom and hammering it with the longer piece. With only one good hand, however, he couldn't get the leverage he needed. He thought about how disadvantaged he was going to be when it came time to escape if his left hand and arm were still useless. Trying another approach, he shoved the longer stick into the wall between logs, and lifted up the blocks so that the end of the stick was pressed against the pin in the bottom. Using his good hand, he pushed down on the blocks until the pin came out the top hole. He slipped his feet out, grateful that he wouldn't have to sleep in the blocks. He would just have to be sure to get himself back into them whenever he heard the guards approaching.

In the morning, a fat guard the prisoners called Jumbo opened the door to Dieter's hut. He released Dieter from the foot blocks, which he had managed to get back on only seconds earlier, with the pin halfway in place. Leaving Dieter's door open, Jumbo went to open up the other hut.

Dieter went into the yard, where he was soon joined by the others.

Gene was full of questions, first wanting to know who had won the last World Series. Dieter, who was not a baseball fan, did not know. Then Gene asked if it was true that President Kennedy had been assassinated. Dieter confirmed this, adding that he had been shot while riding in a motorcade in Dallas, Texas. Next, Gene wanted to know if anyone had produced stainless steel razor blades yet. A bemused Dieter said yes.

"Are you sure about that?"

"Of course I'm sure."

"Well, I'll be," said Gene, obviously disappointed. "That's what I wanted to invent when I got out of this hellhole."

When the guards ordered everyone inside again. Dieter tried to go with the other prisoners but was directed back to his own hut. Duane said not to worry—he would soon be with the rest of them.

Around mid-morning the worst guard in camp—dubbed Little Hitler by the prisoners—announced that the new prisoner was to be interrogated by the North Vietnamese. Prasit, who was fluent in Vietnamese, would go with Dieter to translate. Dieter's heart started beating faster. He could think only of his previous interrogations, which had soon lapsed into beatings and torture.

Little Hitler and several other guards escorted Dieter and Prasit outside the compound, where four North Vietnamese soldiers were sitting on a pile of logs. One of them held a notebook and pencil.

After giving his name and rank, Dieter was asked what kind of plane he flew. He wondered if this was a kind of test, as he was certain that the wrecked Spad had been found. He talked it over with Prasit, and they agreed it would be best if Dieter said something. He told Prasit to say that if they untied him he would draw a picture of his plane.

After being untied, Dieter used a twig to scratch in the dirt the outline of an aircraft with questionable aerodynamics. His creation had nine propellers: four engines on the right wing and five on the left. A concerned

Prasit suggested he add another engine on the right wing to balance the picture, but Dieter decided against making any changes when he saw the man with the notebook carefully copying the design.

When Dieter was asked how many men the plane held, Prasit counseled him, "Tell them the truth. Maybe they didn't believe your nine-engine aircraft."

"I was alone," said Dieter, again thinking that if they had found his aircraft they would know this. "I was the only pilot and there were no crew members."

The soldiers seemed to accept at "face value" everything Dieter told them. His hands were retied and the guards took him and Prasit back to the compound. Along the way, Little Hitler gave Dieter a kick in the back, apparently in retaliation for his being "let off too easy."

Back in his hut, Dieter thought more about escape. Having already learned that "one percent of the problem" was getting away, and ninety-nine percent was "what to do once you are out," he had accepted the practicality of waiting for the monsoons. The other prisoners said that the heavy rain usually lasted for three months, and during the wet season there would be plenty of drinking water in the jungle. Food, however, would be a problem. Sliding over to the wall, Dieter asked Duane if they had ever tried saving some of their rice. They had, Duane explained, but it had soon rotted and turned green. In that case, Dieter said, the rice would have to be dried by being spread out on some material. Duane asked what they would do in the event of a surprise inspection by the guards. Being caught hoarding food would be a serious matter; the guards would suspect that the rice was being saved for a possible escape, and in any case would take it for themselves. Dieter was determined to figure something out—the idea of "rotting away for years" as a POW or waiting until he was too weak to escape was unacceptable. He had been escaping and surviving all his life. So much of what he had done during his life—from growing up in postwar Germany right through his escapes from the simulated POW camp at Warner Springs—was preparation for the survival challenge he now faced.

Shortly after the prisoners were let into the yard that afternoon, the crack of a nearby rifle shot was heard. An ashen-faced Duane came hurrying up the hill from the latrine, with a line of guards behind him. Duane was holding his head above one ear, and his neck was bloody. The guards herded everyone—Dieter included—into one hut. Duane, scared as well as furious, explained that he had no sooner gotten his pants down than a guard nicknamed Nook had yelled at him to get up. Before Duane could stand or even say anything, Nook had fired his rifle. The bullet scraped Duane's head just above his right ear. Upon inspection, the wound wasn't deep and the bleeding had slowed, but another quarter of an inch and Duane would have had a bullet in his brain. Everyone sat back, struck silent. Dieter was sure they all had the same thought: that any minute here "could be our last."

Later that day, Dieter moved his sleeping bag and utensils to his new home, and he became a permanent member of the larger group of prisoners. His cell mates gave him an official welcome by raising their bamboo cups, filled with foul-smelling water, in a toast.

An hour later, the guards put the prisoners in the foot blocks for the night. Also, using old French handcuffs, which had a wrist ring at either end connected by two metal bars, they cuffed the men in pairs. Dieter was locked to Prasit; his left wrist was in the cuff and the metal bars extended across to Prasit's right wrist. As Dieter started to think about a way to release the internal spring that he knew kept the handcuffs locked, Prasit reached down in his skivvies and took out a rolled-up piece of rag that contained a key. Dieter was to learn that anything worth hiding went into one's underwear, as that was a taboo area never searched by the Laotians. All the prisoners had sewn little pockets inside their undershorts to keep contraband. Prasit slipped the key into the keyhole and had Dieter keep pressure on the connecting bars so the spring would not make a loud click when the cuffs opened. Prasit turned the key, and the cuffs snapped open with little noise. The key was passed to the others, who did the same. The other prisoners then deftly slipped out of their foot blocks, having figured out how to do so some time ago.

Phisit explained they had made other keys—one from a quill and another out of wood—but these always broke after being used a few times. About six months after their imprisonment, they got the idea of melting down an empty toothpaste tube—in those days they were at a prison camp where they had been allowed to have a small fire inside their hut. The hot liquid was poured into a mold in the ground. After it dried, an empty ammunition clip was used to "scrape and shape" it so that it would fit inside the keyhole. Their homemade key had worked with all the handcuffs the guards had used since—the Air America crew had been kept in five prison camps in Laos—and from then on they had been able to unlock their handcuffs. With their hands and feet free at night, they could sleep more comfortably. They always kept their handcuffs and blocks nearby so as to get back into them quickly in the event of a surprise visit. But such visits were rare at night, given the lack of lighting in the compound—the guards had no flashlights— and the superstitions of the Laotians, who periodically left offerings at trail heads to satisfy the ghosts they believed roamed the jungle at night. They were deathly afraid of the dark. When one of the guards had to go outside to relieve himself he would not go alone; another guard came along, and they held hands like frightened children. At sunrise, the prisoners made a point of getting back into their shackles before the guards showed up to unlock them.

Days passed with little change in the routine of the prisoners except that their rice portions kept getting smaller, leaving them hungry and steadily losing weight. Dieter was shocked, when a guard let him look into a small mirror, at how his cheekbones protruded from his sunken face, and his "former ruddy complexion was now sallow." The prisoners were always starved for protein. As they circled the compound during their brief periods outside, they could sometimes smell singed hair, which meant the guards were cooking over a fire an animal they had trapped or shot. The mouth of every prisoner watered in anticipation, although the guards seldom shared their bounty. One day, with a barbecue in progress, Thanee went to the fence and asked if there would be any meat that day for the prisoners. No, he was told, the two rats that had been caught were only for the guards. When Thanee told the others, all of them were disappointed except Dieter, who hadn't "yet learned to like rat," although that time would come. He had started eating his toothpaste—peppermint or spearmint— instead of "wasting it" brushing his teeth.

The prisoners tried to keep track of the days and dates, and otherwise bring some normality to their lives. Saturdays were designated hoot-and-holler nights, and they would find songs they could sing together. Every

Sunday they would have a religious service with "Reverend Duane" telling Bible stories, and leading discussions about God. Every other night Duane turned into a teacher of history, a subject he had majored in at college and hoped one day to teach at the Air Force Academy. He would talk for "hours and hours" about history, and the prisoners "loved it" because it gave them something else to think about. Alternating nights were designated as movie night, with everyone taking turns describing favorite films. Dieter enjoyed retelling the zany comedy *It's a Mad, Mad, Mad, Mad World*, starring Spencer Tracy, Jimmy Durante, and Phil Silvers. Invariably, he and his listeners would laugh until their sides ached.

Such activities were the only things that kept them going in captivity; if they just sat back and thought about home all the time it would drive them "nuts." That said, they did set goals. Dieter's was to "get free and come home and be married." Duane wanted "nothing else but to see his wife and girls and have a hamburger." Gene wanted to come home for a tall glass of cold beer, and talked incessantly about a lager's color and taste, and the right amount of foam for a proper head.

When Dieter got to the camp he asked, "What about chess?" He made a chessboard using bamboo and rocks for the different pieces. After everyone learned the game, the prisoners played regularly, and competition heated up between them.

One day Prasit returned from speaking with the guards in the yard and said that Little Hitler had told him everyone was leaving the next day. "We're going to be released!" Prasit said with a big smile.

Dieter pressed Prasit for more details, wanting to know if anything had been said about the Geneva peace talks or about the war being over.

The only thing Little Hitler had said, Prasit explained, was that everyone was leaving in the morning for the headquarters of the province chief in Yamalot. Prasit took this to mean they were to be released.

Gene commented that all Pathet Lao, especially "that little no-good son of a bitch" Little Hitler, were "lying bastards," and that nothing they had told the prisoners had turned out to be true.

Although Duane was excited about the move to Yamalot, pointing out that as a regional headquarters it would have more food and medical supplies, Dieter well remembered Yamalot and the French-speaking province chief. Yes, he had been given plentiful food and had received medical attention, but it had all been for the express purpose of getting him to sign a confession. The wily chief could well have the power in these parts to release prisoners, but given his own experiences at Yamalot Dieter had little faith in that outcome. Still, he knew that the village was much closer to the border of Thailand. If they did end up there, he resolved to escape the first day—with or without the rainy season.

Eventually, the entire group cheered up at the prospect of leaving. After a small portion of rice the next morning, everyone waited in the prison yard for the guards to finish their preparations for departure. Suddenly feeling dizzy, Dieter discovered that he was burning up. All the prisoners experienced the recurrent fever, chills, and nausea of malaria—not surprisingly, given the jungle's infestation of mosquitoes. Dieter—like everyone else—no longer had any antimalaria pills. All the prisoners could do was wait out the troubling spells and try to stay hydrated and rested. Dieter cursed his bad luck; of all the times to be sick, it had to be today.

They were soon on the march, with five guards in front and ten following behind the prisoners. They passed military troops on the move, antiaircraft gun emplacements, and large tractors carving out a road in the middle of the jungle. When the weak and woozy Dieter lagged, Gene pushed him on to save them both from the wrath of the nearest guard, one with prominent buckteeth who had earned the name Crazy Horse for his wild and violent ways.

At the top of a crest they took a trail that Dieter had been on previously. He recalled a junction a few hundred yards downhill, with one direction going to Yamalot. When they reached the fork, they did not head for Yamalot. Dieter counted his steps, in case he ever had to double back in the dark, and reached 6,336 paces from the junction to a fenced compound. The prisoners looked at one another, and it seemed to dawn on them at the same time that this was to be their new home, and they were not going to Yamalot to be released after all.

Gene had been right: the Pathet Lao guards were lying bastards, no doubt intent on breaking the spirit of the prisoners until they lost the will or the physical strength to escape. *Not this guy!* Dieter resolved. *It won't work with this guy! Just wait, I'll get out of here!*

The prison camp looked new, and it was easy to believe what they were told: no prisoners had been kept here before. The site was better camouflaged by the encroaching jungle than the other camp and would be harder to spot from the air. The new camp was closely surrounded on all sides by woods and jungle, and to the south a high ridgeline was visible, covered with an emerald blanket of trees. The prison compound—a clearing studded with six or seven trees—was about forty by forty feet. It was enclosed by a fifteen-foot woven bamboo fence which had one guarded gate that opened onto a dirt path. To the left was a nearby stream and camp latrine, and to the right was the route to the village of Ban Hoeui Het several miles away. Outside the fence at either end of the compound was a thirty-foot guard tower that overlooked the yard from front to back. Also outside the walls were half a dozen guard huts, including one used for food preparation. Inside the stockade were two cells: identical log-and-bamboo huts with thatched, leaf-covered roofs. They were each eighteen feet long and six feet wide. The guards split the prisoners into two groups. Assigned to one hut were the three Thai and Y.C., and in the other hut, a few yards away, were the three Americans.

The separation was fine for everyone involved, as tension had been growing between the Americans and the Thai. Many of the disagreements among the prisoners were typical of men locked up in close quarters under adverse conditions. Dieter learned that Phisit and Y.C. had once had an argument and did not speak to each other for a year; and Y.C. and another Thai were now not talking to each other. Even the two U.S. pilots had clashed early on, owing to what Dieter perceived to be Duane's "religious hard-headedness"—though Duane, a practicing Christian Scientist and teetotaler, had "mellowed" to the point where he promised to get drunk with Dieter when they got out. Duane had been raised to avoid modern medicine, but he now said if anything happened to him he wanted Dieter to see his wife, Dorcas, in Colorado, and tell her to be sure and take their two young daughters, Christine and Cheryl, to a doctor or hospital whenever they were sick because he had decided "that's what they're for."

By the time they arrived at their new camp, the main issue of contention for the prisoners had become the escape plan, with everyone having his own idea of what would and would not work. The Air America crew had previously escaped in May 1964, only to be recaptured six days later. They had not tried an escape since then.

Dieter's plan was to steal weapons from the guards, kill them, and collect all the supplies in camp. After that, they would hold the camp and signal one of the planes that regularly flew overhead—Duane recognized the sound of a four-engine U.S. Air Force C-130 Hercules transport, overhead most nights. If that didn't work they would find a river, either steal a native boat or build a raft from bamboo and banana trees, and float down a tributary to South Vietnam or Thailand, traveling by night and hiding by day.

None of the other prisoners, Duane included, liked the idea of killing the guards. They discussed how under international law a prisoner of war who killed a guard while escaping could be executed upon recapture. The other prisoners did not want to take that chance. In fact, Phisit, the former paratrooper, was opposed to any escape attempt. He announced that he would not assist the others or join them in their planned escape. He said the whole idea was "crazy," and that he didn't intend to get himself killed because of an "escape-happy guy" like Dieter. When Dieter and Duane explained that U.S. military personnel taken prisoner were required by their code of conduct to resist and make every effort to escape, and upon their return home could be court-martialed for failing to do so, Phisit "listened and thought it was funny."

For days, Duane argued with Phisit about the escape, to the point that the two men stopped talking to each other. When Phisit, in a huff, demanded that the escape be shelved because if all the other prisoners broke out he could be killed in retaliation, Dieter blew up. "Go to hell!" he yelled at Phisit. "I'm going even if I have to go alone! I'm not going to rot away the way you've done for three years."

A year earlier, the Air America crewmen had been "forced to write a confession" stating that the Royal Thai government had sent them to "invade Laotian territory and kill Laotians." Gene, as an American, had been singled out, and he "endured more pain" than the others. Passing out numerous times, he was brought back by having water thrown on him, then beaten more. Gene finally wrote out the incriminating statement and signed his name. Now, he was all for the escape, and the three Americans decided they would stick together in the jungle. In fact, they did not share with the

Asians their plans for evasion once they broke out. With Phisit staying behind after an escape, who knew what he might tell the guards? Also, if one
of the other Asians escaped and was recaptured, the Americans had no
faith that he wouldn't "squeal loud and clear to save his own skin."

While discussions continued as to what to do with the guards, everyone
agreed on the timing of the escape: when the monsoons arrived. In addition
to providing drinking water in the jungle, the rains would wash away their
tracks, thwarting any search party of Pathet Lao, who were excellent trackers. Meanwhile, all the prisoners—"except Phisit"—began to save small
amounts of their daily rice ration, which, per Dieter's suggestion, they first
dried for three days, moving it daily to a dry piece of material. Then it was
placed in one of several sacks that Gene had sewn, using scraps torn from
Dieter's nylon bag and a needle Y.C. had found several prison camps ago.
The rice was stored for two more days inside an extra waste container no
one used; the prisoners knew that the guards would never look in such a
taboo place. When they needed room to keep larger amounts of dried rice,
Dieter cut down one of the long bamboo poles holding up the roof of the
Americans' hut—with Duane and Gene "singing to cover the noise." Using
a hardwood stick to break out the thin membranes in the stalk, Dieter
opened a hollow area into which they poured the rice. He then plugged the
end of the pole and carefully put it back under the roof. In the other hut, the
rice-drying operation didn't go as well, and there were so many close calls
with the guards that all agreed the operation had to cease, or the escape
plan would be jeopardized. Everyone at least had some rice to carry now.

The prisoners became keen observers of the camp routine, looking for
any openings or opportunities they might exploit to break out of the compound. Each morning, a group of guards would take the prisoners one at a
time to a nearby stream, where they would dump out their waste containers. Every three days they were allowed to wash their clothes and bathe in
the same stream. The prisoners were not put back into their huts until after
breakfast, and could spend the time walking within the perimeter of the
compound. Most days, guards climbed into the two gun towers. At meal-
time, all the guards gathered outside the compound walls in a kitchen hut
where the food was prepared. This was the only time the guards were
separated from their weapons. Even those on guard duty in the towers left

their guns behind, and others not on guard duty left the guns in their huts located outside the compound. Everyone went to the kitchen and put food onto the turtle shells used for plates, with most returning to the huts or towers to eat.

Inside their own hut, the Americans built a detailed model of the prison camp with twigs and sticks. Pebbles of varying shades and sizes represented different guards, and they began keeping track of every move made by the guards. In a matter of days, they knew each man's routine, and could account for every weapon in the camp. When guards came to their hut, they quickly scattered the miniature model, leaving a harmless-looking collection of sticks and pebbles on the ground.

The wait for the rains continued. The monsoons did not arrive in mid-May, as the men from Air America said had happened the previous year. Dieter's hope to be a free man by May 22—his twenty-eighth birthday—was dashed. The delay also caused a severe water shortage in the camp; the stream from which their drinking water came turned into a "little pool of stinking water filled with wriggling larvae." Water was so scarce that the guards washed themselves and cleaned any game they caught in the water before giving it to the prisoners. When the prisoners filled their cups, they could not see the bottom for the dirt, algae, and worms. With their thirst "putting an end to queasiness," the prisoners drank it anyway.

With the prison camp receiving decreased rations of rice from local villages, the guards organized supply missions to other regions to bring back larger quantities of rice. Typically, the round-trip took at least two weeks. On the journey back, the guards and village porters carrying the loads would eat much of the rice. By the time they returned to camp, there was often only enough to last a week or ten days. Rather than restrict their own portions, the guards ate heartily while cutting back further on the prisoners' rations. When the camp ran low on rice before the next supply party had returned, the guards organized hunting parties, which often returned empty-handed. While the Pathet Lao were excellent trackers in the jungle, many of them "didn't know beans about handling a weapon." When they managed to bag a deer—the species in Southeast Asia were known as muntjac, or barking deer, and they did "bark like a dog"—word spread rapidly and villagers showed up for their share, which custom decreed they were entitled to, since this was their valley. By the time everyone divvied up the meat, usually only the stomach and intestines were left. The gut was sliced open and its contents—mostly undigested grasses—were dumped onto a big banana leaf, which was brought to the prisoners, who wolfed everything down. Once the leftovers included a deer skull, and Dieter hungrily dug out and ate one of the eyeballs.

The guards would keep any leftover meat for several days until it was too rotten to eat. A guard would then bring it to the prisoners, holding a towel over his nose and mouth. Thrown onto the ground, the putrid meat was so moldy it was green; it sat there "moving and bubbling" with crawling maggots. The first time Dieter "chowed down" with the others, he vomited. After that—realizing he would die if he didn't eat—he helped divide it into equal portions for everyone, and kept his own portion down. Not bothering to pick out the maggots, he pulverized them with his teeth before swallowing.

Other unwanted parts of a deer, such as its testicles and penis, were cut off and thrown to the prisoners, who did not waste them. The guards were able to collect tadpoles in the creek with nets. Although Laotians preferred their meat raw, they cooked the tadpoles in a big pot until the mixture was as "black and thick as highway tar." When they brought leftovers to prisoners, it "stunk like heck" but they ate every bite.

The prisoners were getting only a handful of rice daily, plus whatever they could forage. There were rats under the floor of the hut, but they were too fast to catch. One day a snake slithered under the hut; lifting up a floorboard, the prisoners lay on their bellies and watched with eager anticipation. When it struck a rat, the snake was brought up into the hut coiled around a stick. The rat was pried from the jaws of the snake, which was then placed back under the hut to continue its hunting services. The prisoners sliced the rat into equal pieces. Everyone, including Dieter, who had been slow to come around to the idea of eating rat meat, partook of the bonus meal. Rats and snakes became their constant companions. Rats would scamper over them in the dark at night, and snakes were always dropping down from the rattan roof. Dieter awakened one morning to see a snake disappearing down the waistband of his pants, and he calmly waited until it came out his pants leg.

The prisoners felt "dizzy all the time" at the slightest exertion. The hut had three steps down to the ground, and often they "just collapsed right there" trying to get down. Besides suffering from malaria and untold other tropical diseases and parasites, they had bouts of dysentery, which left them acutely dehydrated. As they awaited the rains, they all grew weaker by the day. Dieter began to wonder how many of them would have the physical strength to pull off an escape. Although he had agreed to wait for the rains, he came to realize he had been in a "much better position" to escape when he first arrived. He had been stronger at that time, and familiar with the trails, distances, directions, and terrain. Also, for the first couple of days in camp, he still had his hiking boots, which had subsequently been taken by the guards, who hung them under a hut outside the compound with the other prisoners' shoes. One vital aspect of the escape plan called for recovering their shoes so they would have protection from the thorns and barbs that covered the jungle floor.

The lack of food put the guards on edge. They became meaner, and quicker to beat the prisoners, who worried that the guards might look for an excuse to kill them so as not to have to feed them. The prisoners lost most of their privileges, such as being taken to the stream in the morning and walking freely around the compound. On many days there was no going outside for any reason, not even to the latrine. The guards began locking the prisoners in foot blocks during the day. With the guards in and out of the compound during the day, the prisoners were loath to unlock the blocks and free themselves. They sat in one place all day, "sweltering in the mosquito-ridden heat" and gagging on the fumes of their excrement.

Whenever he had a chance, Dieter made a point of massaging his injured hand and arm, trying to restore the circulation. For a long time it seemed hopeless. Then, one day the unexpected happened: some fingers moved. He undertook a regimen of lifting, stretching, and clenching exercises, and in a week could lift his hand. In two weeks, he could lift it twice in a row. Soon, his left hand and arm—though still weak—were as functional as his right.

Phisit got along with most of the guards and had previously won "special favors"—such as more time outside the compound, coming and going between huts, and extra food—for serving as their medic. He now saw that the guards were getting desperate. No longer concerned only about being punished in the event of a successful escape, Phisit worried that he would not be spared if the guards decided to eliminate the prisoners to end the burden of feeding them. Phisit told the other prisoners he would escape with them on one condition: they must take the guards' guns and be ready to shoot the guards. This was what Dieter had wanted all along, and he agreed. However, the other prisoners were still uncertain about killing the guards.

That attitude changed one night when a group of guards, including Little Hitler and Crazy Horse, taunted the prisoners with a form of Russian roulette. Their rifles—some loaded, some empty—were pointed at the heads of the prisoners. With every click of a trigger, the prisoners would jump with fright, causing much merriment among the guards. That experience solidified the prisoners' final plans for escape. A shaken Duane told Dieter he would go along with the breakout even if it meant killing the guards. The Thai prisoner Prasit seethed: "Just leave me Little Hitler. I want him for myself. That's all I ask."

Everyone concurred that the sound of gunfire would bring reinforcements to the camp, so the idea of dragging the most dangerous and despicable guards into the jungle and strangling them began to catch on. They could keep a couple of the other guards alive for information about the jungle topography or to trade as hostages.

The days proceeded slowly. From the time they awakened at about 5:00 A.M. until they were locked up for the night twelve hours later felt more like forty hours. The nights, when they were finally able to sleep, were the nearest thing they had to freedom. In their dreams, they could envision good things, although at times even their dreams were tainted by their circumstance. Dieter often dreamed of escape. In one nocturnal vision, the whole U.S. Navy came to his rescue, but, alas, without a happy ending. He waved and shouted to a sea filled with ships, but they didn't hear him and "kept on going somewhere else." He awoke in a panic, his heart racing. Whenever he needed extra strength, he thought about his grandfather, remembering the strength of character and willpower the baker had shown in his time of hardship and suffering. Hermann Schnuerle had survived imprisonment by the Nazis; Dieter willed himself to get through his own ordeal.

By mid-June the rains had still not come. Realizing that they were becoming weaker every day, Dieter and Duane decided to make their try before July 4, with or without the monsoons. That seemed to the U.S. pilots an appropriate date to "either be free or dead."

A few days later, Thanee overheard the guards discussing what to do with the prisoners. It was decided that they should be shot, and their bodies dragged into the jungle to make it look as if they had been killed while trying to escape. With their demise, the prison camp would be empty and the guards could return home to their villages, where there was more food.

"That's it!" Dieter exclaimed. "That's the signal. I'm getting out of this joint."

As it happened, Little Hitler and nine other guards were away on a rice-gathering mission, leaving seven guards behind. That meant seven prisoners versus seven guards: "even odds for once," Dieter pointed out.

Without a voice of dissent, the prisoners came to a decision.

They would carry out the escape plan right away.

10

SOUTH CHINA SEA

On March 1, 1966—one month to the day after Dieter's shootdown—*Ranger* lost three aviators "at almost the same time."

Lieutenant (j.g.) Donald J. Woloszyk, twenty-four, of Alpena, Michigan, was flying an A-4 Skyhawk assigned to a reconnaissance mission over North Vietnam. His brother, Ken, twenty-one, an Aviation Electronics Technician Third Class, was working in flight-deck control when his brother's plane was launched.

Woloszyk's flight leader was engaged in a series of steep turns in poor visibility to check a winding road for targets of opportunity when Woloszyk reported losing sight of him and advised that he was climbing above the cloud cover. His location at the time was seven miles inland from the coast. Upon hearing this report, the flight leader climbed above the clouds but did not see his wingman. No hostile fire was reported, although antiaircraft batteries were known to be in the area.

When *Ranger* turned into the wind to recover its aircraft from that afternoon's launch, Ken Woloszyk was visiting a friend in primary flight control—equivalent to the control tower at an airport—located high in the ship's island superstructure with a commanding view of the flight deck below. He saw that his brother's call sign, *Garfish 401*, was not written in grease pencil on the air boss's window, where a list was kept of all the aircraft in the landing pattern. At the time, no one could tell him why his brother wasn't lining up to land with the rest of his squadron. When Don Woloszyk was reported missing by his flight leader, a three-day search was undertaken, but no sign of the missing pilot or his plane was ever found. It would be years before Ken Woloszyk heard anything about his brother's probable fate: "Supposedly he crashed in a farmer's field, and was found with a broken back and died in the field." No remains were ever returned.

While Woloszyk was losing his way in poor visibility, three F-4 Phantoms from *Ranger* were airborne in the same deteriorating weather on a coastal reconnaissance mission—known as a coastal recce in naval aviation parlance—off North Vietnam, about forty miles south of the port of Haiphong.

The commanding officer of VF-143, Commander Walter Spangenberg, Jr., thirty-nine, of Seattle, Washington, was in the lead and had the other two planes in a "tight right echelon" formation with only half a wingspan separating the aircraft. Although Spangenberg had graduated in the top 15 percent of his class at Annapolis (1948) and was the skipper of a "superlative fighter squadron"—VF-143 was known throughout the fleet as the Pukin' Dogs, for its insignia of a winged black panther that resembled a vomiting canine—he was considered a weak stick (a poor aviator) by his own pilots. Flying in tight formation under a low cloud base with limited visibility, Spangenberg ordered a 180-degree turn to the right to reverse course. The tight formation itself—a parade formation good for air shows and other ceremonial events—that Spangenberg had ordered was badly chosen for a coastal recce in reduced visibility over enemy territory; most flight leaders on such missions preferred a combat-cruise formation with 100 feet separating the aircraft. In the low-altitude maneuver ordered by Spangenberg, it was the leader's responsibility not to fly the formation into the water, as the other two pilots would be too busy staying "glued to the lead"—trying not to hit the plane only a few feet in front—to watch their altimeters. The lowest plane on the inside of the turn—"not an easy position to fly"—was particularly vulnerable in such a low-altitude turn; it would have to decelerate quickly while flying a shorter-radius turn than the leader in order to stay in formation. The pilot in that position that day was an "extremely good stick" on his second WestPac cruise, Lieutenant William Frawley, twenty-seven, of Brockton, Massachusetts. A "typical Irish kid from South Boston," Frawley was "a Southie all the way" in personality and accent, and one of the most popular pilots in his squadron. The radar intercept officer (RIO) in the backseat of Frawley's Phantom was Lieutenant (j.g.) William Christensen, twenty-five, of Great Falls, Montana. One of the new crop of RIOs to join the squadron, Christensen was a "big, blond, bright, easygoing kid from America's heartland." (For safety and training reasons, VF-143 attempted to pair an experienced pilot with a new RIO, or a new pilot with an experienced RIO.) In the backseat, Christensen should have been monitoring the instruments and calling out the plane's altitude as a caution to Frawley. Why Christensen apparently did not do so before they flew into the sea could never be determined, although it was speculated that he could have had "his head buried in the radar looking for enemy contacts." It was thought that a more experienced RIO would have noticed the loss of altitude as the flight descended in the turn. Indeed, the RIO in the middle plane did yell out when he realized they were only fifty feet off the water; his pilot urgently pulled up and out of the formation and climbed above the cloud cover. From interviews conducted on *Ranger*, it was clear that Spangenberg took the formation too low while turning. At the point when the other RIO called out the warning, Frawley and Christensen, flying the inside and lowest position in the turn, were "almost certainly in the water." Although interviews were conducted with the four returning aviators, an unofficial inquiry into the cause of the accident was kept quiet, owing to the fact that it involved a squadron CO in a combat environment. Then, the incident was "just covered up" in the interest of maintaining the squadron's morale so early in a combat cruise. Frawley's roommate, the VF-143 pilot Wayne Bennett, who had hung out with Dieter and Spook in Fallon and elsewhere, packed up his friend's belongings. He also wrote a letter to Frawley's wife, Barb, telling her that under the circumstances she needed to understand that "we are not going to find him and he wasn't taken prisoner. Bill is gone." The remains of Frawley and Christensen were never recovered.

In mid-April, the first of two incidents happened that would mean not only the end of the war for Spad pilot Spook Johns, but also the end of his naval service. The first incident, which Spook was positive formed the provoking circumstances that would soon cause him to be removed from the ship, involved VA-145's operations officer, Ken Hassett, with whom Spook had argued with about continuing to look for Dieter on the day he disappeared.

Hassett was leading a flight of four Spads in attacking an enemy supply depot near the DMZ. After expending their bombs and rockets, they went down to make strafing runs with their 20 mm cannons. Spook's guns jammed, and this made him "pissed off." For several more runs Spook followed Hassett down just to make sure the bad guys "kept their heads down," as the enemy had no way of knowing his guns were jammed. On one pass after another, Hassett badly missed the target. Spook kept trying to get him to adjust his errant aim: "You're shooting low" and "You're still low." When Hassett said they were heading back to the ship, the four planes came together in formation. By this time, Spook was so disgusted with Hassett's poor marksmanship and their wasted efforts that he was "steaming in the cockpit." In full view of Hassett he did an aileron roll, an aerobatic maneuver in which the aircraft is rolled a full 360 degrees about its longitudinal axis with no change in altitude or heading. One of the other pilots broke radio silence to exclaim, "Oh, my God!"

Aboard ship, Hassett chewed Spook out in front of others. Then it was Spook's turn; he belittled the senior officer for missing the target every time. "You couldn't hit your ass with a banjo!"

The second incident happened a few days later. Spook was flying as wingman for Lieutenant Commander John Tunnell, thirty-two, of Vista, California. A graduate of San Diego State College, Tunnell was "fit and friendly" and "almost movie-star handsome."

With *Ranger* operating off Dixie Station after eight days in port, the air wing's pilots were warming up on targets in South Vietnam before returning to Yankee Station off North Vietnam.

As was customary in the south, Tunnell and Spook were working with a U.S. Air Force forward air controller (FAC) so as not to hit friendly forces or villages. The FAC, call sign *Cobra Four*, had them bombing a target under the jungle canopy at the Cambodian border. After one run, Spook pulled up and felt a "quick stutter" from the engine. Given the reliability of the Spad's powerful engine, he didn't think much of it and went down for another run. As he pulled off that run, the engine started acting up.

Spook radioed that he had a "rough runner" and was heading for Tan Son Nhut, an airport at Saigon that was the alternative field for *Ranger* pilots that day if they couldn't get back to the carrier operating 100 miles off the coast of South Vietnam.

No sooner had Spook made the announcement than his engine quit. He was able to restart it, but then it died again. What he did not know at the time was that a faulty alternating air-door motor was causing the engine to overheat. Whenever the engine quit, it would start to cool down, and Spook could restart it. But then it would heat up again and die. He dropped his remaining bombs and external fuel tanks, then trimmed the plane for a long glide. He was at 800 feet and steadily losing altitude, with about twelve miles to go to Saigon. He realized he wasn't going to make it.

Spook looked down and spotted a dirt runway a mile or so in front of him. He radioed the FAC, who he knew was following.

"*Cobra Four*, are those guys down there friendly?"

"Yeah. That's my field."

"Good, because I've gotta put in here."

"You better go gear up because you've only got eight hundred feet and a minefield on each end of the runway."

Spook decided to take the FAC's advice. He maintained a fast-clip glide speed of 140 miles per hour until he was sure he was going to make the runway; then he dropped his flaps and popped his dive brakes to lose speed and altitude. The powerless Spad fell from the sky and skidded on its belly for 200 feet, throwing up a plume of dust. A vehicle quickly pulled the plane off the runway so the FAC could land his Cessna L-19 Bird Dog observation plane.

At the field's control shack, Spook got on the radio to Tunnell, who was circling above, to say he was okay.

"Good job," Tunnell said. "See you back on the ship."

The propeller had been "eaten up" by the earth, and the trailing edge of the flaps had "curled up," but otherwise there was little damage to the Spad. After a new engine and propeller were installed and the flaps repaired, the plane was flown back to *Ranger* three days later, ready for more missions.

Spook's Spad after his wheels-up emergency landing. *U.S Navy.*

Spook Johns, on the other hand, had flown his last mission. He was taken that day by helicopter to Saigon, where he spent the night, and was delivered back to *Ranger* the following day. When he stepped onto the flight deck, Spook was told that his presence was required for a debriefing of his mission. He found waiting for him not the usual air intelligence officers with their maps and photographs, but a "bunch of ranking guys" from the air wing and admiral's staff. He told them the circumstance leading up to his emergency landing, and was dismissed with no antagonistic questions or comments. That's why he was blindsided when VA-145's CO, Hal Griffith, stepped into his stateroom a short time later and announced that Spook's career as a naval aviator was finished.

"I don't want you flying our airplanes anymore," Griffith said. "You're done."

Spook reeled at this news. As a veteran of two earlier cruises, he had had only two weeks left before he was due to get out of the navy in the fall of 1965, but extended his naval service for a year so he could go on the *Ranger* cruise, much to the delight of Griffith, who was happy to keep the experienced pilot. And just last month, Griffith had suggested that Spook stay in and make the navy a career. When Spook pointed out he had been passed over twice for promotion to lieutenant, Griffith said he knew someone who had been passed over twice and still made commander. Spook said he wanted to finish the cruise, get out of the navy, and find a well-paying job with an airline. Ironically, Griffith had also recently pinned on Spook his fifth Air Medal for "meritorious achievement while participating in aerial flight." And now he was being told by the same man that he was *done flying*? Griffith said Spook would be permanent duty officer in the ready room until *Ranger* returned to port. He would then be flown home on the first available transport.

Spook suddenly got it: *Hassett had ratted him out to the skipper for that wild-ass aileron roll.* That, combined with a little insubordination thrown in for good measure, as well as always being on the "borderline of trouble" for countless antics in and out of the air, no doubt had done him in. Spook knew he had made the right decision in declaring an emergency and making a gear-up landing, which had resulted in repairable damage to the plane. Would the powers that be have preferred him to end up in the minefield? Or to try for Saigon and crash in the jungle? Or to head for the carrier and crash at sea? Or to crack up on the flight deck? Or to say screw the airplane and bail out to save his own skin?

The next day Spook was in John Tunnell's stateroom complaining about his nonflying status when Griffith entered.

"Skipper, Spook shouldn't be grounded," said Tunnell, who could speak not only as Spook's flight leader on the day in question but also as one of VA-145's senior officers and pilots.

Griffith, who could be as cool on the ground as he was in the air during the heat of combat, said simply, "I told Spook what the verdict was." Without another word, he turned and left the room.

Late in the afternoon of May 12, *Ranger* arrived at the main aircraft carrier pier at the U.S. Navy Base, Yokosuka, Japan. The next morning, Spook, with his heavy gear packed in a wooden box and his uniforms in his seabag, departed from the quarterdeck with a final salute, leaving behind the pilots with whom he had gone to war—some who had already been lost, and others who would not survive the last three months of *Ranger*'s West-Pac cruise.

With his official orders in hand, he took a van to the naval air facility at Atsugi and caught a navy DC-4 heading east. After a refueling at Midway and an overnight stop at Hawaii, he landed at Alameda Naval Air Station the next day. He caught a ride to the naval base at Treasure Island, an artificial island created in the San Francisco Bay for the 1936 Golden Gate International Exposition. There, Malcolm "Spook" Johns was released from active duty.

Within days, Spook was driving his yellow International Scout home to Detroit, with the canvas top rolled back and the wind blowing in his face, just the way he had flown those Spads.

✪ ✪ ✪

On June 20, *Ranger* was back on station in the Gulf of Tonkin.

After daytime flight operations had ceased, the pilots of VA-145 were lounging half-dressed in their rooms or shooting the bull in the ready room following evening chow. The only ones not standing down were the four pilots on an unusual special alert, ready to launch in fifteen minutes. This was the third night of the alert; the first two nights had come and gone without any planes being launched. Four pilots were again designated as Alert 15. They could wait in their staterooms until being called, but they had to be dressed in their flight suits and boots, and wearing special red-tinted goggles to keep their night vision. They had to be able to leave their rooms within 30 seconds and head to the flight deck, where their waiting planes were fueled and armed.

Attack pilots usually did not stand such alerts, although for fighter pilots they were a common occurrence. Whenever the ship was not conducting flight operations and there was no combat air patrol (CAP) aloft to intercept incoming enemy contacts, two F-4 Phantoms remained on ready alert, hooked up to side-by-side catapults with their pilots and RIOs in the cockpits—often reading a book or writing a letter home—prepared to launch on command.

Although only John Tunnell, the senior officer of the four pilots on alert, had been briefed on the details of the special mission, there was scuttlebutt as to why the four Spads were standing by. The northernmost destroyer in the Gulf of Tonkin, positioned there to assist with search-and-rescue operations when pilots went down feet wet, had been reporting small, high-speed boats—believed to be North Vietnamese PT boats—in the area at night. They were operating closer to the destroyer each night, and were being carefully watched. If they were emboldened enough to attack, aircraft would be rapidly launched to get to the scene.

One of the four Spad pilots on alert that night, Bummy Bumgarner, was sure he knew why the Spads and not the A-4 Skyhawks had been given the special mission. In his humble opinion, A-4s "couldn't hit shit." He believed that this had been proved a month before *Ranger* left for WestPac, when an old Liberty ship from World War II was towed fifty miles outside the Golden Gate for the air wing to use as a target for aerial bombing. First the A-4 squadrons came diving down, dropping bombs that fell harmlessly in the water around the ship. Then the F-4s streaked across the sky, launching rockets. With the Liberty ship still unscathed, eight Spads of VA-145 roared overhead. The CO, Hal Griffith, made the first dive-bomb run, with his wingman, Bumgarner, right after him. Bummy managed to thread the eye of the needle, slipping a 2,000-pounder down an open hatch and blowing out the bottom of the ship's hull. When the other Spads arrived, they found the target ship had disappeared "under a mushroom-shaped geyser," which was soon replaced by "just bubbles" where the ship had been. The CO of a squadron following the Spads asked for a target status report, and Griffith responded, "Target is an oil slick." So, deadeye Bumgarner would answer the call to arms if anything had to be blown out of the water this night, although the weather briefing portended a miserable night for flying, with a low overcast and fog.

Shortly after 9:00 P.M., the four pilots received identical calls in their rooms: "Launch the Alert 15. You're go!" Gathering on the flight deck were the flight leader, Tunnell; his wingman, Bumgarner; Skip Armstrong, VA-145's newest lieutenant commander, who one day would captain an aircraft carrier and become a rear admiral; and his wingman, Denny Enstam, who believed the reason the Spads were getting this mission was that neither of the A-4 squadrons wanted its jets up in such abysmal weather and everyone knew the Spads had grit. The night was drizzly and uncommonly dark. The pilots saw their planes parked in their usual spot at the rear of the flight deck. With so many planes parked on the crowded deck for the next day's flight operations, only one of the four catapults was in use: on the bow of the ship, starboard side. Walking to their planes, the pilots found the deck wet and slippery.

Tunnell was first to taxi forward to catapult number one and have his plane attached to the bridle. Behind him came his wingman, Bummy, who was already having difficulties. First, his dragging tail wheel got hung up on the cables that stretched across the deck to catch recovering planes. Once he cleared those obstacles, he found his plane sliding ominously on the slippery deck. It was so dark he had no visibility in any direction; there might as well have been a sheet of black construction paper in front of his eyes. He could see only the yellow lights held by a plane director. The only personnel authorized to move aircraft or give hand signals to taxiing aircraft, plane directors wore bright yellow shirts, which were easy enough to spot in the daytime; at night, they held in each hand a flashlight with a foot-long yellow cone screwed on top. The plane director was off to Bummy's left, in a position that kept him clear of the spinning propeller and also allowed the pilot to see his signals from the cockpit. When the plane director crossed his wands—the signal to stop—Bummy pressed his feet down on both rudder pedals to brake. The plane director waved his crossed wands more frantically. Bummy was standing on the pedals, applying full brake, but the plane still slid on the wet deck before finally stopping. He had no idea how close he was to going over the side into the water. His fate, at this point, was in the hands of the plane director with the yellow cones and the other young men who risked their lives working in the controlled chaos of the flight deck.*

---

* Two enlisted men were killed in the course of their duties on *Ranger*'s flight deck during the 1966 WestPac cruise: Aviation Boatswain's Mate Third Class Clark David Franklin, twenty-three, of Alamogordo, New Mexico; and Airman Douglas Thomas, Jr., twenty, of Columbia, South Carolina. On April 24 and August 4, respectively, Franklin and Thomas were run over by aircraft. Franklin died instantly; Thomas died a short time later in sickbay. Their deaths were classified as nonhostile sea casualties.

When Bummy was finally in place behind Tunnell, the blast deflector wall between them was raised, blocking the powerful prop wash from Tunnell's plane as he ran it up to full power for the catapult shot. Then, Tunnell's Spad was off.

What happened next—before Bummy's disbelieving eyes—seemed to unfold in slow motion. As soon as Tunnell's plane cleared the bow, its left wing dipped. Spad pilots learned early on how to deal with that dangerous tendency of the plane, but this time there was no attempted correction. The wing just kept dropping, and the plane rolled to the left until it was upside down. Then it fell toward the water and dropped from Bummy's sight.

Bummy sat, immobilized by shock but with his mind racing. Tunnell, whom he knew as one of the most experienced pilots in the squadron, had just gone inverted into the water seconds after launch. Bummy knew it was a non-recoverable event; there was no time or altitude for Tunnell to turn upright and get level. And Tunnell would have been killed outright or rendered unconscious by the impact with the water; there would have been no time or opportunity for him to get out. Had there been a failure of the one instrument every carrier pilot stayed glued to on a nighttime catapult shot—the attitude gyro that showed the position of the wings compared with the horizon? Had Tunnell, with no visual references on this dark, foggy night, been unaware that his wings weren't level? Had the gyro given him an incorrect reading and told him his *other* wing was down, causing him to follow the gyro over in the wrong direction? Or, from the jolt of the catapult, had he lost one of the heavy bombs he was carrying under his left wing and had no time to correct for the weight imbalance? There were many questions to which Bummy had no answers. But of this he was certain: John Tunnell had just died in front of him.

Behind Bumgarner, Enstam had also seen what happened. From his vantage point, he saw off the port side of the ship Tunnell's plane upside down in the water, sinking under the glare of a spotlight mounted in the catwalk just below the flight deck.

Bummy wasn't sure how long he froze before the yellow cones of light signaled him to move forward onto the catapult. The blast wall had already been lowered, and he was next.

My, God, he was next! *Holy shit*, he thought. *Can I do this?*

Tunnell—how many hours did he have? The lieutenant commander had 2,500 hours of flight time, but that was not enough to keep him from dying this night. Bummy thought, here he was, a lowly ensign with only 385 hours of total flight time. And he was next?

Bumgarner was more afraid than he had ever been in his life. He could refuse to move forward—he could shut down the engine and climb out—he could go find the skipper and turn in his wings. Had he done so, he knew not many of the guys in VA-145 would have criticized his decision. Carrier aviation in general, and combat flying in particular, required pilots to operate precariously close to their personal and physical limits, but all individuals *did* have their limits.

The yellow cones were getting more frantic again, this time high in the air, forward and back: the signal to come forward.

Bumgarner released the brakes, and moved forward.

Once secured to the catapult, he revved the engine to full power, and signaled the catapult officer he was ready by flipping on his external lights. Then he was off—watching his gyro and making sure to carry out the instrument panel scan taught in flight training for nighttime launches, in case one instrument went bad and gave faulty information.

Bumgarner and the other two Spads rendezvoused at a designated location, then radioed *Ranger* asking if they should continue the mission with only three planes. After a delay, they were advised to go ahead, and someone came over the radio from the ship and gave them the details of their assignment, since Tunnell had been the only one to be so briefed.

Flying in "ludicrous weather" with a 500-foot ceiling and the "moon on the other side of the world," they searched for the wakes of PT boats in the Gulf of Tonkin but found nothing. They never even spotted the U.S. destroyer in the dark. After not more than an hour in the air, they turned around and came back to the ship.

Three of the four Spads that took off that night landed safely.

So VA-145, which had started the cruise with twenty pilots, had now lost three: Dieter Dengler, Gary Hopps, and John Tunnell.

Totaling the operational and combat losses for Carrier Air Wing 14 during *Ranger*'s 1966 WestPac cruise, twelve aviators would take off from the ship and not return—for a variety of arbitrary, cataclysmic, and astounding reasons that carrier pilots go missing. Nine were killed. Three became prisoners of war; one was released in 1973, one died in captivity, and one was about to escape from Laos.

11

ESCAPE

The day before the POWs planned to escape, Dieter received a beating from the guards. His offense: he had used two sticks to drag over to the door of the hut a small corncob that had been thrown to a young pig the guards were fattening. The kernels had already been devoured, leaving only the shriveled cob—filthy with the pig's manure. But Dieter was starving, and he intended to eat it. Before he could begin, the guard they called Moron ran over, yelling and pointing his rifle. He entered the hut, slapped the foot blocks on Dieter, and dragged him outside. A group of guards gathered in the yard. As if prosecuting a court case, Moron waved the corncob as evidence, then flipped it to the pig. For Dieter, the symbolism was clear: *Prisoners are less than pigs.* Then Moron began beating Dieter with his rifle butt. Other guards joined in. When they threw him back into the hut, where all the prisoners had been herded during the beating, the bloodied Dieter stared stony-faced into the yard, saying nothing to the others. Prasit broke the silence, telling Dieter not to forget, when he killed the guards, to kick them in the head "so they'll rot in hell."

For weeks they had been updating their scale model of the camp, marking where the all guards and guns were located from morning until evening. Taking turns peering out between the cracks of their huts, the prisoners had observed every detail, no matter how small, and came to know their captors' routines as well as they knew their own. They had even been able to determine about how long it would take for reinforcements to reach the camp from the nearest village. One morning, the guards spotted strange footprints, and one of them took off to get help; he was back with armed reinforcements a few hours later. The prisoners had considered but rejected a nighttime escape, primarily because it was impossible to venture far in the jungle in the dark and they knew the guards would be on their trail at daylight. The best opportunity for escape remained the period of time when the guards put down their weapons to go to the kitchen around 4:00 P.M. to pick up their evening meal. The prisoners repeatedly timed the interval; the trip to and from the kitchen for those guards returning to the gun towers and adjacent huts took no more than two and a half minutes. In that time, the prisoners would have to slip from their locked huts, get outside the stockade, secure the guns, and be ready to overtake all the guards in the camp.

Everyone had assigned tasks in the escape plan. Dieter was to be the first out of the walled compound; he would then enter the nearest guard hut, where three or four rifles were usually left inside. As he did so, someone unlocked the Asian hut. Two Thai and the other two Americans were to crawl through the hole in the fence. After he had gathered the guns, Dieter was to arm Phisit and Prasit as they emerged from the compound. The three of them were the most capable with weapons. Neither Duane nor Gene was eager to participate in a shootout, and Y.C. couldn't handle a rifle. Gene had a backup role with a weapon, however. He was to head for a guard hut at the back of the compound to retrieve a Thompson submachine gun. As Dieter swung around behind the stockade and proceeded toward the kitchen, Gene was to remain on the porch of the hut with the submachine gun and provide supporting fire if needed. The Thai were to go around the front of the compound, heading for the kitchen where they were to order, in Laotian, the unarmed guards to surrender. With Dieter guarding the back door, they hoped to round up the guards without firing the guns, since the sounds of a shoot-out would reverberate throughout the valley for miles, alerting all villagers and Pathet Lao alike to trouble at the camp. While Dieter, Thanee, and Phisit secured the guards, Gene and Prasit would set up a hand-grenade booby trap on the trail leading up from the village, then hide nearby and ambush anyone heading for the camp. Meanwhile, Duane and Y.C. would search the huts. They would place the guards in foot blocks and handcuffs and lock them in the prison huts until it could be decided what to do with them; killing them one by one was an option. They could then hold the camp and signal aircraft nightly until they were spotted and rescued. If shots were fired in the taking of the camp, however, enemy reinforcements could be expected within hours. In that case, everyone knew that all bets were off and they would have to abandon the camp and head into the jungle.

In Dieter's mind, there was no contingency for failure. If they tried to escape and failed, he expected either to be killed in the attempt—his preference—or executed soon thereafter. There had never been a real alternative for him. Even before the prisoners heard about the guards' plan to kill them, he had not intended to waste away slowly in a jungle prison camp and die from disease, starvation, or beatings.

Weeks earlier, the prisoners had loosened a large support pole in the American hut by pouring water and urine at its base and working it back and forth until they could lift it out. After loosening some logs close to the floorboards, they now had a way to leave the hut quickly. Then, they put everything back and "covered up all traces" of their preparation. Dieter had also dug a hole underneath the fence next to the hut, then covered it up with leaves and bamboo. He had accomplished all this when the prisoners were still being let out of their huts for long periods in the morning, and when the guards in the gun towers were napping or otherwise inattentive, as they often were.

Some hours after the beating over the corncob, the prisoners were let out into the compound. They sat at their wooden picnic table in the center of the yard, slurping down watery rice broth, which had become their only daily meal. The camp dog—as skinny as they were and probably not long for the world, given the guards' own extreme hunger—lingered under the table looking for scraps. There were none, of course, but the prisoners were always willing to let the dog lick any sores on their feet and legs, as they had found that its saliva aided the healing process. Gesturing to the guards that he had to take a leak, Dieter slipped behind the hut to see if the logs were still loose. They moved easily. Also, the hole under the fence looked as if it had not been discovered. Having lazy guards who did not bother to walk the fence line was an advantage.

The prisoners had agreed that if they could not stay at the camp to make contact with planes overhead, they would split into two groups before fleeing overland. Earlier, there had been talk of staying together as one group, but Dieter was opposed to the idea. Such a large group would be easier to track. Also, if they had to hump through the jungle to freedom, Dieter wanted to be with Duane and Gene because the three Americans got along and trusted one another.

The three Thai were a natural team, and given how well Phisit, the former paratrooper, knew the jungle, Dieter figured they had an excellent chance of making it. In fact, Phisit offered tips to the Americans about finding food in the jungle, such as edible ferns that grow along the waterways and figs that could be eaten green or ripe. The three Thai told about the hospitality of their people, especially the monks, and suggested that if the Americans made it across the border into Thailand they should seek refuge at a temple until they could make contact with friendly forces. The Thai and the Americans were in agreement that, with impenetrable jungle, at least two mountain ranges, and North Vietnam to the east, westward was the way to proceed.

The oldest prisoner, Y.C., the Chinese radio operator, was the odd man out. He was set to travel with the Thai group, but he suddenly fell ill with what was believed to be elephantiasis, a tropical disease caused by parasitic worms transmitted by mosquitoes. It left his legs weak and swollen, and his scrotum badly distended. In severe pain, he could barely walk. The Thai balked at taking Y.C. with them.

The Americans talked it over. If they were able to hold the camp, make air contact, and set up a rescue operation from here, Y.C.'s condition would not be an issue. But if they had to head for Thailand and evade enemy trackers en route, there was no way he could keep up. It would be terrible to condemn a fellow prisoner to certain death, and they struggled with the dilemma. Yet everyone knew they would be at a distinct disadvantage carrying a sick man who had trouble walking.

Finally, Gene said he and Y.C. would go together. They would make it over the first ridge to the south, then "lie in wait for air contact."

"Don't be a fool," Dieter said. "We want you with us."

"And I want Y.C.," Gene said, adding that if Dieter and Duane were rescued, "be sure someone looks for us and tell them where to look."

Dieter respected Gene for being "our peacemaker." Whenever there was an impasse among the prisoners, more often than not it was "kind and good" Gene who stepped in to resolve the situation. Now, even though he understood that he was lessening his own chance of a rescue, Gene would not leave behind his Air America crewman, who had become a good friend during their imprisonment. When they divvied up the sacks of dried rice, Dieter and Duane made sure Gene and Y.C. each received "twice the amount" that everyone else got, knowing they might have to hold out longer for rescue.

On escape day, the hours dragged toward the guards' evening meal.

Already, there had been one aborted effort. The day before, after Dieter had crawled out the back of the hut and was ready to slip under the fence, Phisit had called it off from the other hut because two of the guards were unaccounted for in the kitchen. Dieter had to put everything back into place, and get back inside. When he asked later what had happened, Phisit said he didn't think it was the right time. Recalling how opposed to the escape Phisit had long been, Dieter thought he might now be playing mind games. "Boiling mad," Dieter said that if Phisit did this again once the escape was under way he would come back after getting a weapon and shoot him. Dieter could see that Phisit understood there was "nothing idle" about his threat.

As 4:00 P.M. approached on June 29, 1966, Phisit again turned "worried and cautious," sending word that maybe the escape should be put off again. Dieter's response: "Not on your life."

In the Asian prisoners' hut, which was closest to the kitchen, Thanee was counting the guards as they arrived for food. He passed the information to Y.C., who was squatting in the doorway. In English, Y.C. called out in a hushed voice to Duane, stationed in the doorway of the American hut, and Duane passed the word to Dieter and Gene.

"Guards entering kitchen."

"Guards don't have weapons."

They waited for the final count.

"All in the kitchen, but one's missing," Duane said urgently.

They speculated that the missing guard might have gone to check animal traps in the woods.

"Hell, let's go," Dieter said.

Duane and Gene agreed.

"It's on," Duane called out in a stage whisper to the other hut.

Dieter pulled out the loosened pole and logs, and climbed out the opening. Burrowing under the fence like a groundhog, Dieter squeezed through and headed for the nearest guard hut. He leaped onto the porch and crept across the bamboo flooring, which creaked with his every move. Inside, he found two Chinese-made rifles and a U.S. M-1 carbine with a full fifteen-round magazine. While he was with the air force shooting team, he had spent many hours on the range firing M-1s, and had become a skilled marksman with the weapon; he would keep this lightweight, semiautomatic weapon for himself. On the way out he picked up a full ammunition belt with extra magazines.

As he came off the porch, other prisoners were emerging from under the fence. Gene was already making his way down the fence line toward the rear of the compound. Phisit and Prasit came toward Dieter, who gave them the loaded Chinese rifles and some ammo. The two Thai headed off in the direction of the kitchen, with Duane following.

Dieter caught up with Gene. As they rounded the corner under the now empty gun tower, Gene peeled off for the hut where the guard on tower duty routinely left the Thompson submachine gun before going for food. As soon as Dieter rounded the far corner of the stockade, he could see the guards milling about inside the open-walled kitchen hut.

The next instant the guards "realized something was going on" and began yelling at each other and scrambling from the kitchen. They ran not toward the front of the stockade—the direction from which the Thai should have been coming—but toward Dieter.

"*Yute! Yute!*" yelled Dieter. He pressed the butt of the M-1 tightly between his chest muscle and the front ball of his shoulder, tilting his head so that his closer eye looked straight down the top of the barrel. His index finger rested lightly on the trigger.

At that moment a shot rang out. Dieter felt the speeding bullet whiz past his head. He spotted a guard in the kitchen with a rifle pointed his way. So much for the theory that the guards had no weapons! Dieter squeezed the trigger, and dropped with one shot the guard who had fired at him.

Amid excited screams, the horde of guards closed on Dieter, who felt "all alone . . . out in the open." He wondered what happened to the Thai, who were armed with the Chinese rifles, and to Gene, with the submachine gun.

Running for Dieter at full speed, with a machete held menacingly over his head, was Moron. From a few feet away, Dieter fired point-blank at the bare chest of the guard who had beaten him for taking the pig's corncob. The force of the blast lifted Moron off the ground, threw him back several feet, and spun him around. His limp body fell to the ground "dead right on the spot" with a sizable exit hole in the center of his back.

Dieter swung around to see another guard with a machete trying to out-flank him. The M-1 fired only once each time the trigger was pulled, but by rapidly squeezing and releasing the trigger he got off a fast rate of fire. The second guard collapsed on the ground, holding his side and shrieking. With no hesitation, Dieter fired again, to "finish him off."

The remaining guards were now trying frantically to reach the jungle.

"Where the *hell*—is *everybody*?" Dieter yelled.

Then, like a backwoods man on a squirrel hunt, he steadied himself and opened fire. He hit one more guard through the neck as the man ran away. Needing to reload, Dieter slammed home a new magazine. He shot another guard who was just entering the jungle. The guard dropped from sight but then sprang up holding one arm. Dieter kept "banging away" as the guard vanished ghostlike into the thick vegetation.

Duane came running up carrying a carbine he had found in a guard hut. "The clip—the clip," he stammered, explaining that it had fallen out every time he tried to release the safety to fire the weapon.

Dieter showed him why—he had been pressing the clip release, not the safety.

At least one guard had gotten away. There was also still the missing seventh guard, who could be nearby. In spite of all the dead men sprawled on the ground—guards who would never again abuse POWs—the outcome was disastrous, given that the plan had been to capture the guards without firing a shot and without letting anyone get away. The prisoners' bold plan to hold the camp and make air contact was no longer feasible. They had no choice now. They would have to gather whatever supplies they could find and head into the jungle.

When Dieter went to retrieve his and Duane's boots from where they had been hanging under a hut with the other shoes, they were gone. He knew exactly who had taken them: the Thai, who had gotten there first, and had also "picked clean" all the mosquito nets and anything else they thought they could use, without offering to share with the others. Carrying stuffed rucksacks, they had been the first to leave the camp.

Dieter and Gene had an emotional farewell. Gene had found the submachine gun in the guard hut, although when he stepped outside the shooting was over. He now had the weapon slung over one shoulder. As they shook hands, Dieter looked into Gene's face and wanted to say that Gene should come with him and Duane instead of remaining behind near the camp. But Dieter knew Gene had his mind made up and would not leave his sick friend behind. Unable to find the words he wanted to say to his fellow American, Dieter shook Gene's hand warmly.

"Go on, go on," Gene implored him. "See you in the States."

Dieter and Duane took off toward the west and Thailand, although because of the dense foliage, in an hour they had "no more reference" as to direction and could not see more than five feet ahead. In their weakened condition, and unaccustomed to exercise, they started "vomiting right away." They were soon held up by a solid wall of bramble brush. The camp dog had followed them, barking, and they were afraid he would give them away. The dog had his own escape plan, however, and before disappearing into the woods he found a dugout corridor under the thicket; Dieter and Duane crawled through after him. A short time later they reached a ridge. Exhausted, they fell to the ground. When they had recovered, Duane wanted to offer a prayer. They came up on their knees, with eyes closed and hands folded before them.

"God, please help us now. Please let us live."

SHOOT-OUT ←

GUARD
HUT

KITCHEN

GUARD
HUT

OTHER
POWs

15' HIGH BAMBOO FENCE

ESCAPE FROM BAN HOEUI HET POW CAMP
JUNE 1966

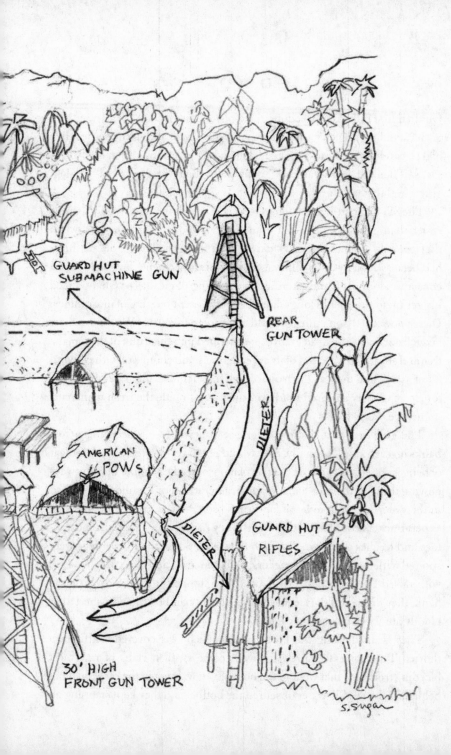

GUARD HUT
SUBMACHINE GUN

REAR
GUN TOWER

DIETER

AMERICAN
POWS

DIETER

GUARD HUT
RIFLES

30' HIGH
FRONT GUN TOWER

S. Sugar

✪ ✪ ✪

On their first full day of freedom, the monsoons arrived.

It rained until Dieter and Duane were drenched, and until the rice they had so carefully dried was soaked, along with everything else in their rucksacks. Then, "it really rained," giving them their "first taste" of the slogging travel that lay ahead.

They found a gully in which to walk. Even with the heavy runoff, it was easier than going through dense jungle and woods. They stopped when they came to a banana tree. Whatever fruit had once hung from its limbs had been swiped by the monkeys, whose vibrant screeches and calls were a constant, along with the intermittent whirring of cicadas—veiled-winged insects up to two inches long—and the ever-present buzzing of mosquitoes. Dieter now tried something he had seen the natives do. With a machete taken from one of the dead guards, he chopped into the trunk of the banana tree and sliced out a section of its core. Eating small chunks of it, they found it not as soft and tasty as the fruit, of course, but moist and nourishing. Before leaving, they smeared mud over the trunk to hide the fresh white cuts in the tree.

The gully led to a shallow creek six or seven feet wide with narrow banks on each side. Normally, they would not have followed a creek for fear of being spotted, but after only a day of monsoons the number of waterways flowing through the area had already proliferated. For a while they walked in the water so as not to leave footprints or break vines and branches that expert trackers could follow. However, they hadn't counted on the mosquitoes and leeches that were drawn to the water. Soon, their lower legs were spotted with the black bloodsuckers, and their arms and faces were covered with raised bites. Around 11:00 A.M., they stopped to rest. Sitting on the bank, they flicked off the leeches with pieces of bamboo, then washed their bloody abrasions as best they could.

They walked along the creek bank, which was covered with sharp thorns. Their bare feet had already become swollen slabs of raw meat bleeding from cuts that went to the bone. Even walking in the creek had not helped, as the muddy water obscured the bottom and they kept stepping on sharp rocks. Dieter cursed the three Thai for the hundredth but not last time for having taken their shoes, which he considered a cowardly, self-serving act that was nothing short of a betrayal of their fellow POWs.

Within an hour it was pouring so hard they could see only a few feet in front of them. They piled up some large fronds and crawled under them. As the rain dripped off the leaves, they opened their mouths and savored the freshest water they had tasted in a long time. They rested for an hour, by which time the rain had slackened. Continuing on, they had no idea how far they had come from the prison camp. The full day of exertion in their weakened state had taken its toll. Duane looked so emaciated that the sight of him frightened Dieter, who knew full well he was also looking at an image of himself. Whenever Duane said he could go no farther, Dieter implored him, "Just one more hour." As dusk descended, Duane, his thin, bent frame close to collapsing with every step, was "gulping air like a distance runner."

They went a short distance into the bush and fought off their fatigue long enough to build a lean-to. The rain and wind soon ripped apart their crude shelter, and did not let up. Soaked and chilled, they talked about how they at least had a dry floor to sleep on and a roof over their heads at the prison camp. Awakened countless times by the rain and cold, they held on to each other for warmth through the long night.

In the morning, they took the lean-to apart and scattered everything in the bushes. After eating a small portion of rice, they hiked along the creek all day in the rain, stopping periodically to listen for anyone following. At one point they realized that they were hemmed in on one side by a solid rock cliff that went straight up, and on the other by jungle so heavy it would "take three days just to go a hundred yards."

It stopped raining briefly at midday, and the sun came out. Entering a clearing, Dieter moved quickly to get a directional fix. He pushed a long stick into the ground, then took a shorter one and placed it at the end of the shadow made by the longer stick. After about five minutes the end of the shadow had moved. He put another stick in the ground at that point and waited a while longer, then did the same thing a third time. He drew a line in the ground connecting the three shorter sticks, and this gave him "an exact east-west line." The good news was that the creek they were following was meandering in the direction they wanted to go, strengthening their hope that it would flow into a river heading west toward Thailand. They continued on, picking leeches off their legs whenever they stopped. Even more exhausted at the end of their second day of travel, they built a stronger lean-to by using vines to tie several bamboo poles to a tree, and a canopy of large banana leaves for a roof. They carpeted the ground with a cushion of leaves, and huddled together as the rain "thundered down from the sky." Duane awakened several times, complaining of cold feet. Dieter rubbed them with his own bare feet.

At sunrise they ate more soggy rice, and although some of it had already turned green from mold it tasted delicious to the famished men. To stretch their supply of food, and needing strength for another long day, they searched under large boulders in the creek for anything edible. They found snails that looked nothing like escargots but turned out to be "pretty good." They cut off the top end of the shell and sucked on it, then turned it around "real fast and sucked the big end," which caused the loosened snail meat to "snap out" so it could then be bitten off.

That afternoon, they arrived at a waterfall that dropped thirty feet into a lagoon. It was a beautiful sight, with a thin veil of mist rising as the falls cascaded into a white-water pool. At another time and in a different world, it would have been Dieter's ideal campsite. But to the weakened pilots, it was just another obstacle, with steep walls on either side that were vine-covered rock faces. They started down, holding onto the vines "just like ropes." Duane, who was a few feet above Dieter, lost his grip halfway down and came crashing into Dieter. The two men tumbled into the churning water below.

Dieter felt himself being pulled down by the current. He had learned a lesson as a boy in Germany when he had fallen under a waterfall and had struggled against the powerful suction, running out of breath. A friend, who dived in and dragged him to safety, later told Dieter that the trick was not to try to surface immediately, but to swim away from the suction until it lessened. Since then, Dieter had used the same technique when caught in a riptide while surfing in the ocean; he swam parallel to the beach and out of the strong current before he turned for shore. Now, he frog-kicked hard underwater, moving away from the falls. As he did, the barrel of the M-1, which was slung over his back on a leather strap, kept hitting his head. Just before he surfaced, his lungs felt as if they would burst. Duane was lying on a flat rock, coughing up water. Dieter floated over and climbed up next to him. After they had recovered, they looked at each other impishly. Realizing the irony of nearly drowning in the middle of the jungle, they "broke out in hysterical laughter."

A few hundred yards away they came to a bigger waterfall. Standing on a rock ledge halfway down another wall of vines, Dieter decided to rid himself of the M-1 because he was tired of lugging the extra weight. Although he would have liked to use the gun to hunt for meat—they had glimpsed a small bear a couple of days earlier—even a single shot would have brought guerrillas down on them. Duane still had the lighter carbine, and Dieter proposed that they keep it for self-defense and take turns carrying it. Duane agreed. Dieter unloaded the M-1 and tossed the gun and ammo into the water below.

When they reached the bottom of the falls, they were too tired to continue or even build a shelter. They bedded down on a pile of leaves under a rocky overhang. The night turned bitterly cold, and again they huddled against each other.

They awakened in the morning trembling from the cold, and helped each other stand up. After being wet and cold for days, they were both badly congested. They continued along the creek, which narrowed into a slippery, rocky gully, over which they "half-walked [and] half-crawled." Blocked by a pile of bamboo in the creek bed, they struggled to get around it. When the gully came to an abrupt end, so did the creek.

Facing a steep divide between cloud-covered mountaintops, they decided to hike over it with the hope there would be a valley with a river on the other side. The ascent, steeper than it looked, was covered by "thousands of years of jungle growth." It was an inhospitable world, with no sun or sky visible through the green ceiling, and thick walls of trees and vines blocking their way. After a few hours they had advanced only about 300 feet in pouring rain. They could see that they would have to climb another 2,000 or 3,000 feet through the dense vegetation to get over the pass. They trudged on a while longer until Dieter called a halt.

"Duane, it's no good," he said. "We can't hack this."

They were both panting, struggling for breath.

"We can't travel—over mountains," Dieter said. "It'd take two days to get over this ridge. Let's go back. Keep looking for a river."

Duane commented that it was going to be a lot easier sliding down the mountain than it had been climbing up. And they did go back faster through mud and muck all the way to where the gully had ended, then retraced their steps a while longer before stopping for the night. The day had involved more exertion than any other since their escape, and at the same time they were rapidly deteriorating physically. And yet, when it was over, they had only ended up back where they had started.

Turning his head away, Dieter quietly let tears of frustration flow.

He had lost track of the date, and did not know it was July 4.

✪ ✪ ✪

In the morning, Dieter and Duane awoke sore, sick, and dispirited.

Still retracing their steps, they were not paying much attention to where they were going; as a result, Duane nearly walked into three bright-coral bamboo vipers hanging from a bamboo cluster right in front of his face. The venomous snakes, considered among the deadliest in all of Southeast Asia, were coiled and ready to strike when Dieter yelled at Duane to duck, which he did at the last second.

At a fork in the creek, they headed away from the falls that they knew were upstream. Eventually, the creek widened and they came to a junction of several waterways. Easing themselves into the cold water, they waded to the opposite bank, hoping to find a bigger river flowing into the basin. Not far away, they came to a river about 300 feet wide.

Excited, they discussed building a raft in the morning and floating to Thailand or out to the ocean. Their spirits were lifted at the thought of no more walking. They built a solid shelter that night, even putting sides on it, and stayed warm and dry for the first time in a week.

Nonetheless, in the morning they both awakened in worse shape. Duane had a fever, chills, and nausea—another malaria attack was coming on. Dieter had a deep, phlegmy cough and his lungs hurt every time he took a breath. Lingering inside before going out to face the cold rain, they ate a little rice and knelt in prayer. Then they took apart their shelter, being careful to hide everything in the bush. For the next several hours they became master raft builders. Dieter cut down about twenty banana trees at the edge of the jungle and hauled them down to the river, while Duane worked at the water's edge interlocking the trunks by driving thin bamboo poles through the soft, fleshy wood. It turned out they did too good a job, because when they tried to drag the solid raft into the water they couldn't budge it. They had no choice but to cut it down in size, leaving room for only one man. Duane was "pretty sick now" from malaria, and Dieter helped him aboard. Duane was lying flat, and Dieter went in the water. Holding on at the back, he kicked to keep the raft going straight in the current. After about a quarter of a mile, they rounded a lazy bend.

The moment they did, they heard the thunder.

Duane yelled and jumped into the water, heading for shore.

Dieter swam his hardest and only barely avoided being swept over the waterfall. Worried, he called to Duane over the roar of the falls. Duane answered, and Dieter found him holding on to some overhanging brush. They helped each other out of the water, and went back to walking. They followed the river for another hour or so before stopping as the shadows grew longer. Too exhausted to build a shelter, they lay down on a rocky shelf and slept.

On their journey the next day down the winding river, they went through forests of vines and over steep rocky overhangs. Dieter was in the lead when he saw something move in front of them. About five feet away was a ferocious-looking lizard or water dragon three to four feet long. Its head was raised, and water dripped from its jaws.

Duane sighed, and Dieter took this to mean the same thing that was on his mind: *meat*. Dieter advanced slowly, raising the machete as the big lizard watched warily. From two feet away, Dieter swung with all his strength. The blow killed the lizard instantly. Dieter turned to see Duane "smiling the biggest grin" he had ever seen on his thin, sunken face. Dieter deftly skinned his kill, as he had done so many times on hunting trips, then sliced up the stringy, snow-white flesh, which they devoured raw. A few hundred feet away they found a second course: a fig tree laden with fruit. Most of the figs were rotten and wormy, but they ate their fill of the sweet fruit and packed what they could fit into their rucksacks.

Dieter and Duane had both been experiencing blurred vision during the past few days, but immediately after they ate the extra food their vision cleared markedly. Their lucky day was not yet over, as they later came around a bend and nearly walked into the middle of a military camp, complete with barracks, a storage area, and huts scattered about. They hit the ground and crawled into the undergrowth. They observed the dilapidated camp for any signs of activity before deciding that it had been long deserted. They rushed to the nearest hut. Once inside, they sat in disbelief over their "good fortune." First they had found food, and now they could spend the night off the ground with a roof over their heads. They ate more of the lizard and the wormy figs.

In their travels the next day, they found the jungle too dense to get through and the streams so clouded from all the rain that they couldn't see the bottom and kept tripping. They had to walk along the banks, stretches of which were infested with leeches. Afterward, they took turns getting the slimy leeches off each other's body. One leech tried to go up Dieter's rectum, and Duane used two sticks like tweezers to work it out. Dieter found leeches on Duane's back so filled with blood that they had turned red, and there were more in his scalp and beard.

That day they decided to get rid of the carbine, which had become too heavy. Duane bent the barrel between two large rocks, then hid the weapon under a log. Dieter tossed the ammunition into a shallow pool.

They spent the night on the ground, "right in the sand and the mud." It rained nearly nonstop, and Duane was getting sicker. When he said he couldn't keep going, Dieter tried to cheer him up. They slept fitfully after eating a small amount of rice and the last of the lizard. By first light in the morning, they spotted the roofs of three huts a few hundred feet away. After they crawled into the bush for cover, Dieter said he would check out the huts and told Duane to stay put.

Dieter crawled through high grass until he was close enough to reconnoiter. He had learned that during the rice-growing season Laotians built labor camps near paddy fields—rice accounted for 80 percent of Laos's agriculture—and after the crop was harvested they went home with the rice. This looked to be such a camp, now deserted.

Dieter went back for Duane, who had fallen asleep in wet leaves. Duane had a high fever, and Dieter was glad to be able to get a roof over his head. With Duane "fighting just to keep from passing out," Dieter draped his arms over his shoulders. With much of Duane's weight on Dieter's back, they worked their way through the bush. Once inside a hut, Duane collapsed. His breathing was ragged and labored, and his eyes were sunk deeply into dark sockets.

"Dieter," Duane said hoarsely. "I'm going to die, I know it. Promise me you'll see that Dorcas is all right."

"Sure, buddy, but you're not going to die. Hell, I'm sick, too, but we'll both be okay."

When they heard planes that night, Dieter tried to start a fire. If they could attract the attention of the pilots with a bonfire, it might lead to an aerial search in the morning. As he had seen the natives do, Dieter split a long bamboo tube in half and laid one half on its side, supported by several sticks pushed into the ground. Inside the tube he placed bamboo scrapings. He cut a notch in the other half of the tube. He rubbed the notched half against the other half, and kept rubbing—back and forth, rapidly—trying to generate the friction needed to get the scrapings to smolder, so he could blow on them to get a flame that could be fed more dry tinder. But it was for naught, as he was too weak to keep rubbing the sticks at the speed required, and Duane was not of much help.

In the morning they were "all of a sudden not hungry anymore." This was just as well, because there was little rice left. Deciding to head back to the river, they had gone about half a mile when they came across a well-constructed native raft made of bamboo. It was covered with rattan, indicating that someone was trying to conceal it. With a pointed bow and stern, it looked much like a canoe. Finding the launch gave them hope that the river was navigable. If so, that meant they could make some distance floating instead of walking. Deciding it would be safer to travel on the river at night, they went into the jungle about thirty feet away and found a place to wait for dark. It was still only mid-morning, so they had a full day of rest, which they both very much needed.

That night was "completely dark, no moon, no stars, nothing," when they pushed the raft into the water. Dieter and Duane both climbed inside. To their surprise, they were sitting in several inches of water. While not watertight, the raft was "very buoyant" and stable. They had difficulty pushing off from shore, even with the long bamboo pole Dieter found in the raft. Once they got into the current, though, they started moving. They heard voices ashore, and knew they were passing a village. They silently floated past two more villages in the dark. Around midnight the moon rose, shining its silvery light across the water.

They heard the rapids before seeing them, and soon were among large rocks, which Dieter was able to keep them away from with the pole. The river began to narrow, and as it did the current quickened. They floated into a wide, slow-moving basin that seemed to offer a calmer ride. That serenity, however, was short-lived. They heard the now familiar thundering of a waterfall, and before they could react, the raft shot over the falls. They hung in the air "completely free of the water," then the raft went down nose-first like a dive-bombing Spad. When they struck the water, Dieter, who was in front, was thrown free, and Duane came flying out close behind. They grabbed hold of the raft, and as it turned slowly in a large pool, they were able to climb back in. The raft had lost pieces of its frame, but it still floated. An hour later, another set of rapids and rocks did it in, and the raft started "splitting into pieces." Before Dieter and Duane could get out, they skipped over more rocks. They heard someone yell, and saw that they had hit a fisherman standing in knee-deep water. When he saw the two ghostly apparitions in the raft, he dropped his net and ran screaming for shore.

As the sun began to rise, Dieter and Duane found a hiding place in dense foliage on the opposite side of the river. They occasionally heard voices on the other bank, and wondered if, based on the fisherman's reported sighting of white men, a local search party had been organized to find them. Then, things quieted down. Although they had lain down in an area full of leeches, they didn't have the strength to move and said "to hell with it." They slept until early afternoon.

When he awakened, Dieter had a new plan. Now that they had been spotted floating down the river, that mode of transportation was too dangerous. He pointed to a ridge to the east, and said that on the other side was

North Vietnam, where there are "bigger rivers" than in landlocked Laos. From where they were, Dieter went on, it was more than 100 miles to Thailand. But once they got into Vietnam, they would be only twenty miles or so from the coast. The more he talked, the more excited they became about heading to the coast.

They even had the "mad idea" that once they reached the coast they could build a raft and float out to Dieter's aircraft carrier in the Gulf of Tonkin. To the two desperate men gamely trying to hold onto hope, the "impossible seemed possible."

They took off for the ridge. It had stopped raining and was hot, and a flying insect—a kind they hadn't seen before, which had inch-long hind legs and was covered with white dots—seemed to be following them. The bugs did not bite them, but buzzed incessantly around their heads, obscuring their field of vision. Only when they got into jungle so dense that the large insects couldn't follow did they lose these unwanted traveling companions.

It was a gentle slope up the ridge, and they made good time. When they reached the summit, a view of many miles stretched out before them. To the east was a succession of ridges like the one they had climbed, and about fifteen miles away was one taller than all the rest.

"That's it!" Duane said joyously. "That's the great divide! We get on top of that son of a gun and we'll see the ocean."

"Okay, let's make it," Dieter said.

The sun had dipped in the west behind them, and darkness came as they went down the other side of the ridge. Losing their footing, they did more "falling and falling" than walking or crawling, so much so that their clothes were ripped to shreds by the time they made it down. The first thing they saw at the base of the ridge was a creek—just a trickle of water only a couple of inches deep—and they both dropped face-first into the stream and drank until their thirst was satisfied.

They followed the creek, which soon led to a wide river.

"A new river," Dieter announced. "Thank God."

Their plan seemed to be working, and they felt they were making progress. They would follow this river to the next ridge, then head over that toward the coast. They even found lodging: a small abandoned village along the river. They crawled into a hut and went to sleep.

The next day they came across a cornfield. They jumped into the field like schoolchildren at a pumpkin patch, and "ate and ate," probably "a hundred ears." The meal gave them renewed strength. When they came to another ridge, they didn't think twice about the climb, even in the heavy rain. It took them until mid-afternoon to go down the other side, this time without any pratfalls. Once down, they walked right into a garden of sugar-cane. They enjoyed another meal, which replenished their energy, then loaded their rucksacks with their spoils.

Dieter decided to scout around, and suggested that Duane rest.

When he came back, Dieter was devastated. What he had found had just about caused him to "drop dead," and he knew it was going to have the same impact on poor Duane. There was no good way to say it.

"You know that first abandoned village we stayed at a few nights ago?"

Duane remembered the place where they couldn't get a fire going.

"Well, it's just across the river over there."

Duane's jaw dropped. "I don't believe you!"

Dieter took him to a spot where they could see the village. They both looked at the familiar layout without saying anything. What more was there to say? Obviously, they had become disoriented. They had floated on the winding river at night, then crossed over a ridge. They thought they had found a new river, but it was the same one. They had followed it back around the same mountain to where they had been days earlier.

They sat in the dark, wrapped in despair, feeling as if they had come to "the end of the line." Duane began crying softly, and Dieter soon joined him. The escape route that was to take them to the coast and freedom had instead kept them deep in Laos. Upriver was the prison camp, and not far away were the Pathet Lao, who were surely out looking for them. In be-tween forces of evil were impenetrable jungles and mountainous terrain.

Suddenly, "an idea flashed" into Dieter's mind. Okay, so they couldn't walk or float out. There was another way—something they had thought of earlier but hadn't done much about since. Being airlifted out was their best hope, and the only way for that to happen was to make contact with planes overhead. Almost nightly they still heard the C-130 transports. Making air contact had been their original plan—and a good one, Dieter thought—had they been able to hold the prison camp.

Dieter, his spirits already lifted, grabbed Duane's arm.

"Duane, the ammo, the ammo!"

Duane looked as if Dieter had lost his mind.

When Duane had gotten rid of the carbine, Dieter had thrown the ammunition into a pool of water. Dieter explained that he would go back and find the cartridges. They could be taken apart for their gunpowder, which could be used to build a big fire—a signal fire.

Duane seemed drained and depressed, unable to bounce back. He was barely listening to Dieter. With another malaria attack coming on, Duane wanted only to get back to the hut, lie down, and sleep. On the way back, he threw up repeatedly. That night he kept waking up, shaking violently, and pleading with Dieter to cover him. Dieter held him closely to radiate body heat. In the morning, Duane was burning up with a high fever.

Dieter knew he couldn't bring Duane to look for the ammo but didn't want to leave him unattended in the hut, in case the Pathet Lao showed up. At sunrise, he woke Duane, half-dragged him into the bush, and covered him with wet leaves, leaving only his head visible. Duane lay "as still as a corpse," and Dieter wondered whether his friend would be alive when he came back. He shook Duane's limp hand, promising to return as soon as possible, and took off.

As Dieter went along the river, he could see that the water level had risen about ten feet, then receded even more. When he came to the spot where he had thrown away the ammo, he had no problem recognizing it. However, the pool of water was now a pit of mud. He dropped to his knees and began digging through the mire. He searched for more than an hour. Then, he saw the tail end of a single cartridge. He was so happy and relieved that he kissed the muddy cylinder, then dug around for more. By the time it was too dark to keep looking, he had found four cartridges. After washing the mud off himself in the river, he crawled into the bush and found a place to sleep.

In the middle of the night he was awakened by a strange noise. Fully alert, he stayed still. Something was creeping closer, and it had a foul odor. The next thing he knew a bear was sniffing him from inches away. Dieter let out a scream and jumped up. The bear let out a growl. They fell over each other and took off, running in opposite directions.

When Dieter returned, Duane was in the same position as before. Fearing the worse, Dieter rushed over and cradled Duane in his arms. Duane's arms clasped him in return. The friends hugged, each grinning at the sight of the other. Duane was less feverish and more alert, and when Dieter told him about finding the cartridges, his eyes lit up.

That night, with clear skies and no rain, seemed ideal to try to make air contact. Dieter decided to get a fire going early enough so he could boil water and cook something for Duane. He prepared the fire pit outside, then set up his fire-making kit. After knocking off the top of a bullet against a rock, he poured out the powder and mixed it with the scrapings. To generate a spark, he rubbed the bamboo sticks together, hard. Duane helped out by blowing gently on any spark, but it still took six failed efforts before they could keep a small flame flickering. Then they carefully added more tinder, and also a few pieces of charcoal they had found in one of the huts. Soon, they had a nice bed of hot embers.

Dieter got a bamboo container from one of the huts and filled it halfway with water. Thinking about his mother's early lessons in the Black Forest, when she had pointed the edible plants out to him—she had called them field salad—he picked some tapioca leaves, which he had seen the Laotians eat. He put them in the pot with a leftover piece of sugarcane, a handful of moldy rice, and tree bark. The "crude stew" boiled for about an hour and was delicious. They both ate well, and felt better after the hot meal.

Their plan was to stay awake next to the fire all night. As soon as they heard a plane, they would light the native torches Dieter had made, using green vines to wrap large, dry leaves around the end of long bamboo sticks. The dry leaves would light quickly over the fire. The plan was for Duane to wave his torch in an S pattern, and Dieter to wave an O—representing two-thirds of the international Morse code distress signal SOS. They hoped that any U.S. pilot seeing a fiery SO on the ground would be curious enough to want to take a closer look.

When the first plane flew over, they did not get the torches lit fast enough. Looking up at the crystal-clear sky—with no overcast or rain—they knew it was a perfect night for keeping a fire going and signaling aircraft. They only hoped they would have another chance. They did, not long afterward; in fact, two more planes flew over in the next hour. They waved their torches, but to no avail.

Fatigue overcame them, and they both fell asleep. Awakened by the sound of C-130 engines, they jumped up. The fire had nearly burned out, but there were enough coals left to light the leafy torches. Duane wildly waved the S and Dieter the O. This time, instead of continuing on, the plane added power and turned. The pilot seemed to have seen them, and was setting up a circle pattern directly overhead.

Duane began yelling loud enough to bring every Pathet Lao within miles to their location. "He sees us! We'll be safe! Oh, God, he sees us!"

Dieter admonished him to "shut up."

"I'm sorry, Dieter," Duane said in a softer voice. "He's circling and taking a bearing and distance reading on this place." Duane said that this was what an air force crew did to help a rescue helicopter find the location at daybreak.

The plane dropped two flares, one after the other. As they swung slowly to earth under parachutes, the flares lit up the night sky as if it were daytime. Duane and Dieter were both struck utterly silent as they watched, trying to come to grips with the fact that they had been seen—really seen— by the U.S. Air Force and would soon be rescued. Their spirits were not diminished when the plane left. *They had been seen!*

To be on the safe side after all the commotion, they hid in the bush the rest of the night rather than going back to the hut. They tamped down the fire to make it less visible. However, Dieter went back about every hour to be sure it hadn't gone out. They had used the last of the gunpowder to start the fire, and he didn't want to take a chance on losing it in the event "something should foul up" in the morning.

Far too excited to sleep, they talked as if they were home free.

"We finally made it," Duane said wistfully.

"In less than four hours, we'll be in a chopper," Dieter agreed.

Duane said he would put Dieter in the rescue hoist first because being a chopper pilot he knew how it worked. Then he'd come up after Dieter. When they got to Da Nang, which is where Duane said they would be taken by the chopper, he was going to have "scrambled eggs and ham for breakfast." But before then, Duane told Dieter, "there's always food on the chopper. So we can have something to eat right away!"

By morning, the overcast had returned, along with light rain. When no helicopter arrived, Duane said, "Don't worry." The ceiling was too low for a helicopter, he explained. They should give it some time.

Part of Dieter wasn't accepting the weather as an excuse, because it didn't look that bad to him. But like Duane, he wanted to keep believing.

By noon, they accepted reality: nobody was coming for them.

The God to whom they had given their deepest thanks during the night now didn't seem so benevolent. They were angry, cussing the pilots who had flown over during the night but had apparently not reported the sighting and had probably sat around "dry and happy in a bar somewhere" talking about the "crazy villagers who waved torches."

"You idiots!" Dieter yelled up to the empty, gloomy sky. "What's the matter with you? Don't you know we've broken out?"

Duane said the other prisoners—the Thai, Gene, and Y.C.—must have not made it either, or rescue aircraft would be out searching.

After a while, Duane moaned. "Goddammit, why don't we just die." He then lay on the ground as if that is exactly what he intended to do. And he did, in fact, become sicker as the day wore on, with a bad cough and a high fever. Dieter realized that Duane was nothing but "skin and bones."

Dieter's vision had started to blur again, and Duane had told him the whites of his eyes were yellow, a sign of jaundice. So were Duane's. Dieter's urine had been "black like tar" for days, and Duane reported his was, too. Dieter had been frightened while relieving himself a few days earlier to see that his feces were laced with wiggling little worms. When Dieter told Duane, he responded, "Yeah, mine's been the same for the past three days." Dieter's lungs were hurting again. But he was not ready to lie down and die. He would keep fighting to get home, and he was determined to bring Duane back with him. That afternoon, Dieter took an empty container to the river, and returned with water, which he began dabbing on Duane to cool him down.

Duane pushed him away. "Leave me alone! I want to die here."

"Hell, no. You're going to get out of here when I get out of here."

"Go on, Dieter. I don't want you around here anymore. I want to die by myself. Just tell Dorcas everything. I'm going to die right here."

"Nobody's going to die here." As Dieter said it, he wasn't sure he believed it. He wasn't even sure they would make it through the night.

✪ ✪ ✪

In the morning, Duane was willing to take a gamble to stay alive.

They had skirted around a village as they came back up the river a couple of days earlier. From what they had seen, it looked peaceful, with locals tending to their gardens, orchards, and livestock.

"I'm going back there to get some food," Duane announced. "Then I'll try to get away." He said he would bring back whatever food he got.

Dieter didn't like the sound of it. "You don't have the strength to make it there and get back. You're not in any condition to pull it off."

"It's all there is left to do. We can't go on like this anymore."

There was logic in Duane's argument. They were keeping the coals burning in the fire pit, and they could keep trying to signal aircraft on clear nights. But to do that they needed food to sustain themselves.

"Okay, Duane, but I'm going with you. We're going to go through this thing together."

It took them two hours to get to the outskirts of the village. Most of the time they stayed low, crawling. They stopped frequently to rest. It was not raining, so it was hot. They each had an empty bamboo container and their rucksacks to carry back their bounty. The first hut they came to had a Jersey cow grazing nearby. No one seemed to be around, so Dieter approached the cow slowly while whispering in a low voice. He went down to milk it but found it dry.

They continued on a trail through waist-high grass, proceeding side by side on their hands and knees. They were both "so exhausted" and "drained" by the physical exertion that Dieter wasn't sure they could even stand at this point, let alone walk. When the trail narrowed, Duane moved ahead. Dieter whispered to him to be careful. Usually, such a caution was unnecessary. By nature, Duane always went slowly and carefully, whereas Dieter was more aggressive in his moves—that was why Dieter thought they balanced each other and made a good team.

"The villagers have to be around somewhere," Dieter added softly as the trail dipped into a small, muddy gully. When they came out of the gully, the path made a sharp right turn around a cluster of tall bamboo.

The next thing Dieter knew, there was a boy carrying water containers who had stopped a few feet off the trail and was watching them.

Dieter and Duane both smiled, and said, *"Sabay."*

At the greeting, the boy nodded and went down the trail.

A few seconds later, Dieter heard someone on his right yell, *"Americali!"* The villagers, who had been nowhere to be found, suddenly seemed to be all around "running and screaming." A wild-eyed young man in a loincloth jumped in front of Duane, swinging a long machete above his head with both hands.

Duane was on his knees, holding the palms and fingers of both hands together in front of him, in a pose of respectful salutation practiced by Buddhists.

"Sabay," said Dieter, also on his knees, clasping his hands together.

The villager hesitated, then dropped the blade on Duane. It landed deep in his thigh, slightly below the groin. Duane bent over, grabbing his leg as the man brought the bloody machete back above his head.

Duane's hideous screams were cut short when the blade fell again, chopping through the back of his neck.

A stunned Dieter watched as his friend's dismembered head fell onto the trail, and blood spurted from his neck in "long, pulsating leaps."

Dieter jumped up as the villager swung the machete at him. He ducked under the blow and threw his hands forward. The villager turned and ran up the trail. Dieter stumbled off in the direction he and Duane had come. He ran through the gully on wobbly legs, and when he made the turn at the cluster of bamboo he stepped off the trail. He had gone only about twenty feet into the jungle when several villagers with machetes ran past on the trail in the direction he had been going.

The "reality and horror" of the situation were still catching up with Dieter, but he knew one thing: he had to run for his life. Only minutes before he had been crawling, unsure that he could even walk, and now he was fully charged, with his body and wits firing on all cylinders. He could feel blood coursing through him and was aware of every beat of his heart, which was so off the chart he thought it "might explode." He dropped into another gully and ran for about 300 yards before reaching dense jungle. Looking back, he realized he had left deep footprints in the mud. He carefully backed up in his own footprints for a distance before leaping onto a rock. Then he moved off in another direction by stepping on rocks and piles of leaves so as not to leave prints. Getting through the dense jungle was hellish, but that didn't matter anymore. He stopped every ten seconds or so to listen for anyone approaching, and was careful not to break off branches that would give away his movements to an experienced tracker.

After about forty-five minutes he came to a wide trail. He stopped and listened but didn't see or hear anything. He quickly jumped across and went about ten feet into the bush, where he sat on his haunches to rest.

"It wasn't ten seconds" before five natives, all armed with rifles, hurried past on the trail. One of them, a woman, stopped right where Dieter had crossed the trail. She faced the other way, searching the bush for any signs of movement, as the others continued down the path.

Dieter recognized that they were setting up a search perimeter, and that by "sheer chance and God's help" he had slipped through with "seconds and ten feet to spare." For a while he worried that the sentry would hear his rapid, deep breathing and alert the others, but she didn't. He began to inch away until he was far enough out of the search area to believe that he had slipped away.

He recognized the area he and Duane had traveled through, and headed for the abandoned village where they had tried so hard to signal the planes. When he reached it, he flopped down on the ground in front of the fire pit, and dug carefully through the ash, trying to find a burning ember. He did, at the very bottom, and added dry tinder until it was a roaring fire. He had a new plan. Since the one plane hadn't done anything about their waving torches, he was going to give anyone flying over "a show they wouldn't forget." He went around the huts tearing off bamboo and other flammables, making a big stack next to the fire pit, and waited.

That night, it was clear again and the stars were out.

And the C-130 came again.

Dieter threw all the fuel he had gathered onto the fire, then ran around like a pyromaniac lighting all the huts until "everything was burning." He wasn't worried about villagers or search parties, because he knew they were scared of the dark. Besides, he was so angry he didn't give a damn. He was pissed off at the damn C-130 pilots for not seeing him and Duane the night before, and he was mad at the choppers for not coming to their rescue while Duane was alive.

The pilots overhead "saw it all right." They made sharp turns over the burning village, and dropped twenty to thirty flares by parachute.

As they did, Dieter screamed at them like a banshee.

In little time, the village burned to the ground, and then the plane left. What would the pilots report this time? Dieter wondered. A village in southern Laos on fire? So what? Who cared? No way they would send a rescue chopper just to check out a burning village.

Dieter, now with no floor under him and no roof over his head, collapsed at the place in the bush where he had hidden Duane when he went to find the ammunition. Everything seemed much different now—colder, darker, lonelier. Dieter sobbed for his dead friend, and for himself, and for the other guys who must not have made it—after all the years of abuse they had endured. He thought of good and kind Gene, trying to take care of poor Y.C. None of it was fair.

He was awakened in the morning by a spattering of rain. He filled up on river water, then found a few small snails to eat. He went searching for a parachute dropped by the C-130 to see if there was anything he could use. His wildest hope was that they had dropped a survival radio or a signal mirror, but all he found with a spent aerial flare was the white canopy of a smaller-size parachute. He picked it up and kept going. Climbing up a hill opposite the burned-out camp, he laid out a "good SOS" in the open using the panels from the chute. Then, he sat and waited for the planes. They came all right—he counted "thirty or forty" of them during the day, as they crisscrossed the sky at thousands of feet in altitude, heading to and from more important places. That night he slept next to his distress signal, which no one saw. In the morning, he rolled up the parachute and put it inside his rucksack.

Back at the river, he heard voices. He quickly moved into the bush for cover. In a few minutes a line of men came out of the jungle. They were a platoon of Pathet Lao, seventeen in all, and each one carried a rifle and machete. They had come from the burned-out village, and were obviously searching for the runaway *Americali*.

He watched them as they looked for footprints and studied the terrain. These guys knew what they were doing. They were following Dieter's exact path even though the footprints by the river were nearly washed away. Dieter continued to watch them, and when they left, he started following behind them.

For some reason, it seemed better to follow the trackers than have them follow him. So, Dieter stayed a safe distance back. There was something else at work here, too. Dieter was getting so weak, and knew he was close to dying, that he had somehow "lost all fear." It seemed "strange and interesting" to watch the trackers track him. Where would it end? Somewhere, he knew, and soon.

Later in the day, Dieter received an unexpected bonus.

After the squad had stopped for a meal and then left, Dieter came out of the bushes and scrutinized the campsite. He found about "twenty grains of rice, a couple of red peppers, a green pepper, a couple of fish heads and a fish bone." Ravenous, he ate everything. Then, his stomach fuller than it had been in days, he crawled back into the bushes and went to sleep.

The next day he had trouble walking. He kept getting dizzy and had to sit down before he fell down. His kidneys and lungs were hurting, and he was coughing up blood. He wasn't sure where he was going, but he thought he should keep moving. And then he passed out. That's when Duane first came to him. *Dieter, my legs are cold. My feet are cold.*

The rest of the day he lapsed into and out of consciousness, and the visions kept coming to him.

The prison camp, with all the shackled men he knew . . .

A golden door in the sky opening and a chariot racing out . . .

His father, Reinhold, wanting to help, pointing the way . . .

Then he saw a black bear. He soon realized from the smell that it was real. The bear watched him from a distance, and followed him, not in a threatening manner, but waiting. Waiting, Dieter knew, for him to lie down and die. Waiting for a meal. Somehow, it didn't bother Dieter.

Many of his conscious thoughts were those of a man making peace.

Was Marina still waiting for him?

Would his mother have to wait seven years for him to be declared dead before she could collect his $10,000 military life insurance?

Would all the people he had ever wronged forgive him?

His thirst drove him back to the river, and the bear followed.

Dieter slipped on the rocks and tumbled into the water. He was so weak he nearly drowned before he was able to climb up on a large flat rock. He saw the bear on the opposite bank, watching him, standing on his hind legs, as if trying to decide whether this was the moment to come for the meal.

Starved and weak, Dieter had very little physical strength left. Dying would be easier than staying alive, and he knew he was close to crossing over. And yet he was not ready to give up. While there was no physical or logical reason for it, his will to live had not yet been extinguished.

Across from him, in the hollow of another rock, Dieter saw a brightly colored snake. Without giving any thought to whether or not it was poisonous, he reached for the snake, taking the head in one hand and the tail in the other. Pulling the snake taut, he bit it in half. The "long brown liver" was hanging out as both ends of the snake coiled around his hands. Dieter ate the liver first, then kept eating until one half of the snake was gone. The other half he put in his rucksack.

He lay on the rock to rest for a minute, or for an hour.

He heard the sound of an approaching truck in the background.

Listening closer, he realized that the familiar sound was not a truck at all. It was a Spad, coming down low, very low, over the river.

12

TO THE RESCUE

So far that morning nothing had gone right for U.S. Air Force Lieutenant Colonel Eugene P. Deatrick, forty-two, of Morgantown, West Virginia. Twice, he and his wingman had taken off from Pleiku Air Base in South Vietnam on an armed reconnaissance mission to Laos, only to be forced back. First, there had been trouble with Deatrick's radio; then his wingman's plane developed a mechanical problem. As maintenance personnel worked on the plane, Deatrick suggested that they grab an early lunch at the cafeteria. Afterward, they returned to the flight line, because Gene Deatrick was determined to get in a mission that day, "one way or the other."

The genial, pipe-smoking Deatrick had been commanding officer of the 1st Air Commando Squadron only four months. After serving as an aide to a four-star general, Howell Estes Jr., for seven years—"the general would never get rid of me because he liked my wife, Zane, so much"—Deatrick pushed for a transfer to Vietnam, convinced that this was his "last chance to go fight." World War II had ended by the time he graduated, in 1946, from the U.S. Military Academy, and he had been an experimental test

Lieutenant Colonel Eugene Deatrick, the Spad pilot who spotted Dieter at the river in Southern Laos. *U.S. Air Force*

pilot in California and Ohio during the Korean War. He was determined not to miss another war. Ironically, after his years of test-piloting the air force's hottest new jets, Deatrick's first combat command was a squadron of A-1 Skyraiders. It didn't take the jet jockey long to become a fan of the old propeller planes, which, like him, had just missed World War II. Deatrick came to regard the rugged Spad as "a hell of a plane." That his squadron would not lose a single aircraft from engine failure amazed Deatrick. A couple of planes were shot down, but the pilots either bailed out or survived crash landings.

When they were finally on their way that morning, Deatrick and his wingman headed across the Thai border to Laos. The area they had been assigned was considered "open," a term that, to Deatrick, meant "we can shoot anything we see because there are no friendlies in the area." They had flown over Laos under such orders before and mostly "worked the trails," catching troops and sometimes vehicles in the open when they were lucky, and otherwise leaving deep bomb craters in roads and river crossings.

About an hour into the flight, they had seen all the usual sights—jungle, scattered woods, and a few rice paddies—but no targets of opportunity. In fact, for the last half hour they hadn't seen a road, a village, or any other signs of life. Deciding to descend and explore a large canyon with a river running through it, Deatrick left his wingman just under the 2,000-foot cloud layer. At that higher altitude, his wingman would have better communication with the outside world via his VHF radio.

Deatrick, a barnstormer at heart, made sure he did "all the buzzing down low" whenever possible. He dropped to a couple of hundred feet. When he came to a sharp bend in the river, he banked ninety degrees to follow it. For the few seconds that his left wing was pointed straight down, he was able to get an unobstructed look at the ground directly below. When he did, he saw what appeared to be a "merry little fisherman" on the river, waving. Passing over at 150 miles per hour, Deatrick went by in a flash and flew upriver for five minutes before something—"I'll never know what"—told him to go back and take another look. He came in steeply banked again so he could look down at the ground. The same guy was on a big, flat rock in the river. He seemed to be waving something white, which Deatrick took to be "fishing nets." On the first pass, the plane could have easily surprised the man in the river, but for him to still be there struck Deatrick as odd. Natives in enemy territory generally did not wave to Spads "fully loaded" with bombs and rockets. More often, they ran like hell for cover.

Given his speed and low altitude, Deatrick was again over the scene only briefly. He now asked what his wingman could make out from the higher vantage point. Circling above, the wingman reported: "It looks like there's an SOS written on a rock."

Deatrick gained some altitude and radioed to the airborne command aircraft for the southern Laos region—a four-engine Lockheed HC-130 orbiting near the Laotian–North Vietnamese border. Call sign *Crown*, the HC-130, a new search-and-rescue (SAR) version of the C-130 Hercules transport, with a crew of seven, was responsible for assembling and managing SAR efforts looking for downed flyers, and for serving as a communications link between the SAR units and other commands.

Identifying himself by his call sign, *Hobo 25*, Deatrick asked: "Anyone been shot down in this area?"

"Negative," the *Crown* air controller reported.

"Nothing? Air force, navy, marines, Thai, Vietnamese?"

"No one is down today."

Damn, this is just not my day, Deatrick thought. Here he was over an area in which "everything is considered the enemy" and he's got a man in a river waving like a fool and laying out an SOS—but *Crown* says there are no downed pilots. Deatrick knew about the enemy's tactics to try to "suck in and take out" rescue helicopters. This could well be a trap. The fisherman could have a grenade under his clothing and wait to be hoisted up to a chopper before pulling the pin. Deatrick knew that if he was duped into calling in a helicopter and it went down, he could lose the combat command he had waited so long to get.

Deatrick got back to *Crown*. "Here's the situation. We've got a nut down here who has an SOS written on a rock."

"What does he look like?" *Crown* asked.

Deatrick had to bite his tongue not to laugh at the question. "Look, I think we ought to try to get this guy out," he said, explaining that he would stay on the scene to direct a rescue helicopter. He had made his recommendation, but he could be overruled by higher-ups.

After several conversations between *Crown* and other commands—including a general as far away as Saigon, Deatrick later heard—*Crown* advised Deatrick that a helicopter was en route.

Now, Deatrick could only wait. He and his wingman made wide circles so as not to pinpoint the man in the river to any enemy forces in the area, "in case he was one of our own." Meanwhile Deatrick hoped that his air force career wasn't about to "go down the drain."

✪ ✪ ✪

U.S. Air Force Captain William "Skip" Cowell, thirty-four, of Honolulu, Hawaii, was sitting in a large tent at the Quang Tri forward combat base near the DMZ in South Vietnam with the crew of his Jolly Green Giant helicopter, awaiting just such a rescue operation.

When the radio call came from *Crown*, Cowell, his copilot, and two crewmen hurried to their Sikorsky-built helicopter, which had already been prepared for flight, with an auxiliary power unit attached to start the engines. Doing the "quick-call checklist," Cowell fired up the two General Electric turbo engines that provided 3,000 horsepower to the five-blade rotor system. Although the helicopter was unarmed, the two crewmen in back—an engineer and a pararescueman—had handguns and carbines, which they could fire from the open cabin door.

Taking off within three minutes, Cowell spiraled the helicopter straight up at seventy miles per hour to gain altitude so as not to fly low over the surrounding rice paddies, where enemy snipers might be lying in wait. Going straight up is not something a helicopter pilot likes to do, because if the engine suddenly loses power the copter will drop straight to the ground. Only when a helicopter has forward speed is it able to autorotate the rotor blades—turning them by the action of air moving up through them rather than by engine power—and thereby allow a powerless helicopter to glide forward as it descends for a safe landing. At 5,000 feet, Cowell lowered the nose to pick up speed and set the dual overhead throttles to cruise speed (140 miles per hour). During their two-minute upward spiral, Cowell had turned to the heading given by *Crown*, so as soon as they were going forward they were on their way to southern Laos.

The helicopter was soon met by two Spads from Gene Deatrick's squadron. Knowing that the planes were on a coastal reconnaissance just north of the DMZ, Deatrick had radioed the pilots and arranged for them to escort the helicopter.

Cowell, who had been flying helicopter rescue missions into North Vietnam and Laos for ten months, liked to look out and see Spads. They were the one combat plane that could fly about as slow as a Jolly Green. Always heavily armed and ready to mix it up, Spads "put the fear of God" into anyone on the ground wanting to harm a helicopter, which was most vulnerable when hovering during a rescue pickup.

So far, Cowell had rescued seven downed pilots. He remembered every one of those missions, and also the ones that weren't successful. Only two months earlier, his and another helicopter had been sent to a location in the Plain of Jars in northern Laos to pick up a downed air force F-105 pilot. When Cowell got there he was told the pilot was hiding by a "red-blossom tree." Cowell made two passes over a red tree but didn't see anyone. On the third pass, he hovered above the tree. That's when the trap was sprung by the enemy, who opened up with gunfire from several locations. It turned out that the F-105 pilot had been killed and was being used as a decoy. The enemy shot out one of the Jolly Green's engines, which caught fire. As Cowell fought to keep control, a bullet—one of thirty-two that hit the helicopter— tore into the bottom of a rudder pedal, knocking his foot off it. Two Spads, one after the other, swooped underneath the helicopter with cannons blazing. The enemy guns were quieted long enough for the crippled helicopter to get away. When they returned to base, the pilot of the backup helicopter said he had seen enough and turned in his wings.

When Deatrick saw the Jolly Green Giant approaching, he radioed that he would take Cowell to the man in the river. Following Deatrick on a low-level pass, Cowell spotted the man on a flat rock with an SOS next to him. At least he was in the open; pickups through dense jungle were trickier, involving lowering a jungle penetrator on a 250-foot cable through the canopy of vegetation. Too, the helicopter had not drawn any ground fire on the first pass. Cowell went upriver a few hundred feet and dropped his two external fuel tanks, making the helicopter lighter and easier to maneuver. Then he came back over the man in the river, setting up a hover 200 feet overhead. The hoist operator lowered the penetrator, which had three metal paddles that folded up. When lowered, the paddles deployed three prongs for seats, complete with a safety belt for what was usually a rough ride up to a hovering helicopter whose whirling blades caused a powerful downdraft.

One thing that struck Cowell as unusual was that they did not have any idea whom they were picking up, since no aircraft were reported down in southern Laos that day. Although Spad pilots had "a lot of credibility" with SAR commanders and helicopter pilots whenever they asked for a rescue pickup, Cowell wondered why he and his crew had been dispatched out here in the absence of any reports of a pilot down.

Cowell received word over his headset from the hoist operator that the penetrator had reached the man but that he seemed to be having trouble opening it up. Finally, the man pulled down one of the paddles and sat on it. With the man hanging on "for dear life," the hoist operator began hauling him up. Some sixty seconds passed. Then: "We've got him!" With that, Cowell pushed the helicopter's nose forward, adjusted the throttle, and climbed out over the river.

In the back of the helicopter, Airman First Class Mike Leonard, twenty-one, of Lawler, Iowa, had reached out and pulled the man into the cabin. Leonard, a husky pararescueman, immediately searched under the filthy man's tattered clothing for any weapons or explosives, and found none. He couldn't tell if the man was white or Asian, but at least he was unarmed. Leonard reached into the man's rucksack. When he pulled out a half-eaten snake, he jumped back and nearly fell out of the helicopter's open door.

Leonard could not make out much of what the man was saying—he had an accent and was "a little excited." The guy "went to pieces," grabbing hold of one of Leonard's legs and crying, "Oh my God, I'm alive!" When he started to shake violently and show symptoms of shock—clammy skin and shallow breathing—he was wrapped in a blanket. Although clearly weak and woozy, the man would not let go of Leonard's leg.

Cowell was heading back to their forward base when his engineer came forward and said the man in back was in "pretty bad shape." He recommended going to Da Nang, which, unlike the forward base, had a fully equipped hospital. Cowell radioed *Crown*, passing along the report of his passenger's condition and asking to proceed 150 miles south to Da Nang. His request was denied. He was told to return to his forward base, and that his passenger would have to wait for medical evacuation to a hospital.

A few minutes later, the engineer was back with a note printed on a piece of paper torn from a flight log. "This is our guy," he hollered over the noise of the whirling rotor blades. "Shot down in February. Been a POW since."

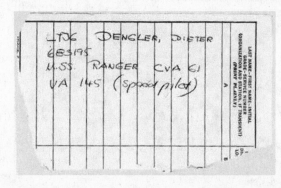

Note passed to rescue helicopter pilot Skip Cowell identifying the man rescued at a river in southern Laos on July 20, 1966. *Family photograph.*

Cowell immediately radioed the identity of their passenger to *Crown*, who cleared him to proceed directly to Da Nang.

As soon as Cowell found out he was carrying a *Ranger* Spad pilot who went down in February over Laos, it "all clicked together." Cowell had piloted the helicopter that had hovered over Dieter's wreckage the day after his crash. It had been his crewman who was lowered to the ground to search the scene. That mission Cowell had flown from the Royal Thai Air Force Base at Udorn, where he had been stationed before being assigned to start up a new rescue helicopter unit south of the DMZ.

Now, six months later, he was bringing out of the Laotian jungle—nearly 100 miles from that crash site—*Ranger*'s missing Spad pilot.

RETURNING HERO

Ranger's C1A carrier onboard delivery (COD) aircraft, *Gray Eagle 057,* was on final approach to the carrier shortly after 4:00 P.M. on July 21, 1966. By far *Ranger*'s most popular plane—it delivered bags of mail and parcels from home during long periods at sea in the South China Sea—the COD was carrying a passenger who was about to receive the welcome of a lifetime.

For Dieter, the last twenty-four hours had been a blur. From his bed at the Naval Support Facility Hospital at the eastern end of the Da Nang Air Base—and through the examinations, blood samples, tests, transfusions, and injections; a hot bath and shave; and "many tears"—Dieter kept wanting to know when he would be taken back to his ship to see his buddies. One of the first messages he received came from his squadron mates:

"SPADS FOREVER" AND SO IT IS WITH THE MEN THAT FLY THEM.
CONGRATULATIONS, RESPECT AND HIGHEST REGARDS FROM MEMBERS
OF VA-145.

That same day, July 20, Dieter was also handed a confidential message from the commander of the U.S. Seventh Fleet:

PLEASE PASS MY PERSONAL CONGRATULATIONS TO LTJG DENGLER
IN RECOGNITION OF HIS HEROISM IN ESCAPING FROM THE ENEMY AND
HIS FORTITUDE AND DETERMINATION IN SUCCESSFULLY EVADING
RECAPTURE AND WORKING HIS WAY TO FRIENDLY FORCES. WELL DONE
AND WELCOME HOME.

VICE ADMIRAL JOHN J. HYLAND

Dieter was allowed to send one message of his own, addressed to Marina
Adamich of Belmont, California:

I ESCAPED FROM PRISON. ALIVE IN HOSPITAL. WILL BE HOME SOON.
LOVE YOU. DIETER.

When he was admitted to the hospital, Dieter weighed ninety-eight
pounds. He was found to have two types of malaria, intestinal worms, fun-
gus, jaundice, and hepatitis. Doctors said he was so malnourished that if
he hadn't been picked up when he was, he would have "died that day or
the next." His condition was listed as fair, with the "prognosis good" for a
full recovery, although it would take medical supervision, time, and rest.
Dieter, with a bone-deep hunger, did his part by eating everything placed
in front of him.

During his first day at Da Nang, Dieter had been questioned by naval
intelligence officers, who reported that the former POW "tired very easily
during [the] interview." When Dieter described Duane's death, he broke
down and had to be given time to recover. He named the other prisoners
who had escaped with him. Shown a map, he found the village of Ban
Hoeui Het, and said the camp was a walk of two hours or so to the west. He
told how Gene and Y.C. planned to hide out on a ridge to the south, awaiting rescue. Dieter was assured that an aerial search would be started immediately. He was surprised to realize that after three weeks of walking in

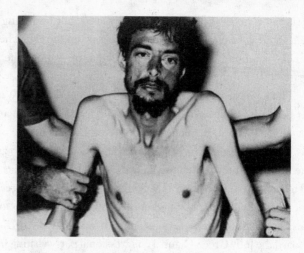

Dieter in the hospital in Da Nang, South Vietnam, on the day of his rescue, July 20, 1966. He weighed ninety-eight pounds. *U.S. Navy.*

the jungle he had been picked up only thirteen miles from the prison camp, and that at one point he and Duane had circled back to within two miles of the camp! Although he had walked eighty-five miles from the site of his crash to the prison camp from which he escaped, he and Duane, in their weakened state, never could have hiked to freedom: from where he was picked up it was 100 miles to Thailand and thirty-five miles to the coast of North Vietnam, with a sizable mountain range in between.

The rescue at the river may have been routine for the experienced helicopter crew used to "hotter pickups" in the face of enemy gunfire, but for Dieter it had been terrifying. After the helicopter's first pass, he heard a single shot echo down the canyon, and feared an enemy patrol was closing in. When there was a large explosion nearby, Dieter thought the helicopter was bombing him—only when he smelled the fuel did he realize that the pilot had dropped the external tanks. With that familiar whiff of aviation gas, he knew for sure that the Spads and the helicopter overhead were not a hallucination. As the helicopter hovered and lowered the penetrator, Dieter heard more shots. When he was finally able to unfold one paddle of the penetrator, he straddled the bar and waved, not bothering with the safety belt. Praying he could keep his "death grip" on the cable, he was hoisted by winch—spinning round and round like a top—above the jungle that had nearly killed him.

The U.S. Navy had been eager to get Dieter out of Da Nang. There had as yet been no public announcement concerning his escape and rescue. Even the officers who were personally notifying Dieter's mother in Germany and his brother in California of his survival were instructed to ask them to keep the news "within [the] family" for the time being. The fact that Dieter had also been interviewed by a U.S. Air Force intelligence officer in Da Nang did not sit well with the navy higher-ups, either—chalk it up to interservice rivalry. A matter of more serious concern was that when Dieter had arrived aboard the Jolly Green Giant, a congressional party visiting from Ohio—with the press in tow—happened to be touring the airfield. After a story appeared stateside about their day at Da Nang, mentioning an unnamed pilot having been rescued near the Laotian border, members of the party were advised that the rescue was classified. The next leak came out of Saigon, where one of the "gruffest of the growling pack" of war correspondents, Joe Fried of the New York *Daily News*, had sniffed out the details—including Dieter's name—and filed a story. The military, however, was able to kill this story, reportedly citing security reasons to Fried's bosses in New York.

Why the tight lid on the breaking news of a navy pilot's successful escape from a POW camp? First, there was concern about the welfare of the prisoners who had escaped with him—no one wanted information released that might aid the communists guerrillas who could still be hunting them. Also, there was the highly sensitive subject of where Dieter had been shot down. Although the entire world knew about the war in North and South Vietnam, the public had not been told about the secret war in Laos. The overall commander in the Pacific (CINCPAC) instructed all commands: "No public announcement about [Dengler's] escape and disposition, or meeting with press authorized until further notice." However, in the face of "considerable bitterness [by] media representatives that higher authority [was] unwilling to release details" after the teaser that had appeared in the published story about the Ohio delegation, it would be only a few days before an assistant secretary of defense in Washington, D.C., issued an official if terse announcement about the escape, naming Dieter.

Close to midnight on July 21, CINCPAC granted authority to the commander of the Seventh Fleet "to retain Dengler in order to obtain information"—most immediately, information that might prove of "value in escape and evasion procedures to aircrews flying over North Vietnam and Laos"—and thereafter to "expedite his movement" stateside, where he was to be admitted to the naval hospital in San Diego and where his "formal debrief" was to be conducted. That high-level authority set in motion Dieter's imminent return to his ship and buddies. The commander of the Seventh Fleet immediately wired the naval support command at Da Nang to "send Ltjg Dengler to RANGER." In the morning, the commander of Carrier Air Wing 14 aboard *Ranger* notified Da Nang: "My C1A, *Gray Eagle 057*, to Da Nang to pick up Ltjg Dengler for return to *Ranger*." Early that afternoon, Dieter had been driven by ambulance to the operations office at the Da Nang airfield, where his rescuer, the helicopter pilot Skip Cowell, happened to be passing through. He saw Dieter, covered with a blanket, lying on a couch waiting for his departing flight. Dieter was in the company of a navy doctor and a two-star admiral. It occurred to Cowell that he had never before seen a "junior naval officer escorted by an admiral."

Waiting on *Ranger*'s flight deck for the COD to land that drizzly day in the Gulf of Tonkin was Lieutenant (j.g.) Robert Montgomery, twenty-four, of Sacramento, California. As the ship's air transfer officer, he planned the incoming and outgoing loads of personnel and mail for the CODs—*Ranger*'s own as well as land-based C1As that flew supplies to the aircraft carriers operating in the South China Sea—and supervised the loading and unloading. He was aware that *Gray Eagle 057* had been sent to Da Nang to pick up Dieter Dengler, and was now returning "the hero to his ship." Montgomery was in an ideal position to be the first on *Ranger* to greet Dieter, and he intended to do just that.

After the COD caught the wire and was being directed off to one side of the flight deck, and while it was "still coasting to a stop," Montgomery ran alongside, opened the door on the side of the plane, and hopped in. The interior of the small plane was cramped and dark, and its limited headroom

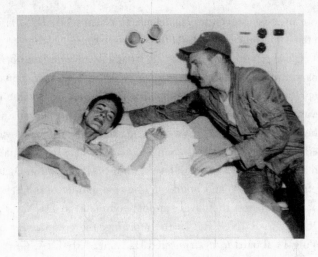

Dieter in *Ranger*'s sickbay, July 21, 1966. Norm "Lizard" Lessard of VA-145 on right. *U.S. Navy.*

required anyone entering to bend at the waist. The first person he saw was a smiling navy doctor. All but one of the rear-facing passenger seats—in single rows on either side of a narrow aisle—had been removed to make room for a metal-wire litter, upon which lay Dieter, who had on a khaki officer's shirt several sizes too big for him. Montgomery's first thought was that the former POW "didn't look like a caveman," and had obviously been "barbered and cleaned up." Then he saw the color of the pilot's skin and realized that "jaundice really *does* make you turn yellow."

"Welcome aboard," Montgomery said.

Dieter returned the greeting with a faint smile.

The COD was rolled onto an elevator, which went down to the hangar deck. There, Dieter's squadron mates, along with hundreds of expectant shipmates, were waiting. When the plane stopped and its wheels were chocked, someone rolled a length of red carpet up to the door.

The red carpet was only the beginning. Dieter would soon be shown to the admiral's quarters, recently vacated when Rear Admiral Weisner and his staff rotated back to San Diego, and a new admiral began flying his flag on another Yankee Station carrier set to relieve *Ranger*, which was due to depart for home in only two weeks.

A grinning Lizard, who couldn't have asked for a better gift for his twenty-fourth birthday the next day, Bummy, Farky, Hal Griffith, and other VA-145 pilots crowded inside the cabin. "Marina's fine, just fine," someone assured Dieter. They brought him out in their arms. When Dieter's weary but joyful face appeared in the doorway, a thunderous roar filled the cavernous hangar bay, followed by hoots, whistles, and clapping.

Against all odds, one of their lost pilots had returned.

U.S. NAMES PILOT IN MYSTERY ESCAPE
BY JOHN G. NORRIS
Washington Post Staff Writer

July 27—The Defense Department identified yesterday the Navy pilot who escaped from a Communist prison camp and was rescued last week after a harrowing 23-day trek through the Southeast Asia jungle. He is Lt. (jg) Dieter Dengler, of Pacifica, Calif., a native of Germany. But official secrecy still shrouded the circumstances under which Dengler was shot down, imprisoned, escaped and was rescued. One reason for withholding all details of Dengler's heroic ordeal and survival is that the locale of the incident was neither North nor South Vietnam.

Reliable sources said that he was downed and imprisoned in neighboring Laos. It is U.S. policy not to admit that it has bombed North Vietnamese troops moving south along the Ho Chi Minh trail in neutralized Laos, just as Hanoi does not talk of operations in that country.

Aside from saying that Dengler "is receiving medical treatment and is being debriefed," the Defense Department would say nothing about the matter. "Security requirements prevent the release of any details at this time," the Department added.

✪ ✪ ✪

The former Spad pilot Spook Johns had always wanted to see Alaska, the only state he had not visited. Embracing the independence of his new civilian life, he loaded up his International Scout with camping gear, and set out from his Detroit home, crossing Canada on the Alaska Highway.

Stopping at one of the way stations that appeared out of nowhere every fifty or sixty miles, he filled the gas tank and went inside for a sandwich and beer. He was casually watching a television mounted above the bar when a still picture of Dieter in uniform filled the screen. The announcer explained that navy pilot Dieter Dengler had escaped from a POW camp—

Spook heard little after that. He put some money on the bar, went outside, started up his Scout, and headed north.

Dieter had been one of the guys Spook tried not to think about. He found he had to do so while flying combat missions, in order to stay focused. There had been little time for grieving over lost squadron mates while he was operating in the South China Sea. And now, there could be no room in his life for ghosts like Gary Hopps, John Tunnell, and all the others who were gone. It was too painful. They had to become "past history."

Yet there had always been something different about Dieter. He was not known to be dead or captured; he was only missing. Too, Spook had been unable to let go of a feeling that he had "let Dieter down" by not staying on the scene against Hassett's orders and looking longer and harder for him. And now, so abruptly that it put a lump in his throat, the news of Dieter's escape and survival "lifted this colossal weight" off Spook's shoulders.

Spook drove on toward Fairbanks, "bawling like a baby."

Dieter had made it back, and Spook couldn't wait to see him again.

14

ALIVE AND FREE

Dieter spent several days on *Ranger.* After his first night in the ship's sickbay, he was moved into the admiral's spacious quarters. One of the first things he did was to pick up the phone and order a "big steak," which was delivered with all the trimmings. A sheet cake decorated with "Welcome Home, Dieter" was also brought up from the galley. Dieter happily popped into his mouth a rosette of red icing. Slices of cake were served to his squadron mates, who crowded into the room for a celebration and a group photograph.

Dieter's proud commanding officer, Hal Griffith, would write in Dieter's officer fitness report for the six-month period ending that month: "Lieutenant (j.g.) Dengler's tenacity and perseverance in escaping from the enemy will remain one of the most amazing feats of the present conflict in Southeast Asia."

On July 25, Dieter was flown to Clark Air Force Base, where he was taken by litter onto a C-141 Starlifter, a four-engine jet transport configured for medical evacuations. The next morning he arrived at Travis Air Force Base in northern California, where he had a brief reunion with Marina and his brother Martin. On July 27, Dieter was admitted to San Diego Naval Hospital, where he was to remain a patient for more than two months. For his first few nights, he found the bed too soft, and slept on the floor. Several

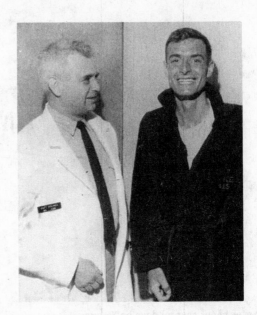

Dieter with his physician, Captain Alden Holmes, during his two-month stay at San Diego Naval Hospital. *U.S. Navy.*

times he awakened in the dark, screaming. When nurses came running, he flailed at them, thinking they were Pathet Lao guards and he was back in the jungle prison camp. He would continue to have such flashbacks for months.

Dieter was still off-limits to the press and public. He was assigned a senior public affairs officer, Captain Gaylord "Hap" Hill, forty-three, of Coronado, California. It was Hill's job, initially, to make sure Dieter stayed off-limits until higher-ups declared otherwise.* In the hospital, Dieter was allowed no unauthorized visitors. One enterprising reporter dressed as a janitor and pushed a broom down the hallway, trying to sneak into Dieter's room, but was halted by a military guard at the door.

---

* Ironically, a few months earlier, Hill had been the navy press liaison for the premiere aboard an aircraft carrier of the movie *Lt. Robin Crusoe, U.S.N.*, about a navy pilot (portrayed by Dick Van Dyke) forced to bail out of his plane and survive on a deserted island in the Pacific.

As his condition improved, Dieter was questioned extensively by naval intelligence officers about his capture, imprisonment, escape, evasion, and rescue. A team from Washington, D.C., administered a polygraph examination. Also, Dieter told close friends that at one point in the debriefing he was "injected with sodium Pentothal," considered a truth serum. What the scrutiny was all about, Hill explained to Dieter, was that the navy wanted to be certain there had been no misconduct on his part during his imprisonment.

Two years earlier, Hill had been the public affairs officer assigned to another U.S. Navy pilot, Lieutenant Charles F. Klusmann, a photo reconnaissance pilot shot down during a mission over Laos, who escaped from the Pathet Lao in August 1964 after two months of captivity. Klusmann spent two days in the jungle and then safely reached a government camp, where he was eventually picked up by U.S. forces. The "glory of his escape," Hill explained, had been "tarnished a bit" when it was revealed that Klusmann, during his captivity, had signed a statement "condemning U.S. operations in Vietnam and Laos."

Dieter was asked repeatedly whether he had signed a confession or any other statement for his captors. Dieter kept giving assurances he had not, although he had been pressured to do so and tortured when he refused. Another issue was that Dieter had carried civilian identification, but given the fact that he was German-born and could have used such identification to explain his accent, this was not seen as a major problem, even when his passport ended up in Moscow, where the state-run newspaper *Pravda* called him "a West German military officer serving in American disguise." At the conclusion of Dieter's lengthy debriefing, it was determined there had been "no misconduct" on his part during his imprisonment. Dieter proved to be "the genuine hero that the navy had hoped for."

Hill and Dieter flew to the Bay Area and were at dockside on August 24 when *Ranger* returned to Alameda after eight months overseas. Besides that trip, Dieter also made a few unauthorized excursions from the hospital. Most notably, he climbed down a fire escape one evening and was not back until the wee hours. The next morning, Hill "practically cut [his] throat" shaving when a local news radio station reported: "Navy escapee slips out of the hospital and ends up dancing with the girls at a go-go bar."

He rushed to the hospital and "read the riot act" to a grinning and unrepentant Dieter.

Dieter finally faced the national press on September 13, 1966, at a press conference held in a banquet room of the officers club at the Naval Air Station, North Island. For his official coming out, the navy had his mother and his brother Klaus flown in from Germany a few days earlier. Their reunion had been tearful and joyous.

Sitting behind a draped banquet table with a battery of microphones and television cameras staring him in the face, Dieter was dressed in crisp tropical whites with his wings of gold pinned above his left breast pocket. He was tanned, handsome, and the picture of health. In the seven weeks since his rescue, he had gained back forty-five pounds.

After being introduced by a senior officer as a "dauntless naval aviator," Dieter looked out at the roomful of print, radio, and television reporters, photographers, and cameramen behind whirring film cameras set up on tripods. "You know, I have been through some terrifying experiences, but

Dieter at the press conference in San Diego, September 13, 1966. At left, public affairs officer Gaylord "Hap" Hill. *U.S. Navy.*

since it is my first experience with the press I am kind of frightened right now. But I am happy to be here." He beamed at the audience. "Man, it's great to be alive and free. I tell you in our moment of desperation, Lieutenant Martin and I decided we would rather die free in the bushes than die at the communists' hands."

In his opening remarks, Dieter thanked Skip Cowell and his rescue helicopter crew, and Spad pilot Gene Deatrick, who "saved my life." About Deatrick, he said, "It was a miracle he spotted me. . . . He may not know it, but he has a great friend for life."

Smiling, Dieter said, "I guess the sooner we get to the questions, the sooner I can get back to the business of flying again."

Jerry Dunphy, a popular news anchor for KNX-TV in Los Angeles, who had been a pilot in World War II, asked: "How did you manage to escape where all the others failed? How do you explain it?"

"I was in the prison the shortest time and maybe I was physically the most able to do so. And my previous background in Germany and naval survival school both helped me do the job."

"What do you mean by 'previous background'?" Dunphy asked.

"I grew up during the war and it was a matter of taking care of yourself, and this did a lot for me. . . . I was able to stand on my own feet."

Pierce Abbott of ABC News asked, "Could you describe to us how Lieutenant Martin was killed?"

Dieter bowed his head momentarily. He knew what he would say, and what he would not say. "We were crawling along on our hands and knees, and all of a sudden somebody jumped out of the bush about twenty feet away, yelling, 'Americali.' He was swinging a machete, and he just started chopping away, and he hit my friend in the leg and then—I turned around and started running." Dieter was not going to give any more details before he had a chance to meet and sit down with Duane's family and tell them everything they wanted to know.

In his answers, Dieter went into graphic details about his own captivity—beaten and tortured, staked out on the ground, hung upside down, dragged by a water buffalo, locked in foot blocks and handcuffs, barely subsisting on scraps of maggot-infested food and resorting to eating rats, snakes, and "anything that crawled."

John Dancy of NBC News homed in on a sensitive area, which Dieter was prepared for after being briefed at length by navy officials. "Were you bombing in North Vietnam or Laos?"

"My target was in North Vietnam," Dieter said.

The way to explain his escape from Laos when the U.S. military was not supposed to be in Laos, the Pentagon had decided, was to claim that Dieter's target had been in North Vietnam, close to the border with Laos, and that after his plane was hit he had crashed in nearby Laos, where he was taken prisoner.

Dancy asked Dieter to describe his escape, which he did.

"What happened to the other men, besides Lieutenant Martin, who escaped with you?" Dancy asked.

"I really don't know, sir."

Dieter was asked what the future might hold for him.

"Well, in prison, all we talked about was food." His smile was now bright enough to light up the room. "We talked about deep freezes and refrigerators, stacking the food up. I decided I am coming back home and I'm going to start a restaurant, a German-type restaurant, and I'm going to stack the food up and never be hungry again."

Hill observed from his seat at the end of the table that all the reporters, even the most seasoned newshounds, were "almost stunned by the story." Dieter was the longest-held American to escape from captivity in the Vietnam War, and this fact itself made for a gripping headline and story. But Hill knew it was more than the tale of a POW's escape. Dieter's story was about an "incredible test and triumph of human spirit and tenacity." As Dieter held the press corps spellbound with his story, Hill understood that Dieter was about to be transformed into not only the most popular military man to return from Vietnam, but the "national hero" that a "hungry country" needed.

The impact of Dieter's story was confirmed when Hill was handed a note soon after the press conference—which had been broadcast live on national radio and television—that Dieter was being summoned by U.S. Senator Richard B. Russell Jr. (D-Georgia), the powerful chairman of the Senate Armed Services Committee, for an appearance before the committee in two days.

Dieter was "surprised by all the attention" he was getting and seemed to feel his story "wasn't a big deal." Hill noted Dieter's "modesty" in talking about his escape and survival; Dieter described his successes as "just doing his job as a navy pilot." Whenever anyone asked Dieter how it felt to be a hero, he was quick to say he didn't think of himself as a hero: "Only dead people are heroes." That attitude, Hill knew, would serve Dieter well personally, not just publicly.

The next day, Dieter and his ever-present escort, Hap Hill, were walking in the corridors of the Pentagon. Word had spread that the dashing navy pilot who had been on television and radio and whose escape and rescue had made headlines across the country was in the building. At almost every office they passed people emerged to shake Dieter's hand and congratulate him. In the office of an assistant secretary of defense, Dieter was instructed as to how he would handle his appearance before the Senate committee.

On their way out of the Pentagon, Dieter and Hill stopped at a shoe-shine parlor. The bootblack working on Dieter's shoes looked up casually after a few minutes, and then with a startled expression exclaimed, "Ain't you the one who escaped from the Cong?"

Dieter smiled and nodded.

The bootblack began snapping the cloth across Dieter's shoes with new gusto. "Man, you gonna get a shine better than Mr. McNamara's!"

In the morning, they took a cab to the Senate office building for the hearing. Dieter was seated alone at a table before the elevated seats of the committee members, with Hill directly behind him.

Senator Russell, one of the most senior members of the Senate, called the hearing to order, saying he had been advised there were areas that would be inappropriate to discuss in public session: first, disclosure of information about "military operations that would jeopardize the lives of any of our fighting men"; second, details concerning the other prisoners in the camp, "except that other gallant American, Duane Martin"; third, tactics and techniques that Dieter had applied to elude his captors.

Russell went on: "The Chair believes that all of us who love this country and who are proud of the competence and dedication of those serving in our armed forces have been impressed and thrilled by the accounts of the extraordinary experiences of Navy Lt. (jg) Dieter Dengler during his imprisonment after his aircraft was shot down while attacking a target in North Vietnam." Russell was a longtime U.S. senator from Georgia, and as head of the Armed Services Committee he certainly knew that Dieter's real target was in Laos, and that U.S. planes had been bombing there for some time.

He continued, "Mr. Dengler was conspicuously courageous in not yielding to torture designed to obtain his signature on untrue statements calculated to reflect unfavorably on the United States. The things that he witnessed and that he endured while a prisoner, and in escaping his cruel captors, and finding a way back to a point of rescue, are ghastly and gruesome. While it is difficult to portray vividly the difficulties he overcame, it is not hard to express our admiration of his dauntless conduct, and I, for one, am proud to see that it was again demonstrated that the spirit of a courageous man is unquenchable.

"The Chair requested Mr. Dengler's appearance here this morning only after being assured that his doctors gave their approval, and in looking at him, as laymen, you can understand why they did. In inviting him here I had two motivations: One, the Chair thought that Mr. Dengler's conduct was deserving of the widest possible publicity and the warmest admiration; and, two, the Chair believes that by hearing firsthand of his experiences we may gain valuable information about the nature of the forces with which we are engaged in southeast Asia, the support they receive, and their motivations; I say, parenthetically, that Mr. Dengler is an American by choice instead of by birth."

Invited to make a statement, Dieter kept it short, pointing out that this was his first trip to Washington. "My friend, Air Force Lt. Duane Martin, spent hours in the prison camp telling me about U.S. history and government procedures. I am truly delighted to be here and see our Congress in action."

Then the questioning began, with Dieter—"his charming self," Hill thought—enthralling another tough audience.

The next morning's *Washington Post* reported:

PILOT WINS APPLAUSE OF SENATE UNIT
BY JOHN MAFFRE
Washington Post Staff Writer

Sept. 17—A young Navy pilot drew a rare standing ovation yesterday after telling a televised hearing of the Senate Armed Services Committee how he survived six months of captivity in Southeast Asia.

"You don't know what freedom is until you have escaped from Communist capture," Lt. (jg) Dieter Dengler, 28, said in a lingering German accent. "I'm German-born but I'm 100 per cent American."

Sen. Margaret Chase Smith (R-Maine) urged the Navy to tell Dengler's story throughout the nation.

"It's important that all Americans should know it," she said.

Newly promoted Lt. Dieter Dengler with chestful of medals. *U.S. Navy.*

Dieter was discharged from the hospital on October 7, 1966.

The next day, he and Marina eloped to Reno. During the ceremony at the Park Wedding Chapel, she switched the gold band he had worn throughout his ordeal from his right to his left hand.

On November 1, 1966, in a ceremony attended by hundreds of guests aboard the carrier *Kitty Hawk* (CVA-63), Vice Admiral Thomas F. Connelly bestowed four medals on Dieter: the Purple Heart, the Distinguished Flying Cross, an Air Medal, and the Navy Cross—the navy's second-highest medal for combat heroism, second only to the Medal of

Honor. After reading aloud the Navy Cross citation, the admiral added: "I've heard the story in the fullest detail and I can say that this citation is a masterpiece of understatement."

THE SECRETARY OF THE NAVY
WASHINGTON

**The President of the United States
takes pleasure in presenting the**

NAVY CROSS

to

Lieutenant (Junior Grade) Dieter Dengler
UNITED STATES NAVAL RESERVE

for service as set forth in the following citation

For extraordinary heroism during an extremely daring escape from a prisoner-of-war stockade on 30 June 1966. Playing a key role in planning, preparing for, and developing an escape and evasion operation involving several fellow prisoners and himself, Lieutenant (jg) Dengler, keenly aware of the hazardous nature of the escape attempt, boldly initiated the operation and contributed in large measure to its success. When an unplanned situation developed while the escape operation was being executed, he reacted with the highest degree of valor and gallantry. Through his courageous and inspiring fighting spirit, Lieutenant (jg) Dengler upheld the highest traditions of the United States Naval Service.

Epilogue

The navy taught Dieter how to fly jets, which weren't nearly as much fun for him as Spads. After spending a year and a half attached to a utility squadron at Miramar Naval Air Station in California flying A-4 Skyhawks—there was "no chance" the navy would have ever sent its most famous escaped POW back into combat—Dieter completed his military obligation in February 1968, and reentered civilian life.

Dieter soon made good on his declaration that he would "never be hungry again," and bought a German-style restaurant near the top of Mount Tamalpais in Marin County north of San Francisco. On the menu of Mountain Home Inn, where one could dine outside on a sunny cobblestone patio overlooking the picturesque bay and its bridges, were all the specialties he loved: bratwurst, schnitzel, spaetzle, German pot roast, and goulash.

Marina and Dieter stayed married for four years. She was a "dedicated career woman," focused on becoming a marine biologist. For his part, Dieter chafed at domestic routine—"buying furniture, having newspapers delivered and all the don'ts that come with marriage." They gave each other their freedom in 1970, divorcing amicably without having had any children.

Dieter resided for a while with his brother, Martin, and Martin's wife, Elaine, in Pacifica, near San Francisco. Dieter told his story of escape and survival in riveting detail to school classes and assemblies, Rotary Clubs, military groups, and anyone else who invited him to speak. At Dieter's urging, the neighborhood kids would collect an assortment of worms and bugs. Sitting on the front porch, Dieter would sort through them, pointing out ones that were similar to those he ate in the jungle. Then he would plop them, one by one, into his mouth, chew pensively, and swallow. Martin once saw Dieter bite into a nasty-looking black bug with a hard shell, then proclaim to the shocked young onlookers, "This one is the best! Get me more!"

Feeling at home atop Mount Tamalpais—in Laos he had always found it better to be "at the top of the mountain than the bottom"—Dieter bought an empty lot next to his restaurant and eventually built a 1,700-square-foot house with his own labor. Hidden beneath the kitchen floorboards was a storage area where he kept 1,000 pounds of rice, 1,200 pounds of flour, 300 pounds of honey, 200 pounds of sugar, and other provisions. He knew he would probably never need his emergency supply, but he found he "slept so much better knowing it's there."

Eventually struck with wanderlust, Dieter sold his restaurant and applied to the airlines. Taking a physical for TWA, he was asked to read a long list of medical ailments and mark yes or no as to whether he had ever had them. He placed a mark in the yes column for almost everything. When the doctor came into the examination room, he said it was obvious Dieter had put the checkmarks in the wrong column. "I've had all those things," Dieter said. "You see, when I was a POW in Laos—" TWA hired Dieter anyway. He flew for ten years as a flight engineer on a Boeing 707. Taking advantage of his bachelorhood and an airline travel pass, Dieter saw the world. He would come off an incoming flight he had worked and stroll down the terminal at San Francisco International Airport, looking to see what flights were leaving for exotic destinations. Often, he hopped aboard an outgoing flight without bothering to go home.

He returned more than once to speak to the staff and students—mostly navy pilots—at the SERE command in San Diego, not only about his escape but also about the lessons he had learned regarding survival. He hoped to pass those lessons on to other pilots who one day might find themselves down in hostile country.

On a return trip to Germany, nearly twenty years after he had left, Dieter looked up his former boss, Mr. Perrot, who had been so tyrannical. Perrot wanted Dieter to know that he had passed his final test and had received his highest grade from Perrot himself. He apologized to Dieter for treating the apprentices so badly, saying he felt he needed to "rule with an iron hand" because the boys of that generation were growing up under such difficult circumstances during and after the war. But if he had it to do over again, the old blacksmith said he would "do it differently." He asked for Dieter's forgiveness. A moved Dieter thanked him—for his disciplined training, and for helping Dieter become more capable, self-reliant, and, yes, "tough enough to survive." Without those qualities embedded in him at an early age, Dieter told Perrot, he "wouldn't be standing here now."

An inveterate adventurer, Dieter had numerous close calls with death— "ten, at least," by his count. He crashed his restored Stearman biplane in Idaho while doing an outside loop, considered one of the most dangerous aerobatic maneuvers. He crashed a helicopter, which "disintegrated" on impact, a couple of motorcycles, and a Jet Ski in the California delta (an accident in which he nearly drowned when he became trapped under a houseboat). Miraculously, he always "walked away without a scratch." His mother, who prayed fervently for him while he was missing in the war, proclaimed, "It was God's will." She always told Dieter there were "lots of good spirits trying to protect him."

On his world travels, he returned often to Southeast Asia, including Vietnam, Cambodia, Thailand, and Laos, where he joined an organized trip in the late 1970s seeking information about POWs still unaccounted for. In spite of his own history in the region, he came to love the area and its people. He had seen, from closer up than most Americans—"the suffering of the villagers" during the war. He would come to regret that he was "sucked into a system" that resulted in so many lost lives on both sides.

All he had ever wanted to do was to fly, since that moment as a young boy when his heart first lifted to the skies. He had wanted to be the pilot he had seen from the window as a child, flying through the sky with such abandon and freedom. It did not occur to him until much later that he had become not only that pilot, but the bomber as well. He had "never wanted to bomb people," precisely because he had "seen it up close" in Germany. He came to believe that the justification for U.S. intervention in Southeast Asia—to stop the spread of Communism—was flawed, and that the war itself was a terrible waste of lives. Although Dieter was not one to back down from a just fight and would have defended his home and new homeland, he would, for the remainder of his life, be "against war—any war."

Dieter went to a VA-145 reunion in Washington, D.C., in 2000, and enjoyed seeing the guys with whom he had flown. He was spotted over in a corner, speaking with his old antagonist, Ken Hassett. In a group picture taken later that evening, Hassett has an arm around Dieter's shoulders. Both men are smiling.

That same year Dieter was diagnosed with amyotrophic lateral sclerosis (ALS), also known as Lou Gehrig's disease. Realistic about his prognosis—he was experiencing a "rapid onset" of the disease—Dieter got busy remodeling his mountaintop home to suit his future needs. He built a lift from the living room to the upstairs bedroom, and ripped out the tub in the bathroom and made a shower that he would be able to roll himself into when he became wheelchair bound. He laid down plywood over the wall-to-wall carpet so he could roll easily from room to room.

After a second marriage and divorce, Dieter was now married to his third wife, Yukiko Ichihashi, a former United Airlines flight attendant of Japanese descent, with whom he seemed to enjoy the happiest years of his life. Dieter refused to wait for the inevitable. The couple flew to Europe; took a four-week motor-home trip through Washington, Idaho, and Montana; and sent Christmas cards with a picture of themselves on a deserted beach in Thailand. They kept going for as long as they could. Toward the end, Dieter told Yukiko how sorry he was that their time together was so short—as it turned out, only a little more than two years. But those years were filled with so much living—the joyous and unpredictable variety that followed Dieter around as if he had a special claim to it—that Yukiko told him they had "equaled what it takes some people twenty years to do and see." She later explained: "Dieter was like a shooting star. All of a sudden he came into my life, then disappeared. Every day with him was a gift."

Dieter had a request of his old buddy, Lizard Lessard, who stopped by for a visit. Dieter wanted to take a flight in his Cessna 182 that he kept parked at a nearby airfield. He would have to be lifted in and out of the plane, Dieter explained. That Lizard did, but once behind the controls, Dieter took over. With Lizard handling the radio because Dieter was becoming increasingly difficult to understand, they took off. They flew all afternoon. Dieter, the pilot, was in the sky that he so loved. It was his last flight.

As the end came near, Dieter lost the ability to eat or speak coherently (only Yukiko could still understand him). He feared ending up "a vegetable," and told Yukiko that he felt "trapped like a tiger in a cage." It was worse than being in prison camp in Laos, he let her know, because this time he couldn't get out. In an e-mail to a friend, typed with the one or two fingers he could still move, Dieter wrote: "I have looked death in the eye, so it is easier for me to handle."

Early on the morning of February 7, 2001, a few months shy of the thirty-fifth anniversary of his escape from Laos, Dieter decided it was time to make his final escape. Yukiko helped dress him in a black long-sleeve shirt, a blue sleeveless vest, blue corduroy trousers, brown socks, and slippers. After he and Yukiko made their farewells, and without her assistance, he guided his electric wheelchair out the front door.

Alone, he rolled down his driveway and out onto Panoramic Highway, deserted at that hour. Three hundred feet up the hill was a fire station. He went into the driveway of the station and stopped. Bringing the barrel of a blue-steel revolver to his mouth, he pulled the trigger.

Dieter was buried on a cool day in March 2001 at Arlington, with full military honors, complete with a horse-drawn caisson, escort platoon, a colors team and band, a firing party, a bugler, and a flyover of U.S. Navy jets in the traditional missing-man formation for a lost pilot.

Postscript

Dieter Dengler's last thirty-five years were a gift.

He had no business surviving his ordeal as a POW. By rights, he should not have made it out of the Laotian jungle, and deep down, he knew this. That death-defying experience strongly shaped his later life. Although it was not the kind of thing he ruminated about, the proof is there: those who knew Dieter agree that no one stuffed as much living into every hour of every day as he did. "One thought is with me always," he often said. "That I am alive and a free man."

Alive and free is how Dieter lived those extra thirty-five years.

Dramatis Personae

ADAMICH, MARINA. Fiancée and later wife (from 1966 to 1970) of Dieter Dengler. Marina received her MA from California State University, San Francisco, and her PhD, in 1976, from the University of California, Santa Barbara, where she taught for several years in the department of biological sciences. Her thesis was a study of "how membranes are involved in telling time in an organism." She later taught in the department of chemistry at Atlanta University (now Clark Atlanta University). The doctors treating Dieter in 1966 advised him to "get back to normal life and not dwell on what he had experienced," but Marina believes he "probably had all the problems and even worse" of what is now routinely diagnosed as post-traumatic stress disorder (PTSD). "He didn't suppress things, and tried to live with them. He was very outgoing, a social-type person, not one to sit and be reflective." Marina had a happy second marriage to a fellow scientist, Dr. Robert Saltman, who died in 2003, after "some wonderful years together." Marina is retired and lives in rural Oregon.

BUMGARNER, WALT "BUMMY." VA-145 Spad pilot. After the *Ranger* cruise, Bumgarner became a flight instructor. He ended up making four WestPac cruises, the last two as catapult and arresting officer on the carrier *Hancock* (CVA-19). After leaving the navy in 1974, he enrolled in crop-dusting school. He eventually owned five crop dusters, and made "good money as long as the environmentalists allowed us." Harking back to the life insurance policy (with no war exclusion) proposed by Dieter that named five bachelors, two of whom—Gary Hopps and John Tunnell—were killed on the cruise, Bummy thinks the premium of $1,800 per man would have been a very good investment; he, Dieter, and Dave Maples would have split $2 million, had the idea not been quashed by the wives of senior officers who thought it "ghoulish." Bummy sold his last aircraft in 1990. Since then he has been a real estate broker in Moses Lake, Washington, where he lives with his wife, Margaret. He misses flying.

COWELL, WILLIAM "SKIP." Captain, U.S. Air Force; Jolly Green Giant helicopter pilot. Five months after rescuing Dieter, Cowell was sent stateside to train other helicopter pilots and work with defense contractors in developing equipment for use in "the real world" of Vietnam. He retired in 1974 after twenty years in the air force, with the rank of lieutenant colonel. Thereafter he and his wife, Rita, moved to the state of Washington, where they bought an apple and pear orchard and became "instant farmers." They are now coffee farmers on the island of Hawaii, where they own ten acres, along with eighty chickens "for bug control." Cowell's only helicopter crash occurred two years before he went to Vietnam, a short distance off Waikiki Beach.

DEATRICK, EUGENE P. Lieutenant colonel, U.S. Air Force; commanding officer, 1st Air Commando Squadron, Pleiku Air Base, South Vietnam. The Spad pilot who spotted Dieter on the river in southern Laos retired from the air force in 1974 with the rank of colonel. Deatrick has long marveled at the fact that had he stuck to his original flight schedule on the morning of July 20, 1966, Dieter would not have been at the river to be sighted at that earlier hour. "If God put me on earth for one reason," Deatrick says, "it was to find Dieter over there in the jungle." As it was, Deatrick describes it as "a million-in-one chance." As Dieter predicted even before meeting Deatrick, he and his rescuer became friends for life.

DEBRUIN, EUGENE "GENE." Air America cargo kicker, prisoner of war in Laos, former Montana smoke jumper. After escaping with his Chinese friend, To Yick Chiu (Y.C.), DeBruin was never seen again, although his family has long sought evidence of his survival. A transcript of a 1971 CIA interview with a source states that the two escapees were probably "killed in the area a few days" after their escape.

DENGLER, MARTIN. Dieter's younger brother. Designated at the age of five by their grandfather to become a baker even though he wanted to "drive trains," Martin has worked as a baker since arriving in America a couple of years after Dieter. Martin owned his own bakery in Santa Rosa, California, for a number of years, and still bakes daily. His and Dieter's older brother, Klaus, still lives in Germany; as a young boy, Klaus showed a talent for music and became a symphonic violinist. Their mother, Maria, died in 1992, at age seventy-two.

INTHARATHAT, PHISIT (aka Pisidi Indradat). Two days after the escape from Ban Hoeui Het prison camp, Intharathat separated from the other two Thai prisoners, Prasit Promsuwan and Prasit Thanee, and continued on his own. The other two Thai were never seen again. After thirty-two days in the jungle, Intharathat was recaptured. He was taken to a Laotian prison camp that held a large number of Royalist Lao pro-western POWs, but no Americans or Thai. On January 7, 1967, a CIA-backed rescue plan succeeded in freeing fifty-three prisoners, including Intharathat. He resides today in Bangkok, Thailand.

JOHNS, MALCOLM "SPOOK." VA-145 Spad pilot. After being sent home from the *Ranger* cruise following his wheels-up emergency landing, Spook flew for the airlines. He admits he isn't "real proud" of his record as a naval officer. Although he is proud of "the way I flew Spads," it always bothered him that he was sent home early. Forty years later, his former CO, Hal Griffith, called to apologize. "I'm sorry about what happened. You were our best pilot." Spook expressed his "heartfelt thanks" for Griffith's "kind words." Spook and his wife, Britt, live in Minnesota.

LESSARD, NORM "LIZARD." VA-145 Spad pilot. When Dieter returned to *Ranger*, Lizard informed him that he owed several hundred dollars for electronics, camera gear, and other items Lizard had bought for him in Japan and elsewhere. Dieter was delighted to make good on the purchases. After two wartime WestPac cruises and two others to the Mediterranean, Lizard retired from the navy in 1985 as a lieutenant commander. He worked for Hughes Aircraft, and later Raytheon, marketing flight simulators for training pilots. He remained a lifelong friend of Dieter's. He lives in Sanford, Florida, with his wife, Cindy, and volunteers for hospice and raises funds for Habitat for Humanity.

MARTIN, DORCAS. Widow of U.S. Air Force Captain Duane Martin. Shortly after his discharge from the naval hospital in San Diego, Dieter traveled to Denver, Colorado, and met with Dorcas, her parents, and Duane's parents to tell them about Duane's last months. The trauma of losing her husband—who had been her college sweetheart—in the war changed Dorcas's life. She was able to remain "high functioning" in raising their two young daughters, Cheryl and Christine, through the formative years, but thereafter she "deteriorated," according to her brother, Chuck Haines, and "fell deeper into psychotic states." She went from a "vibrant, active, fun person on her wedding day," her brother says, to what she is today: "institutionalized, and as much a casualty of the Vietnam War" as Duane, whose remains have never been identified. (The three other crew members of Duane's downed helicopter, captured by North Vietnamese troops shortly after the crash, were taken to Hanoi where they were held as POWs until 1973, when they were returned to the U.S. with other American POWs under the terms of the Paris Peace Agreement. No Americans taken prisoners in Laos by the Pathet Lao were ever released.)

USS *RANGER* (CVA-61). In the fall of 1966, *Ranger* was awarded a Navy Unit Commendation for "exceptional meritorious service" while participating in combat operations in Southeast Asia from January to August 1966, and the Arleigh Burke Fleet Trophy for having shown the most improvement in battle efficiency that year. The *Forrestal*-class supercarrier served in the U.S. Navy from 1957 to 1993. Currently docked in Bremerton, Washington, it is awaiting conversion into a museum ship to be located on the harbor of Portland, Oregon. When it is opened to the public as a floating education center, museum, and memorial, *Ranger* will have on its broad deck a plaque honoring its most famous Spad pilot and former POW: Dieter Dengler.

Source Notes

Complete book publication details are supplied in the bibliography. U.S. Navy ship and unit records such as deck logs, action reports, and war diaries are available at the National Archives II, College Park, Maryland. Other naval documents, such as oral and command histories, communications, and debriefings, are collected at the Naval Historical Center's Operational Archives, and documents relating to naval aviation (1911–present) are available at the Aviation History branch, both located in the Washington, D.C., Navy Yard. Vietnam-era MIA/POW files of the Central Intelligence Agency are located in the Federal Research Division of the Library of Congress. Military personnel records are accessed at the National Personnel Records Center, St. Louis, Missouri. The "Dengler Debriefing," a seventy-eight-page Pacific Fleet/Fleet Intelligence Center document, was obtained following the author's Freedom of Information Act request to the commander in chief of the U.S. Pacific Fleet, Pearl Harbor. The author conducted interviews with Dieter Dengler in 1997 and 1998, and with other individuals from 2007 through 2009.

AUTHOR'S NOTE

xi   "turning point of the war": H. Griffin Mumford obituary, *San Francisco Chronicle*, July 20, 2007.

xi   "most due to": Bowden, *Tales to Noses over Berlin*, p. 17.

xii   "for heroic or meritorious": www.airmedal.org.

xiii   "deep regret": Secretary of War telegram, March 16, 1944.

xiii   "Bob was missing": Jack T. Bradley letter, April 12, 1944.

xiv   "oscillating more-or-less . . . at least 100 feet": Statement of David B. O'Hara, March 4, 1944, in Missing Air Crew Report, March 10, 1944.

xviii*n.*   "made piloting a jet": Grant, *Over the Beach*, p. 129.

CHAPTER 1   "BORN A GYPSY"

1   "under penalty of death": Dieter Dengler interview.

1–2   Conversation between Maria Dengler and SS officer: Dieter and Martin Dengler interviews.

2–4   "born a Gypsy" . . . "an eye on" . . . "talked to all": Martin Dengler interview.

4   Conversation between Maria Schnuerle and Reinhold Dengler: Ibid.

5–6   "Who the hell" . . . "rock refinery" . . . "Now I have" . . . "Since I only" . . . "I'm not fighting" . . . "I may not" . . . "Let's take" . . . "now in God's" . . . "there cannot": Dieter and Martin Dengler interviews.

6–7   "tie the boys" . . . "like an Almighty" . . . "little Dieter" . . . "an entire cartridge": Dengler interview.

7   "ground erupted" . . . "deafening booms": Dengler, *Escape from Laos*, p. 3.

7–8   "Everything is gone" . . . "God's gift" . . . "a million pieces": Martin Dengler interview.

8   "You and the boys" . . . "resettled": Dengler interview.

10   "like a conquering" . . . "wide-eyed and": Dengler, *Escape from Laos*, p. 4.

11   "rolling down" . . . "a herd" . . . "Martin, you go": Martin Dengler interview.

11   "nutrients in the": Dengler interview.

11–12   "the most difficult" . . . "never give up" . . . "the hero of Calw" . . . "nothing getting past" . . . "hero to a" . . . "drive railroad": Martin Dengler interview.

12   "Cold and hungry" . . . "first lesson": Dengler, *Escape from Laos*, p. 5.

12–13   "calloused hands" . . . "We Need Men" . . . "interrupted a hundred": Dieter Dengler, *Escape from Laos*, draft manuscript, c. 1977.

14–15   "nearly froze" . . . "America needs" . . . "all night long" . . . "slave labor": Ibid.

15   "three times to" . . . "the biggest gangster": Martin Dengler interview.

CHAPTER 2   AMERICA

17   "*Auf Wiedersehen*" . . . "had news" . . . "era had come" . . . "strange American" . . . "heaving for" . . . "the most beautiful": Dengler, *Escape from Laos*, draft.

18–19   "You'll end up" . . . "No food allowed" . . . "whole new world" . . . "Will I be" . . . "You will": Dengler interview.

19   "conned" . . . "no way out" . . . "never saw a" . . . "deceiving pictures": Dengler, *Escape from Laos*, draft.

19–20 "every airman should" . . . "surrounded by shooters" . . . "allowed and encouraged": "Sharpshooters from the Wild Blue Yonder," *American Rifle*, January 1985.

21 "more interested" . . . "like corned": Dengler interview.

21 "indiscriminate eater": Mike Grimes interview.

22–25 "fantastic shot" . . . "played survival games" . . . "Martin, what would" . . . "People are chasing" . . . "From Dieter" . . . "This must be" . . . "I like your" . . . "If you want" . . . "got really scared" . . . "If they had booked" . . . "More push-ups!" . . . "Don't *ever*" . . . "I've been watching" . . . "dropped wires down" . . . "My brother is" . . . "This is the same" . . . "flunking to 100 percent" . . . "kind of saved": Martin Dengler interview.

25 "Honorable Dismissal Granted": Permanent Record, City College of San Francisco, February 13, 1963.

26–27 "full of life" . . . "a doctor or" . . . "maybe once" . . . "survived on his" . . . "people magnet" . . . "You couldn't help" . . . "You can bring" . . . "We should be": Grimes interview.

28 "My Volksy is" . . . "Volksy running good": Ibid.

28 "lots of spirit": James Love interview.

29 "popped his head" . . . "a nice icebreaker" . . . "break anything open": Clifford Hoffman interview.

29 "gregarious and innovative": Ann Ryan interview.

CHAPTER 3 TRAINING FOR FLIGHT

31–34 "screaming and yelling" . . . "get guys to" . . . "not one grain" . . . "no hardship" . . . "all fun" . . . "Made a hole" . . . "*Links*" . . . "anyone else would": Dengler interview.

36 "shockingly uncomfortable": Walt Bumgarner interview.

36 "loving every minute": Dengler, *Escape from Laos*, draft.

37 "believe the instruments" . . . "calling the ball": Bumgarner interview.

40 "violent collision" . . . "like a high-speed": Hirschman and Hirschman, *She's Just Another Navy Pilot*, p. 32.

40 "big choice": Bumgarner interview.

42 "carry everything but": Heinemann and Rausa, *Ed Heinemann*, p. 135.

42 "typically cocky Spad" . . . "sleek jets everyday" . . . "Hell, everyone drives": *Navy Magazine*, December 1969.

42 "style and derring-do": Dorr, *Skyraider*, p. 81.

42–43 "first come" . . . "made one beeline": Dengler interview.

44–45 "taxi and abort" . . . "Now jam the": Bumgarner interview.

45–46 "the right leg thing" . . . "That was scary" . . . "pure undisciplined behavior" . . . "good navy pilot" . . . "pretty sharp": Doug Haines interview.

47 "the fastest roller": Hirschman and Hirschmann, *She's Just Another Navy Pilot*, p. 32.

47 "some of hers" . . . "167 degrees off" . . . "stable and steady" . . . "like the wild" . . . "Dieter's mind": Haines interview.

49 "go hunting for": Ibid.

50–51 "pretty miserable" . . . "lumps of coal" . . . "Who's that" . . . "Dieter Dengler" . . . "one size too": Tom Dixon interview.

51–52 "I've got a knife" . . . "Okay" . . . "Take off your": Ibid.

52 "such things to": Harold Griffith interview.

52 "gained three pounds" . . . "everything the guards": Dengler Debriefing, Pacific Fleet/Fleet Intelligence Center, October 5, 1966, p. 64.

52 "in a class" . . . "exasperating" . . . "loved his successes" . . . "astounded and amazed": Dave Maples interview.

52 "make his name": Dixon interview.

CHAPTER 4   THE SWORDSMEN

54–55 "too dangerous" . . . "Okay, you take" . . . "I'll get rid" . . . "Get on my" . . . "buying the farm": Bumgarner interview.

56 "three rounds to warn": Robert J. Hanok, "Skunks, Bogies, Silent Hounds, and the Flying Fish: The Gulf of Tonkin Mystery, 2–4 August 1964," *Cryptologic Quarterly* 19, no. 4/20, no. 1 (Winter 2000/Spring 2001).

57–58 "fleet up" . . . "some problems" . . . "west coast war" . . . "water targets": Griffith interview.

58 "wild evasive maneuvers": Hanok, "Skunks, Bogies."

58 "No boats" . . . "no boat wakes": Stockdale and Stockdale, *In Love and War*, p. 23.

59 "ENTIRE ACTION" . . . "COMPLETE EVALUATION" . . . "over-eager" . . . "freak weather": Hanok, "Skunks, Bogies."

60–61 "non-incident" . . . "excuse to go" . . . "did not want" . . . "quietly removed" . . . "practically useless" . . . "very powerful" . . . "looked like World War": Griffith interview.

61 "airborne and heading" . . . *"Four Eleven"*: Homecoming II Project, May 15, 1990.

62 "no target out": Samuel Catterlin interview.

62 "go straight in": Griffith interview.

62 "just what Johnson": *New York Times*, July 7, 2009.

62 "Where's Vietnam" and other dialogue: Dengler interview.

63 "Ensign Dengler has": Report on the Fitness of Officers, VA-122, February 5, 1965.

63 "couldn't shoot" . . . "still be fighting": Griffith interview.

63 "I don't care": Dengler interview.

64 "everyone wanting" . . . "planning for the": Dengler, *Escape from Laos*, draft.

64 "bombing is quite": Malcolm Johns interview.

64–65 "find women and" . . . "Spad drivers" . . . "loud and clear" . . . "jet jocks" . . . "give up the": Norm Lessard interview.

66 "did something wrong" . . . "damn good pilot" . . . "you can't make": Griffith interview.

66 "very sobering": Daniel Farkas interview.

67 "lots of demanding" . . . "a capable pilot" . . . "a mix of ideal": Clarence Armstrong interview.

67–68 "unbuckling and getting" . . . "square peg" . . . "I'm in the" . . . "a band of " . . . "wild man" . . . "like a bunch": Johns interview.

68 "sweated everything": Frank Schelling interview.

68 "find Soviet" . . . "wasn't the greatest": Johns interview.

69 "not be captured" . . . "shoot it out": Dengler Debriefing, p. 11.

69 "the best one": Dengler, *Escape from Laos*, draft.

70 "a wild guy" . . . "started sobering up" . . . "better have fun": Lessard interview.

70 "wear out" . . . "all the hooligans": Don Martin interview.

71 "Why not?" . . . "ghoulish" . . . "kibosh on it": Bumgarner interview.

71–72 "we didn't believe" . . . "too violent" . . . "Who are they" . . . "liked just fine" . . . "You'll get us" . . . "Come on, Spook" . . . "Goddammit, Dieter": Wayne Bennett interview.

73 "young Elizabeth Taylor": Farkas interview.

73 "in one category": Johns interview.

73 "never stopped pursuing": Marina Adamich Saltman interview.

74 "I've wanted to" and other dialogue: Johns interview.

CHAPTER 5   GRAY EAGLE GOES TO WAR

75 "about a foot": Dengler Debriefing, p. 11.

77 "Dieter, are you" . . . "I never miss" . . . "wasn't into getting" . . . "they wouldn't kill" . . . "gear for survival": Farkas interview.

77 "independent, stubborn" . . . "talking or playing" . . . "many hours": Dennis Enstam interview.

80 "managed by fear": Gary Heck interview.

80 "misused and abused": John Moore interview.

80 "famous red MG" . . . "winning many races": *Daily Shield*, June 5, 1966.

80–81 "in the tank" . . . "new guy was" . . . "really caught on" . . . "lots of ideas": Michael McCuddin interview.

81 "like Dear Abby": Sharon McCuddin Henke interview.

81 "The same leopard": *Navy News Magazine*, February 1966.

82 "unexcelled morale": Legion of Merit Citation, Pacific Fleet, 1966.

84 "had the conn": Ship's log, January 12, 1966.

85 "very close watch" . . . "What's the gun" . . . "Pirates": Stewart Hunter interview.

86 "scopes and radios" . . . "electric ozone smell": Robert Montgomery interview.

87–88 "Call the ball" . . . *"Nine Zero One*, no ball" . . . "You're low" . . . *"Nine Zero One*, ball": Radio message from USS *Ranger*, January 16, 1966.

88 "pickle the trigger" . . . "bright and steady": Bumgarner interview.

88 "high and fast" . . . "Bolter!": Radio message, January 16, 1966.

89 "nightmare" . . . "no moon" . . . "just dropping out" . . . "steel hitting steel" . . . "sucking of metal parts": Lawrence Petersen interview.

90 "failed to climb": Bumgarner interview.

90 "Eject, eject!": Radio message, January 16, 1966.

90 "Airplane in the": Bumgarner interview.

90–91 "nice guy" . . . "Let's have a" . . . "Blow the seats": Petersen interview.

92 "all military in": Lessard interview.

92 "methodical and a": Arthur Windsor interview.

92 "loose cannons": Dixon interview.

92 "went to hell" . . . "fired a pod": Dieter Dengler letter, January 27, 1966.

92 "chicken shitting bombs": Farkas interview.

93 "container full of" . . . "frightened of being" . . . "tumble and tumble": Dengler interview.

93 "find some action": Johns interview.

93–94   "enormous bang" . . . "shake and shake" . . . "couldn't hold them":
Dengler interview.

94–95   "to work over" . . . "infected with VC" . . . "straight scoop" . . . "white
shirts": Norman Lessard journal, 1966.

95   "restock and reload" . . . "get ready to": Lessard interview.

96   "shooting like gangbusters" . . . "without saying" . . . "had it out" . . .
"I'm not flying": Dengler letter, January 27, 1966.

96   "If you want": Windsor interview.

96–97   "red-faced" . . . "I could kill" . . . "more of a": Farkas interview.

97   "restricted to the" . . . "sneak out": Dengler letter, January 27, 1966.

97   "not one" . . . "a little reckless": Griffith interview.

97   "led with his": Bumgarner interview.

CHAPTER 6   SHOOTDOWN

99   "armed reconnaissance" . . . "bridges, truck parks": Operational
Briefing Items for Monday, January 31, 1966.

99   "non-incident": Griffith interview.

99–102   *We shouldn't even* . . . "could take hits" . . . "firing back good" . . . "all
kinds of" . . . "no fluid" . . . "I'm going in" . . . "whole world below" . . .
Electron Lead . . . "Skipper, why don't" . . . "just hanging on" . . . "bigger
than a" . . . "might snap" . . . "Let's take it" . . . "really stupid": Bumgarner
interview.

101   "superb airmanship": Silver Star Medal citation (Harold F. Griffith).

102   "lucky to have": Farkas interview.

103   "like an explosion" . . . "just about had" . . . "I have your": Dieter Dengler
letter, January 31, 1966.

103   "scared shitless": Lessard interview.

103–104   "thought that was" . . . "They caught us": Lessard journal.

104   "Low ceilings and": Daily operations briefing, February 1, 1966.

104–105   "not sublime conditions" . . . "two football fields" . . . "quietly went into
the" . . . "swimming toward California": Sylvester Chumley interview.

106   "seemed endless" . . . "easy": Dengler, *Escape from Laos*, draft.

107   "the V.C. were" . . . "got a couple" . . . "all the way" . . . "Like the LSO"
. . . "The public in": Lessard journal.

108   "worth their weight": Lessard interview.

108   "Secure loose": Dengler, *Escape from Laos*, draft.

110   "700 feet in" . . . "impenetrable": Dengler, *Escape from Laos*, p. 9.

110 "deepest green" . . . "murky and yellow" . . . "great flier": Dengler, *Escape from Laos*, draft.

111 "not making career" . . . "pretty well tuned" . . . "Wild animal": Johns interview.

112 "knew something was": Bumgarner interview.

112 "The heck with": Johns interview.

112 "no side tone": Dengler, *Escape from Laos*, p. 10.

113 "like a lightning" . . . "tumbling through the": Dengler interview.

113 "wild gyrations": Dengler, *Escape from Laos*, draft.

113–114 "shiver from nose" . . . "wobbled": Dengler, *Escape from Laos*, p. 11.

115 "boresighted": Ibid., p. 12.

115 "continuous grinding": Dengler Debriefing, p. 13.

116 "stumbling and falling": Dengler, *Escape from Laos*, p. 13.

116–117 *"Zero Four"* . . . "rendezvous circle" . . . *"Electron Five"* . . . "Time to get" . . . "We've got a" . . . "Got our charlie" . . . "by-the-book" . . . "I've got the": Johns interview.

118 "brought up the" . . . "disappeared on purpose" . . . "dropped out of " . . . "just disappear": Griffith interview.

118 "off the wall": Enstam interview.

118 "good way to": Farkas interview.

118–119 "fifty-fifty whether" . . . "go on a" . . . "wasn't out of ": Enstam interview.

119 "a little different" . . . "the end of " . . . "another flying job": Lessard interview.

119 "real cool guy": John McGrath interview.

119–120 "real nose high" . . . "incapacitated in the" . . . "dead before he": Jeff Greenwood interview.

120 "wasn't uptight and" . . . "liked Dieter" . . . "square search": Lessard interview.

123 "nuts enough to" . . . "ditch in the" . . . "could escape from": Farkas interview.

CHAPTER 7   WILL TO SURVIVE

124 "tearing metal": Dengler, *Escape from Laos*, p. 16.

124 "no time for": Dengler interview.

125 "so close": Dengler Debriefing, p. 15.

125 "no sweat" . . . "walk right out" . . . "forgotten all about": Dengler, *Escape from Laos*, draft.

125 "Really, really" . . . "squared away": Dengler Debriefing, p. 14.

125–126 "at least 120" . . . "had it beat" . . . "nearly mad" . . . "bag a helicopter": Dengler, *Escape from Laos*, pp. 16–17.

126 "they'll call in" . . . "within five minutes": Dengler Debriefing, p. 14.

127 "impossible to get": Dieter Dengler, GE Lecture Series, Smithsonian Air and Space Museum, Washington, D.C., March 23, 1989. Hereafter cited as Smithsonian lecture.

128 "staring up" . . . "big, round": Dengler, *Escape from Laos*, draft.

128 "think right away": Dengler Debriefing, p. 15.

128 "tasted wonderful": Dengler, Smithsonian lecture.

129 "about 30 pounds": Dengler Debriefing, p. 15.

129 "so clear" . . . "lay low for" . . . "take a train": Dengler, *Escape from Laos*, draft.

129 "getting familiar": Dengler, Smithsonian lecture.

129 "a miniature waterfall": Dengler, *Escape from Laos*, p. 21.

130–131 "practically tore off " . . . "ready to do" . . . "So happy" . . . "sickening" . . . "middle of nowhere" . . . "deeper in the": Dengler, *Escape from Laos*, draft.

131 "stolen goods": Dengler, *Escape from Laos*, p. 24.

132 "*Yute, yute*": Dengler, Smithsonian lecture.

132 "came alive" . . . "comically": Dengler, *Escape from Laos*, pp. 27–28.

132 "*Nicht schiessen*" . . . "waited for the": Dengler, *Escape from Laos*, draft.

134 "dead by now": Ibid.

134 "real good ears" . . . "stopped dead": Dengler Debriefing, p. 17.

134 "not having the guts": Dengler, *Escape from Laos*, draft.

135–136 "smashed to pieces" . . . "more and more" . . . "drink anything": Dengler interview.

137 "fell most of" . . . "angier and angier" . . . "dirty looks" . . . "*This is to be*": Dengler, *Escape from Laos*, pp. 33–35.

137 "simple, ten-cent": Ibid., p. 43.

137 "out of pure": Ibid., p. 45.

137 "looking for a": Dengler Debriefing, p. 23.

138 "spell in the" . . . "a newfound plaything" . . . "almost happy": Dengler, *Escape from Laos*, pp. 41–42.

138 "like and respect": Ibid., p. 59.

139 "evidently a province": Dengler Debriefing, p. 18.

140 Dialogue between Dengler and the province chief: Dengler, *Escape from Laos*, pp. 55–56.

140   "genuinely good man" . . . "poor mother" . . . "alive and well": Ibid., p. 57.

141   "in good hands": Dengler Debriefing, p. 19.

141–142   Dialogue between Dengler and the province chief: Dengler, *Escape from Laos*, pp. 59–60.

142–143   "one of his" . . . "just short of" . . . "ashamed of his": Ibid., p. 62.

143   "murderous policies": Dengler Debriefing, p. 19.

143   Dialogue between Dieter Dengler and the Laotian province chief: Ibid., pp. 19–20.

143   "blurry feet and": Dengler, *Escape from Laos*, p. 63.

144   "threw it at": Dengler Debriefing, p. 21.

145   "sudden surge of": Dengler, *Escape from Laos*, p. 52.

146   "very heavy sleepers": Dengler Debriefing, p. 22.

146   "fake snoring": Dengler, *Escape from Laos*, p. 69.

146–147   "series of hundreds" . . . "*Americali*": Dengler Debriefing, p. 23.

147   "just beautiful": Dengler, Smithsonian lecture.

147   "dipped a wing": Dengler Debriefing, p. 23.

147–148   "an injection" . . . "vision": Dengler, *Escape from Laos*, p. 74.

148   "brownish, scum-filled": Ibid., p. 75.

148   "drank and": Dengler Debriefing, p. 23.

148   "like a madman" . . . "never known" . . . "as large as" . . . "thousands of" . . . "only numbness": Dengler, *Escape from Laos*, pp. 75–76.

149   "endless night": Ibid., p. 78.

149   "There will be": Dengler, *Escape from Laos*, draft.

CHAPTER 8   "WE'LL RUN OUT OF PILOTS"

150   "Evidence of death": Radio message from USS *Ranger*, February 7, 1966.

151   "rough copy" . . . "Time of Death": Certificate of Death, c. February 1966.

151   "could do anything" . . . "if anyone could": Algimantas Balciunas interview.

152   "There was no": Daniel Farkas journal, 1966.

152   "with pilot fixation" . . . "squared-jawed" . . . "give you the" . . . "Not much": Farkas interview.

153   "in the hopes" . . . "hoping for good" . . . "still no sign" . . . "Still no word": Lessard interview.

153n.   "in the basket": Bumgarner interview.

153–154   "suspected truck" . . . "target of opportunity" . . . "got down really" . . . "hit in the" . . . "straight in" . . . "waste": Dixon interview.

154   "so the navy": Johns interview.

154   "mysteriously" . . . "screws and bolts": Bumgarner interview.

154   "That's two pilots": Lessard journal.

154   "At this rate" . . . "engendered a whole": Farkas interview.

155   "great-sounding": Hunter interview.

155   "Gary and I": Commanding Officer's Comments, Memorial Services, February 12, 1966.

156   "about 12 miles" . . . "nothing firm": Lessard journal.

156   "good guy" . . . "90 percent chance" . . . "running around out": Lessard interview.

CHAPTER 9   PRISONERS OF WAR

157–158   "different breed" . . . "running the show": Dengler interview.

159   "food for the" . . . "long prayer" . . . "construction of bamboo" . . . "filth and blood": Dengler, *Escape from Laos*, draft.

159   "only remaining link": Dengler, *Escape from Laos*, p. 83.

160   "cut up to": Dengler, *Escape from Laos*, draft.

160   "Steve McQueen movie": Dengler, Smithsonian lecture.

161   "down the sights" . . . "dead and deserted": Dengler, *Escape from Laos*, p. 91.

161–162   Dialogue between Dengler and Duane Martin: Ibid., pp. 92–93, and *Escape from Laos*, draft.

162   "Not gonna get": Dengler, *Escape from Laos*, draft.

162   "slamming the door" . . . "Don't worry": Dengler, *Escape from Laos*, p. 93.

162   "Hey, you guys" . . . "Don't be stupid": Dengler, *Escape from Laos*, draft.

164   "just to keep": Dengler, Smithsonian lecture.

164   "by two girls": Dengler Debriefing, p. 61.

164   "Take it easy": Dengler, *Escape from Laos*, p. 95.

165   "no sign or" . . . "in a giant": Phisit Intharathat, "Prisoner in Laos: A Story of Survival, Part I," *Smokejumper*, October 2006.

166   "started to believe": Dengler, *Escape from Laos*, draft.

167   "Are you sure" . . . "Of course" . . . "Well, I'll be": Dengler, *Escape from Laos*, p. 100.

168   "Tell them" . . . "I was alone" . . . "face value" . . . "let off too" . . . "rotting away": Ibid., pp. 102–103.

168   "one percent" . . . "what to do": Dengler Debriefing, p. 62.

169   "could be our": Dengler, *Escape from Laos*, p. 105.

170   "scrape and shape": Intharathat, "Prisoner in Laos: A Story of Survival, Part I."

170   "former ruddy complexion": Dengler, *Escape from Laos*, p. 129.

170   "yet learned to" . . . "wasting it": Ibid., p. 108.

171   "Reverend Duane" . . . "hours and hours" . . . "loved it" . . . "nuts" . . . "get free" . . . "nothing else" . . . "What about chess?": Dengler Debriefing, p. 60.

171   "We're going to" . . . "that little no-good" . . . "lying bastards": Dengler, *Escape from Laos*, p. 110.

172   *"Not this guy!"*: Ibid., p. 113.

173   "religious hard-headedness" . . . "mellowed": Ibid., p. 115.

173   "that's what they're": Dengler, *Escape from Laos*, draft.

174   "crazy" . . . "escape-happy guy": Dengler, *Escape from Laos*, p. 114.

174   "listened and thought": Intharathat, "Prisoner in Laos: A Story of Survival, Part II," *Smokejumper*, January 2007.

174   "Go to hell!" Dengler, *Escape from Laos*, p. 118.

174   "forced to write" . . . "invade Laotian territory" . . . "endured more pain": Intharathat, "Prisoner in Laos: A Story of Survival, Part I."

175   "squeal loud and": Dengler, *Escape from Laos*, p. 132.

175   "except Phisit" . . . "singing to cover": Ibid., p. 115.

176   "little pool" . . . "putting an end": Ibid., p. 116.

176   "didn't know beans": Ibid., p. 126.

176–178   "bark like a" . . . "moving and bubbling" . . . "chowed down" . . . "black and thick" . . . "stunk like heck" . . . "just collapsed": Dengler Debriefing, pp. 49–50.

178   "dizzy all the": Dengler, *Escape from Laos*, p. 127.

178   "much better position": Dengler Debriefing, p. 61.

178   "sweltering in the": Dengler, *Escape from Laos*, p. 117.

178–179   "special favors" . . . "Just leave": Ibid., pp. 125, 126.

179   "kept on going": Dengler interview.

180   "either be free": Dengler, *Escape from Laos*, draft.

180   "That's it!" . . . "even odds": Dengler, *Escape from Laos*, p. 143.

CHAPTER 10   SOUTH CHINA SEA

181   "at almost the": Hobson, *Vietnam Air Losses*, p. 51.

182   "Supposedly he crashed": Ken Woloszyk interview.

182–183   "tight right echelon" . . . "superlative fighter" . . . "glued to the" . . . "not an easy" . . . "extremely good stick" . . . "typical Irish" . . . "a Southie all" . . . "big, blond" . . . "his head buried" . . . "almost certainly" . . . "just covered up" . . . "we are not": Bennett interview.

184   "pissed off" . . . "kept their heads" . . . "You're shooting" . . . "steaming in the" . . . "Oh, my God!" . . . "You couldn't hit": Johns interview.

184   "fit and friendly" . . . "almost movie-star": Ray Hanzlik interview.

184–185   "quick stutter" . . . "rough runner": Johns interview.

185   Dialogue between Malcolm Johns, *Cobra Four*, and John Tunnell: Ibid.

185–186   "eaten up" . . . "curled up" . . . "bunch of ranking" . . . "I don't want": Ibid.

187   "meritorious achievement": Air Medal citation, c. 1966.

187   "borderline of trouble": Bennett interview.

187   "Skipper, Spook" . . . "I told Spook": Johns interview.

189   "couldn't hit shit" . . . "just bubbles" . . . "Launch the Alert": Bumgarner interview.

189   "under a mushroom-shaped" . . . "Target is an": Johns interview.

192   "ludicrous weather" . . . "moon on the": Bumgarner interview.

CHAPTER 11   ESCAPE

194   "so they'll rot": Dengler, *Escape from Laos*, p. 144.

196   "covered up all": Intharathat, "Prisoner in Laos: A Story of Survival, Part II."

197–198   "lie in wait" . . . "Don't be a" . . . "And I want": Dengler, *Escape from Laos*, p. 147.

198   "our peacemaker" . . . "kind and good" . . . "twice the amount": Dieter Dengler letter to the family of Eugene DeBruin, October 24, 1966.

198–199   "Boiling mad" . . . "nothing idle" . . . "worried and cautious" . . . "Not on your" . . . "Guards entering" . . . "Guards don't" . . . "All in the" . . . "Hell, let's" . . . "It's on": Dengler, *Escape from Laos*, pp. 150–151, 154.

199   "realized something was": Dengler Debriefing, p. 31.

199–200   "Yute! Yute!" . . . "all alone" . . . "finish him": Dengler, *Escape from Laos*, p. 155.

200   "dead right on" . . . "banging away": Dengler Debriefing, p. 32.

200   "Where the hell" . . . "The clip": Dengler, *Escape from Laos*, pp. 155–156.

201   "picked clean" . . . "Go on, go on" . . . "God, please help": Dengler, *Escape from Laos*, pp. 156–157, 159.

201   "no more reference": Dengler Debriefing, p. 33.

201   "vomiting right away": Dengler, Smithsonian lecture.

204   "it really rained" . . . "first taste": Dengler Debriefing, p. 33.

205   "Just one more" . . . "gulping air like": Dengler, *Escape from Laos*, p. 164.

205–206   "take three days" . . . "an exact east" . . . "pretty good" . . . "real fast" . . . "snap out": Dengler Debriefing, pp. 33–34.

206   "thundered down from": Dengler, *Escape from Laos*, p. 165.

206   "just like ropes": Dengler Debriefing, p. 35.

207   "broke out in" . . . "half-walked" . . . "thousands of years": Dengler, *Escape from Laos*, pp. 166–167.

207–208   "Duane, it's no" . . . "We can't travel": Dengler Debriefing, p. 35.

209   "pretty sick now": Ibid.

209–210   "smiling the biggest" . . . "good fortune": Dengler, *Escape from Laos*, p. 170.

210   "right in the": Dengler Debriefing, p. 36.

211   "fighting just to" . . . "Dieter" . . . "Sure, buddy": Dengler, *Escape from Laos*, pp. 172–173.

211–213   "all of a" . . . "completely dark" . . . "very buoyant" . . . "completely free" . . . "splitting into pieces" . . . "to hell with" . . . "bigger rivers": Dengler Debriefing, pp. 36–37.

213   "mad idea" . . . "impossible seemed": Dengler, *Escape from Laos*, pp. 175–176.

213–214   "That's it!" . . . "Okay, let's" . . . "falling and falling" . . . "A new river" . . . "ate and ate" . . . "a hundred ears" . . . "drop dead": Dengler Debriefing, p. 37.

214–215   "You know that" . . . "Well, it's just" . . . "I don't believe" . . . "the end of" . . . "an idea flashed" . . . "Duane, the ammo" . . . "as still as": Dengler, *Escape from Laos*, pp. 180–181.

216–218   "crude stew" . . . "He sees us!" . . . "I'm sorry" . . . "something should foul" . . . "We finally made" . . . "In less than" . . . "scrambled eggs" . . . "there's always": Ibid., pp. 183–185.

218   "Don't worry" . . . "Goddammit, why" . . . "skin and bones" . . . "black like tar" . . . "Leave me alone!" . . . "Hell, no": Dengler Debriefing, p. 39.

218   "Yeah, mine's been": Dengler, *Escape from Laos*, p. 180.

218–219   "dry and happy" . . . "crazy villagers" . . . "You idiots!" . . . "Go on, Dieter" . . . "Nobody's going": Ibid., pp. 186–187.

219 Dialogue between Dengler and Martin, Dengler Debriefing, p. 40.

219–220 "so exhausted" . . . "drained" . . . "The villagers'": Ibid.

220–221 *"Sabay"* . . . *"Americali!"* . . . "running and screaming" . . . *"Sabay"* . . . "long, pulsating" . . . "reality and horror" . . . "might explode" . . . "sheer chance" . . . "seconds and ten feet" . . . "a show they": Dengler, *Escape from Laos*, pp. 189–91.

221–222 "It wasn't ten" . . . "everything was burning" . . . "saw it all" . . . "good SOS" . . . "thirty or forty": Dengler Debriefing, pp. 41–42.

223 "lost all fear" . . . "strange and interesting": Dengler, *Escape from Laos*, p. 196.

223 "twenty grains": Dengler Debriefing, p. 44.

224 "long brown liver": Dengler, *Escape from Laos*, p. 201.

CHAPTER 12 TO THE RESCUE

225–228 "one way" . . . "the general would" . . . "last chance" . . . "a hell of " . . . "we can shoot" . . . "worked the trails" . . . "fishing nets" . . . "fully loaded" . . . "everything is considered," and dialogue between Deatrick and *Crown*: Eugene Deatrick interview.

227–228 "all the buzzing" . . . "merry little fisherman" . . . "I'll never know" . . . "It looks like" . . . "suck in and" . . . "in case he" . . . "go down the" . . . and dialogue between Deatrick and *Crown*: Eugene Deatrick, GE Lecture Series, Smithsonian Air and Space Museum, Washington D.C., March 23, 1989.

229–231 "quick-call checklist" . . . "put the fear" . . . "red-blossom" . . . "a lot of" . . . "We've got him!" . . . "pretty bad shape": William Cowell interview.

230–231 "for dear life" . . . "a little excited" . . . "went to pieces": *Oakland Tribune*, July 28, 1966.

231 "Oh my God": Dengler, *Escape from Laos*, draft.

231–232 "This is our" . . . "Shot down in" . . . "all clicked together": Cowell interview.

CHAPTER 13 RETURNING HERO

233 "many tears": Dengler, *Escape from Laos*, p. 205.

234 "died that day": Ibid., p. 210.

234 "prognosis good": Report of Casualty, July 20, 1966.

234 "tired very easily": Radio message from COMNAVSUPPORT DANANG, July 20, 1966.

235 "hotter pickups": Cowell interview.

236 "death grip": Dengler, *Escape from Laos*, p. 204.

236 "within [the] family": Radio message from BUPERS, July 22, 1966.

236 "gruffest of the": *Time*, June 10, 1966.

236 "No public announcement": Radio message from COMSEVENFLT, July 22, 1966.

236 "considerable bitterness": Radio message from COMNAVSUPPACT DANANG, July 26, 1966.

237 "to retain" . . . "expedite his movement": Daily operations briefing, July 21, 1966.

237 "value in escape" . . . "formal debrief": Radio message from COMSEVENTHFLT, July 24, 1966.

237 "send Ltjg Dengler": Radio message from COMSEVENTHFLT, July 21, 1966.

237 "My C1A": Radio message from CAG SEVEN SEVEN PT FOUR (*Ranger*), July 21, 1966.

237 "junior naval officer": Cowell interview.

237–239 "the hero to" . . . "still coasting to" . . . "didn't look like" . . . "barbered and cleaned" . . . "jaundice really *does*" . . . "Welcome aboard" . . . "Marina's fine": Montgomery interview.

240 "past history" . . . "let Dieter down" . . . "lifted this colossal" . . . "bawling like a": Johns interview.

CHAPTER 14 ALIVE AND FREE

241 "big steak": Balciunas interview.

241 "Ltjg. Dengler's tenacity": Report on the Fitness of Officers, VA-145, October 27, 1967.

243 "injected with sodium": Deatrick interview.

243 "glory of his" . . . "tarnished a bit" . . . "condemning U.S." . . . "no misconduct" . . . "the genuine hero": Hill, "Just Below the Angels," pp. 1019, 1021.

243 "a West German": *New York Times*, July 30, 1966.

243–244 "practically cut" . . . "Navy escapee" . . . "read the riot": Gaylord Hill interview.

244–246 Quotes and dialogue during press conference: Transcript of press conference, U.S. Naval Air Station, North Island, San Diego, September 13, 1966.

246   "almost stunned" . . . "incredible test of " . . . "national hero" . . . "hungry country": Hill, "Just Below the Angels," pp. 1022, 1026.

247   "surprised by all" . . . "wasn't a big" . . . "modesty" . . . "just doing his": Hill interview.

247   "Only dead people": Dengler interview.

248   "Ain't you" . . . "Man, you gonna": Hill, "Just Below the Angels," p. 1024.

247–248   Quotes and dialogue during Senate hearing: Testimony of Lt. (jg) Dieter Dengler, USNR, before the Committee on Armed Services, United States Senate, September 16, 1966.

248   "his charming self ": Hill interview.

250   "I've heard the": Hill, "Just Below the Angels," p. 1028.

EPILOGUE

251   "no chance": Hill interview.

251   "never be hungry": Martin Dengler interview.

251   "dedicated career woman" . . . "buying furniture": Dengler, *Escape from Laos*, p. 210.

252   "This one is": Martin Dengler interview.

252   "at the top" . . . "slept so much" . . . "I've had all": Dengler interview.

252–253   "rule with an" . . . "do it differently" . . . "tough enough" . . . "wouldn't be standing" . . . "ten, at least" . . . "disintegrated" . . . "walked away" . . . "It was God's" . . . "lots of good" . . . "the suffering" . . . "sucked into a" . . . "never wanted to" . . . "seen it up" . . . "against war": Dengler interview.

254   "rapid onset": Coroner's report, Marin County Coroner, February 21, 2001.

254   "equaled what it takes" . . . "Dieter was like": Yukiko Ichihashi-Dengler interview.

254   "a vegetable": Lessard interview.

254   "trapped like a": Ichihashi-Dengler interview.

255   "I have looked": Dieter Dengler e-mail to author, August 15, 2000.

POSTSCRIPT

257   "One thought is": Dengler, *Escape from Laos*, p. 211.

Bibliography

Bowden, Ray. *Tales to Noses over Berlin: The 8th Air Force Missions.* London: Design Oracle Partnership, 1996.

Bridgeman, William, with Jacqueline Hazard. *The Lonely Sky.* New York: Holt, Rinehart, and Winston, 1955.

Bradley, James. *Flyboys.* New York: Little, Brown, 2003.

Burgess, Richard R., and Rosario M. Rausa. *U.S. Navy A-1 Skyraider Units of the Vietnam War.* New York: Osprey, 2009.

Cawthorne, Nigel. *The Bamboo Cage.* New York: S.P.I., 1994.

Colvin, Rod. *First Heroes: The POWs Left Behind in Vietnam.* New York: Irvington, 1987.

Cressman, Robert J. *USS Ranger: The Navy's First Flattop from Keel to Mast 1934–1946.* Washington, D.C.: Potomac, 2003.

Dengler, Dieter. *Escape from Laos.* Novato, Calif.: Presidio, 1979. Paperback edition printed 1996.

Dorr, Robert F. *Skyraider.* Illustrated History of the Vietnam War, no. 13. New York: Bantam, 1988.

Drury, Richard S. *My Secret War.* Fallbrook, Calif.: Aero, 1979.

Fey, Peter. "The Effects of Leadership on Carrier Air Wing Sixteen's Loss Rates during Operation Rolling Thunder, 1965–1968." Master's thesis, U.S. Army Command and General Staff College, Fort Leavenworth, Kans., 2006.

Fields, Kenny Wayne. *The Rescue of Streetcar 304.* Annapolis, Md.: Naval Institute Press, 2007.

Foster, Wynn F. *Captain Hook: A Pilot's Tragedy and Triumph in the Vietnam War.* Annapolis, Md.: Naval Institute Press, 1992.

Francillon, Rene J. *Tonkin Gulf Yacht Club.* Annapolis, Md.: Naval Institute Press, 1988.

Grant, Zalin. *Over the Beach: The Air War in Vietnam.* New York: Norton, 1986.

Gray, Stephen R. *Rampant Raider: An A-4 Skyhawk Pilot in Vietnam.* Annapolis, Md.: Naval Institute Press, 2007.

Heinemann, Edward H., and Rosario Rausa. *Ed Heinemann: Combat Aircraft Designer.* Annapolis, Md.: Naval Institute Press, 1980.

Hill, Gaylord "Hap." "Just Below the Angels." Unpublished manuscript, 1982.

Hirschman, Loree Draude, and Dave Hirschman. *She's Just Another Navy Pilot.* Annapolis, Md.: Naval Institute Press, 2000.

Hobson, Chris. *Vietnam Air Losses.* Hinckley, England: Midland, 2001.

Holloway, James L. III. *Aircraft Carriers At War.* Annapolis, Md.: Naval Institute Press, 2007.

Hubbell, John G. *P.O.W.: A Definitive History of American Prisoner-of-War Experience in Vietnam, 1964–1973.* New York: Reader's Digest Press, 1976.

Johnson, Frederick A. *Douglas A-1 Skyraider.* Atglen, Pa.: Schiffer, 1994.

Macdonogh, Giles. *After the Reich: The Brutal History of the Allied Occupation.* New York: Basic Books, 2007.

McConnell, Malcolm. *Into the Mouth of the Cat.* New York: Norton, 1985.

McGrath, John M. *Prisoner of War: Six Years in Hanoi.* Annapolis, Md.: Naval Institute Press, 1975.

McNamara, Robert S., with Brian VanDeMark. *In Retrospect.* New York: Times Books, 1995.

Morrocco, John. *Thunder from Above.* Boston, Mass.: Boston, 1984.

Nichols, John B., and Barrett Tillman. *On Yankee Station.* Annapolis, Md.: Naval Institute Press, 1987.

Rochester, Stuart I., and Frederick Kiley. *Honor Bound.* Annapolis, Md.: Naval Institute Press, 2007.

Sharp, U. S. Grant. *Strategy for Defeat.* Novato, Calif.: Presidio, 1998.

Sherwood, John Darrell. *Afterburner: Naval Aviators and the Vietnam War.* New York: New York University Press, 2004.

Stafford, Edward P. *The Big E: The Story of the USS Enterprise.* New York: Random House, 1962.

Stockdale, James Bond, and Sybil Stockdale. *In Love and War.* New York: Harper and Row, 1984.

Talbot, David. *Brothers: The Hidden History of the Kennedy Years.* New York: Free Press, 2007.

Turner, Richard E. *Big Friend, Little Friend: Memoirs of a World War II Fighter Pilot.* New York: Doubleday, 1969.

Webb, Kate. *On the Other Side.* New York: Quadrangle, 1972.

Index

BOOKS BY BRUCE HENDERSON

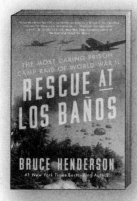

RESCUE AT LOS BAÑOS
**The Most Daring Prison Camp Raid
of World War II**

Rescue at Los Baños tells the story of a remarkable group of prisoners—whose courage and fortitude helped them overcome hardship, deprivation, and cruelty—and of the young American soldiers and Filipino guerrillas who risked their lives to save them. The Los Baños raid was hailed, years later, by General Colin Powell: "I doubt that any airborne unit in the world will ever be able to rival the Los Baños prison raid."

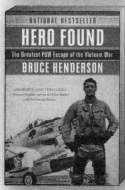

HERO FOUND
**The Greatest POW Escape
of the Vietnam War**

In 1966, German-born POW Dieter Dengler proved to be no ordinary prisoner. With a heroic impulse to free not only himself but also other POWs—some of whom had been held for years—Dengler returned to his ship after six months of captivity—emaciated and ravaged with tropical maladies, but alive and free. Bruce Henderson, who served with Dengler aboard the USS *Ranger*, offers this riveting account of Dengler's story.

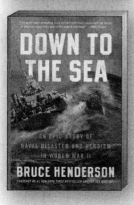

DOWN TO THE SEA
**An Epic Story of Naval Disaster and Heroism in
World War II**

Beginning on December 7, 1941, Bruce Henderson follows four U.S. Navy ships and their crews in the Pacific until their day of reckoning three years later with a far different enemy: a deadly typhoon. Drawing on extensive interviews with nearly every living survivor, many of their rescuers, families of lost sailors, personal letters, and diaries, Henderson offers the most thorough account to date of one of the greatest naval dramas of World War II.